Squandering Billions

Squandering Billions

HEALTH CARE IN CANADA

Gary Bannerman
Don Nixdorf, DC

Illustrations by Kerry Waghorn

hancock

house

ISBN 0-88839-604-X (hardcover)
ISBN 0-88839-602-3 (paperback)

Cataloging in Publication Data

Bannerman, Gary, 1947–
    Squandering billions : health care in Canada / Bannerman, Gary,
Don Nixdorf ; illustrations by Kerry Waghorn.

Includes bibliographical references.
ISBN 0-88839-604-X (bound). — ISBN 0-88839-602-3 (pbk.)

    1. Medical care — Canada. 2. Medical care — Canada — Finance.
I. Nixdorf, Don, 1949– II. Title.

RA410.55.C35B36 2005   362.1'0971   C2005-902237-X

Printed in Indonesia — TK PRINTING

Cover illustration: Kerry Waghorn
Cover design: Rick Groenheyde
Author photos: Patricia Bannerman
Production: Ingrid Luters

For a record of permissions obtained for quoted material
used in this book contact Don Nixdorf.

*We acknowledge the financial support of the Government of Canada through the
Book Publishing Industry Development Program (BPIDP) for our publishing activities.*

Published simultaneously in Canada and the United States by

HANCOCK HOUSE PUBLISHERS LTD.
19313 Zero Avenue, Surrey, B.C. Canada V3S 9R9
(604) 538-1114 Fax (604) 538-2262

HANCOCK HOUSE PUBLISHERS
1431 Harrison Avenue, Blaine, WA U.S.A. 98230-5005
(604) 538-1114 Fax (604) 538-2262

Web site: www.hancockhouse.com
Email: sales@hancockhouse.com

Contents

Dedication

To the memory of two outstanding "Bills" in my life, and the many fine health professionals who cared for them at the end: William MacDonald Bannerman (Moncton Hospital and New Brunswick Extra Mural Hospital); and, William Eric Walrond (Parkside Hospital, Wimbledon, U.K.).

— GB

As always, for my parents, daughters and loyal friends, but also for my colleagues — chiropractic doctors — and the public they serve. My message to all health professionals is that the only worthy path to success is when we put patient interests first.

— DN

For my parents and brother who brought sandwiches and encouraging distraction throughout this project; to the late Len Norris whose drawings, especially of doctors and hospital situations, were an inspiration; and to Roy Peterson whose art has always been a guiding light.

— KW

The Authors

Gary Bannerman is a veteran journalist, publisher, public affairs broadcaster and the author of several books. He has served on the board of directors of corporations of various sizes, and as a communications consultant to CEOs and senior management of many companies. He has been published in scores of magazines and newspapers and, for 16 years, he hosted Western Canada's most successful news talk radio show. His work has been honored with numerous prestigious awards. (*www.bannerline.net*)

Dr. Don Nixdorf has been among Canada's most prominent health professionals for more than a generation, a member of national and provincial agencies and a participant in numerous studies and commissions. The Executive-Director of the British Columbia Chiropractic Association since 1985, he is also a veteran of countless encounters in all forms of media on behalf of his profession, including his own open-line radio health program. His work on behalf of the chiropractic profession keeps him in frequent contact with health ministers, other professionals, media, insurance companies and community organizations. (*www.bcchiro.com*)

The Illustrator

Canadian **Kerry Waghorn** is one of the most accomplished caricaturists in the world. His *Faces in the News* feature is a 28-year journalistic legend. He is represented by Universal Press Syndicate and featured regularly in scores of North American and international journals. He has been or is currently published in the *Chicago Tribune, Denver Post, Miami Weekly News, Boston Globe, Baltimore Sun, Tokyo Japan Times, Montreal Gazette* and *Ottawa Citizen*. (*www.kerrywaghorn.com*)

Authors' Note

The book is intended to be provocative, informative and entertaining, hopefully to generate a healthy debate. It is not — in any sense — designed to be academic in nature, but we are grateful to the many scholars whose work has been of help. A partial bibliography at the back lists the most significant text references. We have been deliberate in the avoidance of footnotes and references for specific text items. With respect to the Internet, wherever appropriate in the text, without distracting readers, we have given web site addresses. As the text progressed, the authors attempted to record URLs but eventually gave this up as an impossible task. The number of sites, sub-sites and links that evolved from them were visited and referenced at such high speed and in a volume that became enormous and constant, often for no more than the correct spelling of a person's name. Our appreciation of the resource goes far beyond being grateful. Those curious as to sources of our information and quotations should be able to find them quickly with appropriate keywords in their Internet browsers.

The authors are particularly grateful to Frances McLafferty, MA, of Simon Fraser University in Burnaby, B.C., for outstanding research in the early stages, and solid ideas that proved instrumental in the text; and to Shirley Stocker, a noted Canadian journalist and broadcast producer, whose investigative and interviewing skills were instrumental in the preparation of two chapters.

Finally, readers are advised that we have attempted to make each chapter as much of a stand-alone item as possible, sensing that many people within the health industry may focus predominantly or exclusively on the subjects most relevant to them. This has necessitated some repetition, in order to reinforce the central themes throughout. But we have also tried to make the content flow smoothly from cover to cover for those who honor us by reading it all. We trust the occasional redundancy will not prove to be too much of a burden.

Introduction Gary Bannerman

As a 1950s' child in Sydney, Nova Scotia, one of my favorite things to do was to stick my foot into the X-ray machine at Bishop's Shoe Store. Groups of kids would hover around the machine as the lucky one got to wiggle his or her toes, while everyone else watched the movement of foot bones. This was a big deal on Charlotte Street, in this most modern of shoe stores. It was even more exciting than the donut-making machine at the Metropolitan Store, and that was saying something. By the time I had my first plantar wart on a foot years later, it came as no surprise to me that my family doctor was able to use the magic of X-rays to burn this menace away. It was a spectacular success and, thankfully, the foot and I survive a lifetime later. Others, I gather, were not so fortunate.

Family doctors are like that: happy to accommodate whatever fad comes from approved pharmaceutical companies and equipment suppliers. The priority is that the parade of patients must keep moving. Nothing in the Canadian medical system rewards or encourages quality. Quantity pays. Speed pays. The per-patient fees are niggardly. If a doctor can encourage a "procedure," the realm of "value added" will prevail. An ingrown toe nail or wart removal might increase revenue of a patient visit from $25 to $200, if it's done right. An appropriately solemn consultation may even result in profitable revisits.

Then there are the bonuses from pharmaceutical companies and equipment suppliers. Drug companies can often be convinced to buy the "Docs'" bowling team a dinner every game night, as long as the local "detail" representative (salesperson) gets to give a fifteen-minute talk and drop off free samples. Often, the drug companies pay an "honorarium" to compensate for the bowlers' time while the sales pitch is delivered. And it's no trick to get one of them to fly an MD and spouse to some interesting city for an "educational/scientific opportunity." Medical and biomedical conventions tend to be so influenced by drug company dollars it makes the financing of political parties seem miserly by comparison — and a little suspect in view of the published ethics of both medical associations and the congresses themselves.

Nothing in Canadian law requires the periodic review of medical doctors' competency, or an upgrade to their certification. Physicians' provincial regulatory colleges encourage it, but it is purely voluntary. Few medical professionals do anything other than study whatever might increase their income. Many general practitioners study to attain "specialist" credentials. The typical MD, qualified a generation ago, has never formally studied anything again, except the sales pitches from drug salespeople, health journals, and the general rhetoric around the coffee room. Nor is he or she required to do so.

This helps explain why I got to wiggle my toes in an X-ray machine at a shoe store in the 1950s, and why today the public is subjected to whatever the current equivalent may be. Are middle-aged women at all surprised that the same doctor who so enthusiastically put them on hormone replacement therapy (HRT) pills a few years ago now tells them that these same pills may be fatal? Are they angry that only a few years ago they were shamelessly sold on the cosmetic benefits of breast implants yet are now suffering serious side effects and having the implants removed? Given the recent history experienced by women, men might be wise to pay more attention to the propaganda surrounding prostate cancer.

■ ■ ■

When I explained the premise for this book to a learned friend recently, he told me of a Yale University colleague who says unequivocally that the best thing he can do for his own health is to avoid hospitals until such time as he is unable to enter in a vertical position. The statistics are simply alarming. The number one cause of death in North America is medical misadventure. Dumb mistakes. Wrong diagnoses. Needless drugs. Questionable surgery. Viruses contracted in hospitals. A study by the Canadian Institutes of Health Research and the Canadian Institute of Health Information, released in 2004, concluded that 185,000 patients out of 2.5 million admitted to acute care hospitals suffer death, disability, or extended hospitalization as a result of "adverse" effects of treatment. Between 9,250 and 23,750 of these people die because of preventable errors. Motor vehicle accidents kill 3,000 a year in Canada. Despite dramatic television footage and newspaper headlines reporting highway tragedies, driving is a much safer activity than hospitalization.

A United States report documented that there were 783,936 deaths caused by conventional medicine in 2001 overtaking heart disease as the number one killer (699,697 deaths). The Canadian research focused on acute care hospitals only, while the U.S. work studied all medical care.

The late Dr. Robert Mendelsohn of Chicago, once chairman of the licensing committee for physicians in the State of Illinois, was among the doctors the American Medical Association most enthusiastically promoted. President Lyndon Johnson appointed him to a commission that addressed health care inequities in American ghettos. But Mendelsohn later became outraged by the incompetence and pomposity of his profession, evolving into one of the AMA's fiercest opponents. His book, *Confessions of a Medical Heretic*, became a nuclear bomb within American health care.

"When you go to a doctor, you are seen not as a person who needs help with his or her health, but as a potential market for the medical factory's products," Mendelsohn wrote in 1979. "Modern medicine cannot survive without our faith. Medicine is neither an art nor a science. It is a religion."

After my journalism career had moved me from the east to the west coast of Canada, and from newspapers to radio, I had the pleasure of hosting Dr. Mendelsohn on several occasions. The air became supercharged when he was amidst a debate with anyone defending the status quo of health care monopolized by medical doctors, likely the most powerful trade union on earth.

During one 1980s visit, we were on the eve of what the United Nations promoted as the "Year of World Peace." I asked Mendelsohn what MDs could do to assist the cause. His reply: "Go out of business." This was his sense of humor, and then he explained that the tragedy of the era was that the "business" of being a doctor had little or nothing to do with patient health.

■ ■ ■

As a young reporter in 1967 and 1968, I attended conferences of the Canadian Medical Association (CMA) and provincial medical associations, in which the prevailing theme was that medicare and Bolshevik communism were synonymous. MDs seemed to overlook the views of Prime Minister Lester Pearson, and see in the unlikely figure of kindly, intelligent and sincere Rev. T. C. "Tommy" Douglas, who pioneered Canadian medicare in Saskatchewan, as some kind of pernicious threat to their profession. This baffled Pearson and just about everybody else.

Douglas and other pioneers had been promoting universal health care for decades and an inconsistent hodge podge of provincial approaches was the result. Pearson and Opposition Leader John Diefenbaker both believed that the time had come for national standardization, to ensure universal coverage, including the poor and working poor. How could this possibly be seen as an assault on health? The CMA thought it was. Or was it something other than public health that concerned them?

The CMA's foresight with respect to medicare in 1967 is consistent with their posture today. They invariably defend the indefensible — unfortunately, very successfully.

It's likely apocryphal, but I'm told that at a Halifax conference during this era, one speaker laboured on endlessly to the point that the Chair interrupted him with the comment, "You've been looking up backsides so long you have finally become one." The bore was a proctologist.

■ ■ ■

At the outset of this book, and in view of the foregoing, I feel compelled to report a personal health care history of unfailing excellence. Three times in my life I had near-death experiences: once by virus, once by car accident, and, most worrisomely, once as a byproduct of professional stress and lifestyle. In every instance, I emerged with unreserved admiration and gratitude toward the many medical doctors, registered nurses, health technicians, and institutions that provided care. I also believe that these people are the norm, not the exception, superbly skilled and dedicated.

It will be documented in this book that the most astonishing advances in health care have been in the field of public health, not just the elimination of plagues and epidemics worldwide, but the systematic control of local environments. Monitoring water supplies, sewage disposal, sanitation in food services, immunization programs, and constant research of new threats, does more for humankind than anything that ever happens at local hospitals or clinics. The fact that we are living longer and better, with less fear of infant mortality or terrorizing diseases, has everything to do with the poorest paid doctors in the world — public health officials.

The other area of amazing, consistent success is in emergency services, where we are led to believe most of the work is done by rookie doctors and other stressed-out personnel, nurses, and paramedics. There are stunning results at just about every hospital emergency room throughout the world. Why is this? Where the situation is so prone to accidents or less-than-sophisticated care, why are the outcomes so good?

More tragedies and misadventures occur as a result of routine doctor visits and scheduled procedures. Most observers believe that when our health professionals, in all of the accredited specialties, respond instinctively to obvious emergencies and trauma, they do what is necessary with uniform brilliance, and unconsciously so. It may be cruel to suggest that when a medical doctor has time to think, or when he or she allows himself to believe that the patient's visit is routine, all of the problems begin, but the evidence seems to indicate that is precisely the case. The outcome of that routine visit, too often, is less than beneficial to the patient. I expand on these points throughout the book

■ ■ ■

It was a unique privilege for me in my broadcasting career to have met and interviewed scientists and doctors who changed society forever. Among these were the renowned vitamin and nutrition pioneers, all of whom were vilified in their era by the medical establishment: two-time Nobel Prize winner Dr. Linus Pauling (vitamin C); Dr. Abram Hoffer (vitamin E and megavitamin therapies); the Shute brothers, Dr. Wilfred and Dr. Evan (vitamin E and multivitamins as therapy, particularly for heart disease), and others such as "The Codfather," Dan Dale Alexander, who traveled North America promoting the value of natural cod liver oil, and Dr. Earl Mindell the best-selling author of *Vitamin Bible*. Also among these guests was Dr. Robert Atkins, the New York doctor whose first book generated a world shortage of litmus paper during the 1970s, as millions of people tested their urine for changing ph levels associated with fat metabolism due to the absence of carbohydrates in the diet. I would like to emphasize that every one of these people, whether they were as distinguished as Dr. Linus Pauling or merely a best-selling author, was condemned by the medical establishment. Patients were warned that they would be killing themselves if they opted to create "very expensive urine." This advice came from doctors who rarely spent even a few minutes studying nutrition during medical school, let alone whole courses. Who won? Walk into any drug or grocery store today, or big box wholesaler, and look at the vast amount of space devoted to vitamins and supplements. It usually commands more territory than the entire area occupied by dispensing pharmacists.

Medical doctors argue that they hold a public trust to protect the public from quacks, fads, and products that have not been thoroughly tested. Their argument is most ingenuous. How do they explain today's wonder drug that becomes tomorrow's nightmare? What about the X-ray fad a previous generation so thoroughly promoted? Where do they learn about anything new, except from sales people, medical literature, and conventions dominated by drug money and the manufacturers of equipment? There is little unbiased in-service education. It seems clear that the establishment opposes anything it does not control, but the vitamin story aptly demonstrates that the true power is with the people.

■ ■ ■

It was also in my broadcast studio, 25 years ago, that I first met the co-author of this book, Dr. Don Nixdorf. Don and various colleagues over the years introduced me to chiropractic. I became aware of another health paradox. Chiropractic is so popularly accepted as a profession and treatment option yet it still suffers from mind-numbing discrimination from government, public institutions, and the health establishment. As years passed, what I found most remarkable about Dr. Nixdorf — in the face of this Everest of ignorant opposition — was his consistent support for all of the accredited, established health professions, and his advocacy of multidisciplinary care. This message dominates this book.

There is a strong chiropractic component to the book because we believe this may be the most outstanding example anywhere about how care can be improved for millions of patients, pain reduced or eliminated without drugs or surgery, and billions of dollars saved for society, freeing up resources for other purposes. But it is not just about chiropractic. The bottom line is that the health system must find ways to bypass expensive gatekeepers who add no value to the health care process and frequently promote remedies that do more harm than good. Patients must more expeditiously be routed toward the most-effective, efficient, and economical solution for whatever ails them.

Introduction Don Nixdorf, DC

Rarely a year goes by that there is not some big-budget, high-profile federal or provincial commission of inquiry into health care and, most notably, health budgets. Political clichés fill the air about efficiencies, more billions of dollars, wait-lists, and the availability of qualified professionals. Nothing ever changes in a substantive way, except the public perception that Canada's health care system has gone steadily downhill for a quarter century. We used to quietly boast that we had the best universal coverage in the world.

You cannot get the right answer if you consistently fail to ask the right question. We do not need a Royal Commission to understand the phrase "evidence-based care." Before investing in a specific treatment, facility or professional, ask what "facts" exist to demonstrate that this is potentially the most effective approach? Here are questions, virtually never asked by health ministers:

- Is the goal health care, illness care or wealth care?
- Does a patient have the right to choose appropriate care, and, if so, why are medical plans not equitably covering all accredited and regulated health professionals?
- Since 30 percent of all visits to medical doctors and health professionals are for spine-related illnesses and injuries, why does the system not insist that primary diagnoses and care is delivered by those most thoroughly trained to recognize and treat these problems?
- Is there a strategy to avoid or minimize, where possible, the use of drugs or surgery?
- What is the precise nature of the relationships among pharmaceutical companies, medical conventions, hospitals,

universities, and individual doctors? Why do medical licensing boards not investigate and intervene in these relationships? This is a study that should involve expert auditors from the Canada Customs and Revenue Agency, able to scrutinize both direct and indirect subsidies, including all travel, entertainment, and gift benefits associated with all sales, events, and undertakings.

- Are we more concerned about incomes for professionals than outcomes for the public?
- Why is it that the "health crisis" seems to disappear from headlines as soon as health professionals' and staff contracts are signed?"
- Is the real issue a matter of protecting monopolies or is it serving the public?
- Why is the system so afraid to implement evidence-based treatment as determined by past and current "outcomes" and hard, irrefutable data?

Much of my professional life as a chiropractor involves representing my profession to government, other health professionals, insurers, compensation boards, the media, and wherever invited in public — locally, regionally, and nationally. We present briefs and reports wherever we feel our views may be helpful. But to keep myself in perspective and focused upon the point of it all, I still treat patients every week, constantly reminding myself and my chiropractic colleagues that if we put the best interests of the patient first, and ourselves second, we cannot help but to also benefit.

Most studies indicate that Canada is not keeping pace with other western nations in either qualifying health professionals or properly equipping hospitals. Waiting lists are longer than ever, governments are cutting back on coverage, and if there is a consistent theme to both the criticism of the Canadian system and the proposed solutions, it is that we spend sufficient amounts of money, but we do not manage or use the system effectively. This is a responsibility shared by every group and professional involved in the health field. If those managing the health funds — corporations, insurers, public officials, and even patients themselves — start by first examining the desired outcome, and then seeking immediate access to the most effective way of getting there, fortunes will be saved.

■ ■ ■

We, in Canada, have a long and mostly distinguished health care history. Saskatchewan became the medicare pioneer in 1947 but every province had moved in that direction prior to the enactment of *The Medical Care Act* of 1966, implemented in 1968 (replaced by the *Canada Health Act* in 1984). Debates and studies since 1984 have been partially in response to changes in technology, disease patterns, and population growth. However, health reform has tended to be obsessively focused on governance and management structure rather than the delivery of service. Quality care should be the issue, not governance, fee negotiations or turf wars among administrators, professionals, institutions, and insurers.

Public education about health services is vital to the provision and understanding of good care. Government must ensure high ethical standards among practitioners, but individuals and health plans should be encouraged to choose within a system free of either direct bias or the perception of bias. Empowering the public would improve outcomes. Prevention must be part of any prudent planning, but there will always be patient/provider interaction. Here are some additional thoughts and questions that are discussed at length in this book.

- Structural changes to the health delivery system, administrative infrastructure or redesign of items covered by an insurance plan, does not improve healing — getting patients better, faster does. Can we get injured or ill people back to productive lives and work more expeditiously, with less cost for them and the system?

- How can we end the shell game of cutting specific costs and services from one budget, and then transferring these responsibilities to other insurers, employers, and the public? Moving problems does not treat the patient, and never generates any net savings to the public purse. The problem — and cost — just pops up somewhere else.

- Has patient care become merely an excuse to enrich health professionals, equipment manufacturers, administrators, pharmaceutical companies, consultants, insurers, contractors, and suppliers?

- Political and bureaucratic managers of the health system are frequently more concerned about catering to professional and employee monopolies than they are with quality, economical patient care.

- According to the Canadian Medical Association, 40 cents of each payroll dollar is attributable to health costs, including lost employee time due to illness and injury.

- The gatekeeper role exclusively held by medical doctors frequently puts them in the position of diagnosing and/or treating conditions for which they have little or no qualifications or expertise. Often, the "referral" role of MDs with respect to specialists, dietitians, physiotherapists, and other professionals, simply compounds the costs, delays treatment, and extends patient suffering.

- The specialized health professionals such as podiatrists, naturopaths, chiropractors, and nurse practitioners must be used more effectively where evidence indicates patient recovery times are shorter and costs are lower. Expanding medicare coverage to encourage the use of these services would actually save substantial amounts of money.

- As much as 50 percent of all the drugs prescribed in Canada are wasted. Dramatic action is necessary to more accurately prescribe the proper pharmaceutical for each patient and each condition, and to curtail a tendency to keep experimenting "until we get it right." Misuse of drugs has become a major contributor to disease in Canada, and an alarming factor in "cause of death" and morbidity statistics.

I hope that in the pages to follow, we will adequately provide the background for all of these issues and more, and present convincing evidence of how we can make health care better in Canada, and as good or better than any in the world.

"You cannot get the right answer if you consistently fail to ask the right question."

" What's wrong with this picture? "

1.

The Gatekeepers

The medical establishment has become a major threat to health. The disabling impact of professional control over medicine has reached the proportions of an epidemic . . . . It must now be understood that what has turned health care into a sick-making enterprise is the very intensity of the engineering endeavour that has translated human survival from the performance of organisms into the result of technical manipulation.

— IVAN ILLICH, PhD

The most outstanding testament to Ivan Illich's landmark 1976 work, *The Limits of Medicine, Medical Nemesis*, is that it is still in print — unrevised — and selling respectably almost thirty years after its publication. It is among the volumes the better bookstores must carry in their permanent inventory. Almost nobody ever quotes Illich in context. Critics of medicine latch onto quotes such as the one that begins this chapter and others that follow. Medical doctors, health bureaucrats, and biological scientists rise in defense, citing parades of miracles and achievements for which they have been responsible. Illich's target is modern society itself. We, the public, have sacrificed our autonomy and our integrity to the myth of medical infallibility, eagerly spurred on by those within the system who profit most greatly from it. Politicians are merely a reflection of public irresponsibility, a collective Pavlov's dog earning votes by shoveling favors and resources in directions that even they know to be ridiculous.

"Iatrogenesis," or illness caused by medical care, is an important word in health literature and a concept that is used throughout this book. "Iatros" is the Greek word for *doctor* and "genesis" means *origin*. Illich says: "More people die now because crisis intervention is hospital-centred than can be saved through the superior techniques the hospital can provide. . . . Until proved healthy, the citizen is now presumed to be sick. In a triumphantly therapeutic society, everybody can make himself into a therapist and someone else into his client."

The difference between an itch and an allergy depends upon the thickness of the patient's wallet. The media bombards us with information about cures and therapies. There is rarely a television advertising break or page in a publication that does not propose an over-the-counter or prescription treatment for something. It is a standard show biz formula followed by reporters to make sure there is a medical story in every newscast or journal, either proclaiming a miraculous breakthrough for science (invariably years away) or warning of some new disaster (invariably requiring professional consultation). How could we not be neurotic about aches, pains, and disabilities, real or imagined? How can you sit through twenty minutes of television without wondering if you have a disease? Need an excuse for anything? Modern health propaganda will provide you with a smorgasbord. The mere fact that you are going to a doctor gives your medical complaint legitimacy. Poor me. Government to the rescue, irrespective of cost — a right of citizenship.

Illich argues that there is no longer such a thing as a "social disorder." Everything is a disease and income-generator for the health industry. No one is "absolutely" responsible anymore for alcoholism, drug addiction, sleeping-on-the-job, inattention, violence, or unacceptable behavior of any kind. The catch phrases "mental disease" or "stress-related" and many others make the intolerable explainable and highly profitable for self-appointed saviors with their questionable remedies. "The pain, dysfunction, disability and anguish resulting from technical medical intervention now rival the morbidity due to traffic and industrial accidents and even war-related activities, and make the impact of medicine one of the most rapidly spreading epidemics of our time," Illich said.

Diagnostic bias
We prostrate ourselves on the altar of what the late Dr. Robert Mendelsohn of Chicago described as "the Church of Medicine," and invite physicians to prospect all over our body in search of work. Report after report in modern times demonstrates that routine "check-ups" with the local doctor are a waste of time and while advanced warning of certain illnesses can save lives, these scavenger hunts most often miss the serious and discover the unimportant, turning the latter into discomfort and, sometimes, disaster for the patient.

Illich says medicalized prevention "turns the physician into an officially licensed magician whose prophecies cripple even those left unharmed by his brews . . . . the mass hunt for health risks begins with dragnets designed to apprehend those needing special protection . . . the United States proudly led the world in organizing disease hunts and, later, in questioning their utility." Public health programs promoting chest X-rays, with mobile units roaming through cities, was a practice that is now remembered with a sense of horror. No one knows for sure how much cancer this routine, ubiquitous service caused within the populace. Our society diagnoses illness, rather than health. All practitioners are warned about "diagnostic bias," the tendency to discover something within the examiner's area of expertise and source of income. This bias is cited by health critics to decry what they see as needless surgery for cosmetic purposes or reasons of expediency: tonsillectomies, hysterectomies, Caesarean sections, and a long list of other dubious practices, unnecessary if not in specific instances, then certainly in the volume.

Illich reports this anecdote:

> The classic demonstration of this bias came in an experiment conducted in 1934. In a survey of 1,000 eleven-year-old children from the public schools of New York, 61 percent were found to have had their tonsils removed. The remaining 39 percent were subjected to examination by a group of physicians, who selected 45 percent of these for tonsillectomy and rejected the rest. The rejected children were reexamined by another group of physicians, who recommended tonsillectomy for 46 percent of those remaining after the first examination. When the rejected children were examined a third time, a similar percentage was selected for tonsillectomy so that after three examinations only sixty-five children remained who had not been recommended for tonsillectomy. These subjects were not further examined because the supply of examining physicians ran out. This test was conducted at a free clinic, where financial considerations could not explain the bias.

"Diagnostic bias in favour of sickness combines with frequent diagnostic error. Medicine not only imputes questionable categories with inquisitorial enthusiasm; it does so at a rate of miscarriage no court system could tolerate," Illich concluded.

The pervasiveness of Ivan Illich's theories was demonstrated in an important Australian study in 2003. Conducted by Professor Jeff Richardson and Dr. Stuart Peacock of Monash University in the State of

Victoria, for the Centre for Health Program Evaluation, the report systematically compared mortality rates to the number of doctors in a population. They too, selected Ivan Illich quotes as a philosophical premise
for their work.

The report was titled *Will More Doctors Increase or Decrease Death
Rates? An econometric analysis of Australian mortality statistics*. It concluded:

> Systemic evidence is surprisingly consistent. It implies an association
> between mortality and an increase in the doctor supply which is not
> easily attributed to reverse causation or to a spurious correlation with
> some other attribute of the population. The cross-sectional evidence
> seems to be stable. The present results are largely consistent with those
> obtained from data 20 years ago. Ideally, further research is required
> using panel data. However until this is completed and the evidence pre-
> sented here is contradicted, then the hypothesis that iatrogenic effects
> may more than offset the direct beneficial effects of additional, and
> largely unregulated, medical services must be contemplated seriously.

The birth of medicare

American icon Martin Luther King once stated, "Of all forms of inequality, injustice in health care is the most shocking and most inhumane."
Today, the United States remains the only nation in the so-called "first
world" without universal health care. The roots of what we call
"medicare" in the western world date back to Germany in the nineteenth
century and efforts elsewhere, notably New Zealand and the American
state of Wisconsin, before World War II. But the acknowledged author of
universal coverage was a kindly English intellectual and economist,
William Henry Beveridge, whose 1942 report, *Social Insurance and
Allied Services*, ultimately changed the world. Vilified by conservatives
as the architect of "the welfare state" and honored by socialists as the
ultimate defender of the common man, Lord Beveridge was neither. He
was a Liberal, a party that diminished into obscurity during the years of
his greatest influence.

The Canadian health care system evolved into its present form over
five decades. Saskatchewan, in 1947, was the first province to establish
public, universal hospital insurance, and by 1962 became the first to take
the giant step by covering physicians' services. By the late 1950s, however, all provinces had some form of blanket hospitalization coverage

and the Government of Canada began to share some of the costs. By 1961, all 10 provinces and two territories had public insurance plans that provided universal access to hospital services.

Prime Minister John Diefenbaker, in 1961, became concerned that health issues were splitting the nation. People were making decisions about where to live and work on the basis of their health coverage and needs, wearying of disputes when they submitted receipts from one jurisdiction for reimbursement in their home province. Diefenbaker reached out to a distinguished friend and colleague, the Chief Justice of Saskatchewan, Emmett Hall, to head a national study. Within a year, Hall not only became Chairman of the Royal Commission on Health Services, he was elevated to the Supreme Court of Canada. The Royal Commission report in 1964 led to the proclamation of *The Medical Care Act* at the end of 1966. Canada's medicare commenced on July 1, 1968. By 1972 all provinces and territories were participating in the program.

Any historical review of universal health care worldwide inevitably leads to the inescapable conclusion that the authors were hopelessly naive. They all genuinely believed that quality care for everybody would actually be profitable for both government and society. Lord Beveridge argued that when people were healthier they were able to be more productive; therefore, they could contribute more to the economy and become more affluent purchasers of British goods. Business would proceed more smoothly as fewer worker-days would be lost due to illness, or other health-related family crises. He said this would enhance the competitiveness of British industry in the postwar period by shifting labor costs such as health care and pensions out of corporate ledgers and onto the public accounts.

A key architect of Canadian medicare, Mr. Justice Hall, said in a 1964 CBC interview, "From a humanitarian standpoint, there is — we believe — an obligation on society to be concerned with the health of its individuals. But on the economic side, investments in health are investments in human capital, and just as investments in engines and railroads are investments in capital, so are investments in people. They pay off in the economic area and they pay great dividends to the nation that looks after the health of its people."

The visionaries did not anticipate the consequences of making unlimited health care a right of citizenship. They ignored the potential among the public for limitless consumption, hypochondria, misuse to disguise other failures and the ability of a multidimensional health industry to manufacture needs. Consider these consequences:

- The ballooning of health bureaucracies. The power of these fiefdoms and the income of those within them depends upon the growth of budgets, regulations, studies, and controls.

- The growth of university medical schools, scientific research centres, and schools of public administration. While incessantly pounding the drum for more money, institutions crank out graduates in search of diseases that they can treat, cure, and build careers upon.

- Powerful mass media breathlessly dispatch medical stories, alternating between announcements of wonder cures and alerts to terrifying diseases.

- Hypochondria. The multi-billion dollar advertising industry propagandizes people to be ever cognizant of aches, pains, infirmities, and imperfections.

- Recreational health care. Elderly people make regular doctor visits as much out of loneliness as medical necessity. As one ages, there are few moments when something does not hurt, predominantly minor irritations. There is always a reason to see the doctor.

- The disincentive to productivity. The media culture advertises illness as the norm, not an anomaly, and generates its own mythologies, such as the impact of stress on human biology. Labor contracts usually specify numbers of "sick days" as a right of employment, and some contracts — in order to keep people from malingering — encourage employees to bank their sick days and take extra holidays or pay instead.

- The pervasive investment by pharmaceutical companies and medical equipment suppliers in, and the ethically questionable acceptance by, universities, research labs, health congresses, and individual doctors. Abuse of pharmaceuticals has become an epidemic tragedy. Since universal health care rewards physicians only for quantity of care, the prescription is the easy way to keep patients moving fast, feeling that they achieved something as a result of their medical visit.

- Advertising and promotional investments by pharmaceutical companies and other manufacturers of health supplies — encouraged by too many doctors — is aimed at manufacturing patients where no real medical need exists.

- The cost of modern cures: the increased use and manufacture of drugs and the high cost of the technology.

- The diminishment of the family doctor and a holistic relationship with the patient-family. Economic pressures make house calls inadvisable; public mobility; patients' multiple job changes and therefore changes in medical plan coverage; medical specialization; office visits being restricted to one health problem per visit; the growth of other health professions; and, most pervasively, family break-up.

- Diseases of affluence haunt major industrialized nations: obesity, drug addiction, pollution-caused respiratory conditions, motor vehicle accidents, and reckless recreation.

- Iatrogensis: illness, disability, and death as a consequence of treatment, and not the condition that precipitated the medical attention.

Could anyone have imagined all of the above? Both British National Health and Canada's medicare were in crisis by the late 1970s and the concerns continue to this day. Governments consistently react to these issues with expensive studies, inquiries and commissions, often as a substitute for political action. The lack of follow-up on most of these investigations demonstrates the political insincerity of their original assignment.

A 1999 debate in the British House of Lords illustrated both the naivety and the decency that propels universal health care. The late Earl of Longford (author, historian, Conservative Frank Pakenham) rose to discuss Lord Beveridge.

> He did wonderful work with the foundation of the welfare state. The morning after it was completed I went into a news agent to try to buy a paper. The lady said, "It's no good trying to buy a paper here. That Sir William Beveridge is going to abolish want, so all the papers were sold out." Later that day or the next day I asked him to come to lunch. I was meeting with Evelyn Waugh, an old friend and famous writer. They did not get on at all well. Evelyn Waugh said to him at the end, "How do you get your main pleasure in life, Sir William?" He paused and said, "I get mine trying to leave the world a better place than I found it." Evelyn Waugh said, "I get mine spreading alarm and despondency" — this was in the height of the war — "and I get more satisfaction than you do." So he did not meet with universal acclamation, but nearly everyone admired Beveridge at that time. He was a wonderful man.

The Canada Health Act

Justice Hall was recruited again in 1979 to the position of Chair of the Health Services Review Committee. Portability and the accessibility of care, and discrepancies in coverage, had become the focus of federal-provincial disputes. From the outset, the federal treasury contributed funds for hospitalization and physician care, but it remained a provincial responsibility to determine how these were spent. Provincial programs expanded in the field of pharmacare, dentistry, chiropractic, optometry, physiotherapy, other alternative services, and in a growing attempt to build home care. If the *Medical Care Act* and its regulatory infrastructure did not compensate the provinces, the *Canada Assistance Act* was often brought into play to pay for services for any persons who could not afford their provincial health insurance premiums.

But what ultimately led to Emmett Hall's 1979 appointment was the difficulty all provinces were having in their negotiations with medical doctors. "Balance billing" or "extra billing" became a rallying cry of physicians. They argued that if the public treasury could not afford to pay adequate compensation, then they should be free to surcharge their patients. This was anathema to Hall. He could not have been more blunt in his report. Doctors could opt in or opt out, not a combination of the two. He defended the right of physicians — indeed all professionals — to set their own fees, but added that there is no obligation upon government to pay them. Similarly, he said government should not even consider imposing a system of government-salaried doctors. The 1979 Hall report was predominately condemned by the hospital and medical establishment, but largely applauded by the public. Hall told an interviewer: "The only people who seemed to be in favour of the report were the people themselves."

Following the Hall report, planning began for modernizing the national health legislation. The *Canada Health Act* was passed in 1984, replacing the *Hospital Insurance and Diagnostic Services Act* (1957) and the *Medical Care Act* (1966). The new legislation retained and entrenched the criteria, or basic principles, underlying the national health insurance program that had been contained in the earlier legislation.

A key ambition of medicare's authors was that the plan would insure the patients, not the income of professionals. It is the health condition that is covered. Therefore, a "comprehensiveness" clause was crafted to read, in full:

In order to satisfy the criterion respecting comprehensiveness, the health care insurance plan of a province must insure all insured health services provided by hospitals, medical practitioners or dentists, and where the law of the province so permits, similar or additional services rendered by other health care practitioners.

But, the *Canada Health Act* web site states the five principles as follows:

- **public administration:** the administration of the health care insurance plan of a province or territory must be carried out on a non-profit basis by a public authority;
- **comprehensiveness:** all medically necessary services provided by hospitals and doctors must be insured;
- **universality:** all insured persons in the province or territory must be entitled to public health insurance coverage on uniform terms and conditions;
- **portability:** coverage for insured services must be maintained when an insured person moves or travels within Canada or travels outside the country; and
- **accessibility:** reasonable access by insured persons to medically necessary hospital and physician services must be unimpeded by financial or other barriers.

Otherwise, how funds are spent and the delivery of service is entirely a provincial concern. The "comprehensiveness" bullet is the fatal flaw in management of health care, because it is a misnomer. The principle should more accurately be titled, "monopoly." The phrase "medically necessary services" is not in the act, but rather a term created by the Canadian Medical Association and its sycophants in government. It awards to hospitals and medical doctors, professions exclusively engaged in and rewarded for illness care, not wellness care, an absolute monopoly on federal funds. By making the focus of medicare hospital-based, it ignores the reality that the vast proportion of Canadian health care occurs outside of hospitals, and by making physicians the only publicly funded caregivers, the plan ignores a vast range of other health professionals, most of whom are less expensive than medical doctors and, within their defined specialty, more able.

The *Canada Health Act* covers hospitals, physicians, hospital-based dentistry, and "others." The latter requires provincial medicare legislation. If a physiotherapist, podiatrist, chiropractor, acupuncturist, or other specialist provides treatment at a hospital, the federal plan covers the cost. Beyond that, the provinces and private insurers are free to cover whatever services they wish. Although provinces seem to be consistently cutting back on the number of professional services they cover with extended benefits (chiropractic, optometry, physiotherapy et al.), often based upon individual income levels, and the extent of the coverage when they do, medicare has always been far broader than the apparently narrow definitions in the federal legislation.

The gatekeepers

The presumption of infallibility of medical doctors — disastrous economically and in terms of patient health — underscores medicare. It assumes a level of brilliance, selflessness, and integrity that would make Florence Nightingale blush. Increasingly, general practitioners are becoming brokers for lab services and specialists. Most of the valuable information gained by annual check-ups is through blood and urine tests performed elsewhere. Computers interpret the basic results and flag for consultation any problem areas. If the GP is merely a broker, why add the cost of another professional consultation and if there is value, surely the specialist or the lab should pay a sales commission to the doctor-as-agent, rather than billing the customer's medical plan?

Perhaps the most absurd example of misplaced monopoly was the advent of acupuncture in western society. For years, practitioners of ancient Asian therapies had to hide from the authorities and some were prosecuted for practicing medicine without a license. Some of them had outstanding credentials from China and Chinese societies elsewhere, including academic credentials. The American and Canadian medical establishments did everything in their power to warn people away from acupuncture and to encourage prosecutions of those who persisted in providing these treatments.

The public and media backlash against governments, particularly from Asian communities, finally brought a political reaction and an even more bizarre result. Acupuncture was made legal, but only upon referral from physicians, who were not only ignorant about it but publicly opposed to the practice for reasons of ideology or competition. Scores of Canadian doctors took crash courses in acupuncture. Government started paying fees to MDs who took quickie courses masquerading as training, but continued to condemn — if not prosecute — those who had devoted their lives to it. Gradually, Chinese acupuncturists who were also medical doctors, persisted in their quest for a reasonable public policy and compromises were gradually reached to also accommodate skilled technicians.

The largest health profession ignored by the *Canada Health Act* is chiropractic. There are more than 6,600 practicing doctors of chiropractic in Canada, up from 1,200 at the time of Justice Hall's 1961–64 commission, and they treat five million Canadians each year. The growth and success of chiropractic has occurred in spite of relentless, monumental abuse and discrimination by medical doctors, the health establishment, and governments. The greatest possible tribute to chiropractic is that almost all new patients are refugees from the "free" services of medical doctors. They usually arrive after long periods of disability, pain, and treatment with drugs and surgery. They arrive with considerable dissatisfaction, irrespective of whether part of their chiropractic fees are covered by medicare or their charge cards. And they stay with chiropractic. The only equivalent free-market test faced by Canadian medical doctors took place when a few accepted Emmett Hall's challenge and opted out of provincial medical plans, billing their patients directly. All failed. Most desperately climbed back aboard the comfortable vehicle governments had created for them.

In the United States, the American Medical Association made such a determined effort to stamp out chiropractic it found itself the target of antitrust litigation. The AMA had a policy actively condemning chiropractic care, requiring that its members never refer a patient to a chiropractic doctor nor accept a referral from a chiropractor. It vigorously opposed public support for chiropractic education at accredited universities, and then used "insufficient education" as an argument against chiropractic. This practice was so pervasive and illegal, as the court ruled, the AMA was found guilty in 1987 of running a predatory monopoly. The AMA's attempt to appeal this judgment was rejected by the United States Supreme Court in 1991.

As Emmett Hall was writing his 1964 Royal Commission report, a major inquiry into chiropractic was taking place in Quebec: the Royal Commission on Chiropraxy and Osteopathy, chaired by Mr. Justice Gerard Lacroix. Hall had many supportive things to say about chiropractic, but he concluded that he found it impossible to adjudicate the gap between the medical doctors' opposition and the arguments in favor of the chiropractic profession. Hall added that if Justice Lacroix determined that "the claims of the chiropractors are found to be valid, they then should be incorporated into and integrated with the teaching of health sciences in universities. No good can come from warring factions between competitors in the health field. It is, in our view, fundamental to good health care, that all who labour legitimately in the field should do so in harmonious co-operation."

Justice Lacroix not only found chiropractic to be a valid form of treatment, he commented on the medical establishment's persistent opposition to it: "When I first started this study, it came as a surprise to me to learn that so much of the opposition by traditional medicine was based on bias and prejudice, ignorance and refusal to learn about chiropraxy." The Quebec Commission totally discredited the arguments of the Canadian Medical Association, encouraging the acceptance and independence of chiropractic, and added, "The idea of providing chiropractic under medical referral has been rejected as being impractical." Despite Justice Hall's deference to Justice Lacroix's endorsement of chiropractic care, the medical monopoly and its anti-chiropractic stance remain intact 40 years later.

Not only have the American courts condemned the AMA's monopolistic practices as contrary to the public interest, Canadian authorities have commented as well. Appearing before a British Columbia Royal Commission in 1991, Jim Bocking, then the Acting Director of Investigations and Research for the Department of Consumer and Corporate Affairs in Ottawa, said, "In areas such as health care, unrestricted competition may not be the best alternative; that there may be a necessity for trade-offs and other concerns. Nevertheless, competition, or the absence of it, can have far reaching and important implications for both the quality and cost of health care." Bocking cited the United States antitrust case against the AMA with respect to chiropractic, as an example of traditional professions "engaging in practices that frustrate the growth of segment professions and that may result in higher health costs." He also cited the attempts by optometrists to control eyeglass sales and dentists to control the dental-related services of denturists and hygienists. Bocking concluded: "General powers to professions should be clarified so as not to unintentionally permit anti-competitive conduct."

One of Canada's foremost health economists is Dr. Pran Manga, a professor at the University of Ottawa, who played a key role in the creation of the *Canada Health Act*. The author of numerous important studies for governments, Royal Commissions, the United Nations, the World

Health Organization, and several sovereign states, he has also conducted studies concerning the use of chiropractic services. A 1993 study led by Dr. Manga demonstrated that the Ontario Health Insurance Plan (OHIP) would save hundreds of millions of dollars per year if more effective coverage of chiropractic was provided. These findings were reviewed and recommended to government by an expert panel chaired by the Hon. Tom Wells, a respected former cabinet minister. Dr. Manga revisited the study in 1998, concluding that the savings to the Ontario government would likely be $548 million per year. Extrapolated on a national basis, it could mean a savings of $2 billion a year.

Manga points out that medical doctors receive "little or no education at all about the back. Mistreatment results in needless and damaging use of both surgery and pharmaceuticals." Although Ontario has been one of the provinces that has included chiropractic services, OHIP did not aggressively embrace Manga's recommendations and accrue the benefits, and, in 2004, the province took a retrograde step. The new provincial Liberal government enraged the federal Liberal Party, on the eve of a national election, with dramatic increases to OHIP premiums, contrary to promises made during the Ontario election campaign. Among the other changes to the provincial medical insurance plan was a complete cancellation of patients' chiropractic coverage.

The Ontario government reported that eliminating chiropractic would save $47 million during the remainder of that fiscal year and almost $100 million for each year thereafter. Dr. Manga, who analyzed this announcement, was amazed by the breathtaking stupidity of the arithmetic. He pointed out that the alleged savings claimed by the Ontario bureaucrats — 100 percent of current chiropractic payments — assumed that the disenfranchised chiropractic patients would simply disappear. They would grudgingly pay the fees previously covered by insurance, irrespective of the rules of extended benefits plans or their personal financial means.

Obviously, Manga said, many of these patients and potential new patients who would benefit from chiropractic care, would seek relief through government funded medical services. The pain does not go away because a politician changes the regulations. Dr. Manga used words such as "ridiculous" and "unbelievably naive and simplistic" to characterize aspects of the Ontario decision. With confidence, he prophesied that the delisting of chiropractic services would cost Ontario at least $200 million to provide alternative health services (doctor fees, X-rays, drugs) to replace the $100 million worth of chiropractic services the government thought they would save. Patients would go to medical doctors instead, who are more expensive and less able to treat the condition.

The reasons for the overall increase in health care costs due to the delisting, and therefore marginalization, of chiropractic services include the following:

- it increases the queues and waiting times for government-insured medical care;
- it increases expenditures on drugs;
- it increases the use of emergency care services in hospitals;
- it increases the direct and indirect costs of treating neuro-musculoskeletal disorders and injuries;
- it imposes a heavier regressive financial burden on the low and middle income groups; and,
- it inhibits access to treatment of the disorders and injuries chiropractors treat.

In a 2004 interview, Dr. Manga said, "Indeed, the only beneficiaries of this retrograde policy is the medical profession and, through it, the pharmaceutical companies."

Romanow and Kirby
In 1994, the Prime Minister's Forum on Health spent $12 million and achieved nothing. Commissions, conferences, and inquiries have become one of Canada's most vibrant health industries. There have been countless provincial investigations and regular meetings of first ministers with health at the top of the agenda. The amount of time, energy, and money invested by every significant organization in the health field, employers' groups, chambers of commerce, unions, insurers, and compensation boards cannot possibly be measured. Not one patient has been made to feel better as a result of this ongoing and suffocating process.

Between 2000 and the end of 2002 the country was entertained by an estimated $20 million worth of federal investigations into health care in the form of parallel sorties by Senator Michael Kirby's Senate Standing Committee on Social Affairs, Science and Technology and former Saskatchewan Premier Roy Romanow's one-man commission on the "Future of Health Care in Canada." Ottawa admits to spending $15 million on the Romanow exercise. Kirby's committee spent a fraction of that amount and produced a report that had much more substance. (The oft-maligned Senate frequently assembles distinguished minds at virtually no cost and often trumps the value of outrageously expensive, politically motivated, and inevitably useless government extravaganzas. Senate salaries, travel expenses and much of the infrastructure are absorbed by routine budgets.)

The Senate Committee began its work during 2000 and made periodic reports, concluding in October 2002. Romanow was assigned in April 2001, and issued the commission's final report in November 2002. During the course of the work it often appeared as if the high profile national figures were dueling for attention. Kirby appeared to be more willing to break with health finance traditions, while Romanow preached a relentless stream of platitudes about protecting the public, the glories of the Canadian health system and the need to defend the status quo. They both advocated more money, albeit with improved accountability.

Boasting about one of the most "exhaustive" inquiries ever conducted into health care, Romanow said, "Our health outcomes, with a few exceptions, are among the best in the world." He advocated $15 billion more federal investment, including:

- a minimum of 25 percent of insured health services transferred to the provinces;
- a $2 billion national home care program;
- funds to improve access to care in rural areas;
- funds to improve services to aboriginal people;
- $1 billion to help those with huge drug bills;
- support for efforts to reduce waiting lists for diagnostic services.

Romanow urged more accountability and evidence-based decision-making. These are meaningless objectives unless facility managers can move patients to less expensive institutions (some of which will not meet the definition of a hospital under federal law), or home, with funding to support medical, nursing, and technical care in the home environment. Furthermore, without moderating the physician-patient control of costs, how can accountability be achieved? Doctors and patients are the principal determinants of costs to the medical plan. Presently, the merchant-doctor faces no competition, and the consumer-patient has a blank cheque for unlimited shopping.

"In their discussions with me, Canadians have been clear that they still support the core values on which our health care system is premised — equity, fairness and solidarity," Romanow wrote. "These values are tied to their understanding of citizenship. Canadians consider equal and timely access to medically necessary health care services on the basis of need as a right of citizenship, not a privilege of or status of wealth."

Although Kirby was as enthusiastic as Romanow in defending Canada's medicare program, his report was far more courageous and creative. Romanow proposed administrative solutions to systemic and structural problems, as well as additional dollars to be vested with the same bureaucrats, managers, and professionals who have dominated the process from the beginning of medicare. Neither Kirby nor Romanow touched the Holy Grail of the existing medical monopoly. They failed to acknowledge the patient's right to choose the most appropriate care for their own condition. Paying for one service and not another, without evidence to demonstrate optimal value and outcomes, rewards waste and incompetence.

The fact that Kirby's report was applauded in Alberta and was more controversial elsewhere are clues to its summary recommendations. In addition to an immediate $5 billion injection into the health care budget, and $10 billion over the next decade, Kirby touched off a debate by urging the option of more private health care services. His committee proposed deadlines for the public system to provide necessary care for specific cases, or a court could order coverage of private treatment elsewhere.

Other highlights of Kirby's report:

- a proposal to link health-care cash transfers to the GST, committing 3.5 percent of the tax to achieve a stable long-term flow of funds
- a National Health Care Council, independent of government control, to monitor the dispersal of funds
- $10 billion of federal funds to upgrade equipment for hospitals and community clinics
- a supplementary national insurance plan, costing nothing for those earning less than $31,677 and from $185 to $1,400 a year for others, depending on income, to cover recovery at home, prescription drugs and palliative care

Kirby, in public speeches, expressed alarm that some Canadians suffering long-term illnesses might be losing their homes and facing bankruptcy because of the rising costs of pharmaceuticals. The report proposed a catastrophic prescription drug program to assist individuals whose drug costs exceed $5,000 per year or three percent of their income. The proposed drug program also included a cost-sharing plan with the provinces to cover the drug costs for up to three months of post-surgery home care and palliative care.

Chiropractors, acupuncturists, optometrists, naturopaths, physiotherapists, massage therapists, nutritionists, nurse practitioners, paramedics, are part of a long list of professional caregivers who were patronized when they presented thoughtful briefs. Ultimately they were ignored and insulted in both Kirby's and Romanow's final reports. How could they possibly do anything but urge the millions of people they treat each year to question the reports and the process that generated them? The concept of patient-empowerment envisaged by the authors of the *Canada Health Act* — the freedom to choose among accredited health professionals — was ignored. The perversion of the "comprehensiveness" clause became more entrenched than ever. And predictably, the provinces unanimously endorsed the reports. They clearly advised Ottawa that they wanted more money and less meddling. End of story.

It is hard to read these 400-page tomes without asking why it cost $20 million for the sole purpose of promoting the health establishment's agenda. Virtually all of the witnesses — as well as the commissioners and support staff — whose recommendations made it into the final report, were on the public payroll anyway, paid handsomely to write briefs recommending more funds for themselves and their issues. How much thought could it have taken to recommend more money for the provinces and basic health coverage, pharmaceuticals, home care, diagnostic services, rural communities, and native health programs? The memo recommending Roy Romanow's appointment must have covered all of that.

The high cost of death

At the time of Ivan Illich's book, in the mid-1970s, few could have imagined how expensive the cost of modern medicine would become. While old epidemics have been conquered, AIDS, Alzheimer's disease, and the ailments of a large aging population seem to demand an inexhaustible source of funding. As taxpaying citizens, we demand access to every option of treatment or drug therapy for ourselves or our loved ones — if only to soothe our troubled conscience. Everything possible must be done. If this were purely humanitarian, there might be moral justification for such zeal and thoroughness. In fact, every remedy or procedure inflates the importance of those who provide it: the institutions, the people who run them, the suppliers of equipment and chemicals and, most notably, the physicians who attend each hospital death.

In *The Limits of Medicine*, Ivan Illich wrote, "Therapy reaches its apogee in the death-dance around the terminal patient . . . . conjuring doctor perceives himself as a manager of a crisis. In an insidious way he provides each citizen at the last hour with an encounter with society's deadening dream of infinite power. Like any crisis manager of bank, state or couch, he plans self-defeating strategies and commandeers resources which in their uselessness and futility, seem all the more grotesque."

"We prostrate ourselves on the altar of what the late Dr. Robert Mendelsohn of Chicago described as 'the Church of Medicine' and invite physicians to prospect all over our body in search of work. Report after report in modern times demonstrates that routine 'check-ups' with the local doctor are a waste of time and while advanced warning of certain illnesses can save lives, these scavenger hunts most often miss the serious and discover the unimportant, turning the latter into discomfort and, sometimes, disaster for the patient."

"People must be really sick here in Rosedale."

"Why is that Dearest?"

"It says we have five times as many doctors per capita than the national average."

2.
Faith and Miracles

Our health outcomes, with few exceptions, are among the best in the world, and a strong majority of Canadians who use the system are highly satisfied with the quality and standard of care they receive.

— ROY ROMANOW

Surveys and Statistics

An old joke reports a survey in which 80 percent of respondents said they believed most lawyers were crooks, but 92 percent were convinced that their lawyer was the exception. If the same questions were asked concerning the health professions, and most notably nurses and medical doctors, the apparent popularity is such that 80 percent or more would say they were great, and 92 percent would say the doctors and nurses they deal with are "the best."

In fact, in 2004, Leger Marketing surveyed Canadians' opinions of a large selection of professions and reported that 94 percent of Canadians believe nurses are doing excellent work, and 89 percent have the same opinion of medical doctors. Only firefighters received a higher rating.

American consumers must be tougher critics. A similar 2003 United States Gallup Poll surveyed Americans' opinions and reported lower approval ratings for all professions compared to the Canadian Leger survey results. Nurses topped the list with 79 percent, pharmacists scored 67 percent, and medical doctors scored 63 percent, which represented another drop in a continuing decline in their approval rating.

The faith in medical professionals is such that people spend more time doing research prior to their next car or cell phone purchase than they do before choosing a physician. There are no *Consumer Reports* rankings of doctors, there is no star-rating system as you find for hotels in a travel guide, and there are no Internet resources to guide us. It is difficult to find a GP who is taking new patients, and the wait-time for an appointment with a specialist can be months. People seem grateful be able to see anyone, never mind indulging in the luxury of researching relative levels of competence and expertise among practitioners.

Health care is broadly criticized in Canada these days, but the targets of criticism are rarely ever the professionals. People, both within and outside the professions, focus on flaws in the "system," presumably meaning governments, budgets, and bureaucracy. In the interactions between caregivers and their patients, positive energy prevails. The caregivers focus on the immediate task or problem and they approach their work with confidence and enthusiasm. However, when these same people are forced to deal with the business and political sides of medicine, this is not the case. Just about everybody is depressed.

There are turf wars everywhere. Registered Nurses are locked in a struggle with medical doctors who are doing everything in their power to prevent cost-effective nurse practitioners — nurses with advanced accreditation — from delivering some of the more basic care now greedily guarded by the MDs' monopoly. Doctors complain about the shortage of physicians, often seeking incentives to serve remote communities or to be "on call" by local hospitals. At the same time, they oppose anyone else stepping into the breach. Practical nurses and other caregivers in hospitals feel that they carry a disproportionate share of the workload, but receive insufficient pay and respect. Just about all of them are stressed-out by the pressures of the job, mostly due to the bureaucratic environment they have to work in rather than their patient caseload.

Studies for the past 20 years have advocated "closer to home" approaches to care, recognizing that home care is not only cheaper to deliver, but can actually enhance healing. Huge savings are projected if the system would finance only the level of care people need: home care rather than a rest home; a rest home rather than a nursing home; a nursing home rather than a private hospital; a private hospital rather than acute care; outpatient rehabilitation centres rather than hospitals; and, ambulatory care whenever appropriate.

The stakeholders are intransigent. Turf wars among health bureaucrats and professionals conspire to maintain the status quo. For example, health care unions strive to keep 100 percent of their members' jobs. Transferring blocks of patients from acute care to less costly neighborhood facilities often becomes a union negotiation focused on jobs, not patients. If the transfer does not result in any job losses, unions usually agree; if it does, there is a fight. Governments usually cave in. Once all the deals are made to protect the vested interests, the formerly cheaper facility has become just as costly as whatever it was supposed to replace.

"Home Care," may become the new front line of health delivery. There seems to be a template of phraseology, which has been used in every political speech and health study for the past 20 years, that speaks about how much we would save and how much healthier people would be, if we could care for them in their own home. But ask the home nurses, physiotherapists, occupational therapists, domestic care assistants, and health technicians who work in this field what they think about these pompous, cliché-ridden political speeches. They will tell you that the words are never backed up by money. This is because the money has to be extracted from budgets of the powerful (hospitals, bureaucrats, doctors, and unions) and transferred to the weak (home care infrastructure).

Another barrier to walking the talk is the spectre of private home care delivery. An entrepreneurial approach has made private home care service dazzlingly more effective — and appropriate —than the public system. The small business management model is successful where the service involves occupational or physiotherapy, respiratory equipment and oxygen technicians, domestic care workers, dieticians, or nurses. The traditional approaches of government and unions usually end up making home care just as expensive and insufferably bureaucratic as an acute care hospital where more time is spent on processing paperwork than caring for patients.

General practitioners feel they are getting the butt end in the health care debates and initiatives, including less support for their fees and working conditions than seems to be accorded the more glamorous specialties. The communities they serve are aging before their eyes. Most who remain in general practice will eventually become geriatricians. When they move or retire, there will be little or no equity value in their practice. When doctors retire at an older age, their practice tends to be comprised of fewer young patients and fewer patients in total; therefore, the practice has a lower billing volume.

The so-called "family physician" has become an anachronism. The traditional general practitioner took a holistic view of a patient. The doctor cared for parents, delivered babies, and comforted dying grandparents with the understanding that treating the individual meant treating the whole family. Often the intangibles were as important to health as any specific condition. This became so profoundly recognized that by the 1960s "Family Practice" had become an accredited specialty of medicine, requiring as much extra study as other specialties. However, family life has changed dramatically since the 1970s. Families break up and disperse. Patient mobility is a fact of modern life. People simply move a lot more than they used to. The family doctor has been left behind in the wake of all this change.

The walk-in clinic appears to be where we are headed. These no-appointment offices in shopping centres and other convenient locations dispense impersonal medical care that focuses more on the complaint than the individual. These clinics lend themselves to privatization — even within the rules of the *Canada Health Act*. Clinic owners (often doctors themselves) provide the facilities, equipment, receptionist, accounting, and management, while clinic doctors bill for the patient care and insured services. The doctors pay back either fixed charges or a percentage of billings to the owner.

The depersonalization of health care and the diminishment of family practice cannot possibly be a good trend. Three professors from the University of Toronto's Faculty of Medicine, Oswald Hall, Merrijoy Kelner and Ian Coulter, in a 1980 book titled *Chiropractors, Do They Help?* wrote:

> At the individual level, a person may discover that medical care is so highly specialized that it becomes necessary to seek out a different physician for each troubled organ, and no single practitioner is concerned about the totality of his health problems. The person may come to feel that there are numerous health practitioners who are prepared to deal with his illnesses, but none who are concerned with his health.

Another challenge to GPs comes from hospital management. Every time the political jurisdiction has a reorganization or rationalization of facilities GPs suffer dislocation. This happens with such frequency in every province, it may serve only to make bureaucrats and politicians feel needed. The hospitals where the doctors have visiting privileges may not be where their patients end up. They either have to waste professional time driving from hospital to hospital or hand off the patient to others. If a doctor has privileges at hospital A and government closes A then the doctor's patients must travel to hospital B. The continuity of the doctor-patient relationship is disrupted if the doctor has no attending privileges at hospital B.

The GP, more than anyone else in the health care field, suffers from the byproduct of the information age: the patient who arrives for a scheduled 10-minute appointment with 15 pages of information about their particular ailment downloaded from the Internet. Our present medical system rewards doctors for quantity, not quality. Therefore, the self-educated patient becomes an impediment to productivity and bottom-line economics.

Many doctors are angering their patients who ask for help about a problem other than the one for which the appointment was scheduled. "One issue per visit," is an annoying rule in too many doctors' offices these days. Can a system that rewards only quantity expect any better? "One issue per visit" is an abomination contrary to every principle upon which a quality, universal system is built. The only purpose of this practice is to generate more income for the physician. Instead of a comprehensive doctor-patient dialogue taking place, patient care ends up being fragmented by multiple visits.

Chats with patients cost money. This is a problem far easier to manage in the regimented environment of a hospital than in a physician's office. By the time a patient gets to a specialist or a hospital, the assignment is more structured and specific.

Nevertheless, the informed patient adds useful educational pressure, encouraging doctors to be better informed. Some health professions, such as doctors of chiropractic in some jurisdictions, require mandatory continuing education, but this is unusual for medical doctors. The relentless pace of emerging scientific developments, and changing standards of care, has forced specialists to keep current within their specialty. Conscientious doctors study the latest medical literature, track patient outcomes, and attend conferences and lectures — but most are not required to do so.

In an important 1993 study, Morris L. Barer, PhD, an economist and professor in the Department of Health Care and Epidemiology at the University of British Columbia, said:

> It had struck us as peculiar that, on the one hand, everyone seems to agree that the pace of medical knowledge and medical technology is indeed pretty remarkable. Yet on the other hand, everyone seems relatively complacent about the fact that we train physicians over periods of five to ten years, then we set them loose on patients for up to forty years and sometimes longer without even requiring that they demonstrate that they are keeping on top of this constantly changing knowledge and skill-base.

Regional distribution of services is a major challenge to health planners.

Like just about every other professional group, doctors congregate in urban areas, or anywhere else perceived to have either a superior lifestyle, affluence or, preferably, both. Interestingly, however, evidence indicates that the relative level of health of a population has little to do with the number of physicians that serve it. Health statistics in communities that appear to be short of physicians do not vary significantly from those that have too many. But doubling the number of doctors in an area can multiply health costs fourfold due to doctor-prescribed diagnostic procedures and pharmaceuticals. Where there is a shortage of doctors, optional but beneficial procedures such as hip replacements may not get done and people will suffer. On the other hand, they are spared the downside of modern health: dangers inherent in any form of treatment.

In his book *The Limits of Medicine: Medical Nemesis*, Ivan Illich discredited claims of the medical profession in sophisticated society for the conquering of disease and improved general health. He wrote:

> The fact that doctor populations are higher where certain diseases have become rare has little to do with the doctors' ability to control or eliminate them. It simply means that doctors deploy themselves as they like, more so than other professionals, and that they tend to gather where the climate is healthy, where the water is clean, and where people are employed and can pay for their services.

Much of the literature today, and a key thrust of this book points to failures within our health system:

- problems of bureaucracy
- unevenness of services
- the appearance that there is more concern for health professionals and workers than their patients
- overuse and abuse of pharmaceuticals
- the insensitive warehousing of seniors
- the paucity of home care programs
- malpractice
- greed
- questionable ethics by professionals with respect to drug companies and suppliers
- insufficient professional development

This all begs the question: if there are so many problems with our health care system, why does the public have so much faith in the professionals that run it? The answer can be found by exploring any of these issues to find heroes working diligently to make things better. If some of the medical doctors and health professionals are exploiting the system and exacerbating the problems, a far greater number of them are at the head of the pack in the quest for solutions. Name the problem and then search the web sites and libraries of professional associations, medical schools, and public agencies, and it can quickly be seen that the insiders know more about the problems than we do, and they are working toward solutions. Unfortunately, the ethicists and evangelists with respect to standards of care and best professional practices are far removed from the front lines of health care.

Therefore, there is a basis for faith in health professionals — certainly for many of the most accomplished practitioners — but the ideals get too easily discarded by the "business" of medicine. The "intent" of both government and practitioners cannot be faulted, but the practice leaves much to be desired. The "system" must be to blame then, and ultimately, in a democracy, that means all of us. We tend to demand too much of medicare and do too little in terms of optimizing our own health. But health professionals are people too, with all of the human frailties: a tendency to be self-serving, jealous, territorial, complacent, and quite capable of making serious errors. There is too much central control and too many monopolies within health care. In business, competition makes good things happen. The more we empower the public to make decisions about their own health — including the freedom to choose among a broader range of health care providers — and the more we use modern educational and promotional media to inspire good health habits, the better it will be for society.

Who are the champions?

One need only look at global population statistics to realize that the investment we make to extend our own lives by a year or two, and to make daily life more enjoyable, is — statistically speaking — a rather irrelevant extravagance. Were it not for the occasional plague and famine in third world nations and major international wars, we would already have lost even the theoretical ability to feed and serve a global population. Plagues and epidemics that decimated populations well into the twentieth century were defeated but, contrary to myth, in broad statistical terms, modern medical science has not achieved much with respect to the morbidity rates of the major killers: most cancers, heart disease, AIDS and more rare, but equally vexing, human conditions.

The real champions of health care are the people who work in public health. These include doctors, nurses, lab scientists, food inspectors, and water and sewer engineers. It is the global public health infrastructure — including the cities and towns of Canada — that has been responsible for improving the health of the greatest number of people at the lowest cost.

The recent Canadian experiences with the Walkerton water scandal, SARS, BSE (mad cow), and the avian flu epidemic thrust this usually low profile aspect of health care repeatedly into the headlines, not in a uniformly favorable light, but sufficiently so that we were reminded about their importance.

What has raised the rankings of the nations of western economies above other countries in terms of low infant mortality rates, longevity, and quality of life, are the following:

- improvements in water purification and sewage disposal
- better housing, clothing, and nutrition
- safe management of the food supply
- control of the infectious diseases of infancy and childhood
- development of vaccines and public immunization programs that protect against certain communicable diseases
- eradication of tubercular cattle
- incident reports, case studies, follow-up and education activities of health officers

Amid the politics of health care, we forget that many medical professionals never treat a patient, but often make contributions of greater worth. Among these are public health doctors in many agencies of local, provincial, and federal government; health and biological scientists; educators; pathologists; writers and broadcasters. The daily work of physicians in patient-practice interactions primarily treats a patient's symptoms but not their environment. Physicians who choose careers in public health instead of private practice can affect social and health policies resulting in a large scale prevention, reduction, or eradication of the cause of symptoms.

Other Ivan Illich excerpts emphasize this:

> . . . two things are certain: the professional practice of physicians can-
> not be credited with the elimination of old forms of morbidity, nor
> should it be blamed for the increased expectancy of life in suffering
> from new diseases. For more than a century, analysis of disease trends
> has shown that the environment is the primary determinant of the state
> of general health of the population. . . . One third of humanity survives
> on a level of undernourishment which would formerly have been lethal,
> while more and more rich people absorb ever-greater amounts of poi-
> sons and mutagens in their food.

The major breakthroughs of medical science and public health,
throughout recorded history, are remarkably few. In a 1998 Yale
University book *Medicine's 10 Greatest Discoveries*, MDs Meyer
Friedman and Gerald Friedland listed the following:

1. Andreas Vesalius and Modern Human Anatomy
2. William Harvey and the Circulation of Blood
3. Antony Leeuwenhoek and Bacteria
4. Edward Jenner and Vaccination
5. Crawford Long and Surgical Anesthesia
6. Wilhelm Roentgen and the X-ray Beam
7. Ross Harrison and Tissue Culture
8. Nikolai Anichkov and Cholesterol
9. Alexander Fleming and Antibiotics
10. Maurice Wilkins and DNA

Reading any chapter of the Friedmand/Friedland book, it becomes
apparent that each of these landmarks in medicine actually represents a
family of discoveries and discoverers. The theory and practices of sterile
medical procedures took several generations to evolve, led by Britain's
Lord Lister and France's Louis Pasteur, whose work in microbiology
became more famous than the discoverer, Leeuwenhoek. The development of medical equipment such as the microscope and the stethoscope
was revolutionary in its day. Canadians Frederick Banting and Charles
Best appear on most lists for the discovery of insulin.

No matter how much time one spends trying to add items to the list
of spectacular discoveries that changed the course of mankind, the list
still remains remarkably short. How can it be then that just about every

magazine and television newscast we view these days seems to be proclaiming some new wondrous discovery? Today's scientists may indeed
be as prolific as they seem, but we ought to keep a skeptical eye on the
media. Scientists need money to keep their research going. Publicity
helps. Each little advance justifies a news release. Pharmaceutical companies pump up sales of their products by promoting their brand names.
New biomedical companies raise capital and hike up their stock values
by constantly feeding the media with research updates.

The list of discoveries fails to mention the spectacular advances
made by surgeons. Patients and even fellow professionals marvel at the
dexterity and talent of the best surgeons, particularly as they perform
such delicate work as neonatal and neurosurgery. Beginning with Dr.
Christiaan Barnard in 1967, the transplant age has given many additional
years of productive life to tens of thousands of people. Heart, eyes, kid-
neys, lung, and liver — each successful transplant is a miracle. Others
who work in reconstructive surgery, those who reattach severed limbs, or
who achieve wonders in prosthetics, are also among the stars of medicine
who earn for their entire profession public admiration and respect. New
technologies and surgical methods have turned major surgeries into
minor procedures. Laser surgery and probes with microscopically thin
devices, guided by computer imaging, have become the source of new
miracles.

One of the most surprising areas of consistent medical excellence has
been the hospital emergency department. Despite overcrowding, relentless pressure, and often less experienced physicians than one would find
elsewhere in a hospital, the quality of work is usually outstanding. The
number of adverse events in emergency departments and outpatient services are disproportionately low compared to non-emergency based care
provided by hospitals. Here triage and the processing of patients occur
instinctively. Modern technology and the training of staff, paramedics,
and emergency workers throughout society have advanced significantly.
A Harvard study on adverse events in routine patient care recommended
that the philosophy of triage, used in emergency rooms, may be advan-
tageous everywhere. Start with the most serious issue that could produce
the obvious symptoms, and work backwards, doing only what is necessary to stabilize a patient. This was contrasted with routine doctor care
that typically featured speculative diagnoses and the liberal use of high
risk procedures.

The Canadian Association of Emergency Physicians is proud of the
performance of their members despite their having to deal with the

perennial problems of underfunding of emergency departments and over-crowding. Often patients get stored in the corridors of hospitals because there are no other beds for them to move to. People who have difficulty accessing medical care near their homes are using the hospital emergency room as a drop-in clinic, frequently for trivial matters.

Responding to a recent Ipsos Reid poll, which reported that 74 percent of Canadians were concerned about prolonged ER waits and deteriorating service, the association emphasized the following:

- On average, one patient "warehoused" in the ER denies access to the emergency department for four patients per hour.

- Between 1991 and 1997 the occupancy rate of acute care beds in Toronto hospitals exceeded 90 percent and peaked at 96 percent in 2000. Overcrowding in emergency departments exists only when bed occupancy rates exceed 90 percent.

- Estimates are that 10 to 25 percent of available, funded hospital beds are taken by so-called "bed blockers" — people who should be receiving care outside a hospital (e.g. in a long-term care facility or even at home). This blockage in hospital wards contributes to the backlog of patients waiting for admission in the emergency department.

- During 1999 there was a two percent increase in the number of patients who left the emergency department of an Ontario hospital without having been assessed by a physician.

- A Canadian study, by Dr. Michael Schull, of overcrowding and ambulance transport delays for patients with chest pain in Toronto has documented delays in the treatment for myocardial infarction patients and suggests that there is a correlation with the shortened survival of these patients.

- Statistics that track the incidence of ambulance redirects (also known as critical care bypass) in Toronto show a dramatic increase. This means time looking for alternate beds when the most obvious destination is unavailable: 49 hours (January 1996); 180 hours (January 1998); and 290 hours (January, 2000).

- The emergency department is a major access point to the health care system. In Ontario, in 1990 there were an estimated 3.4 million annual visits to the province's emergency departments. In 1993 that statistic rose to over 4 million visits, and in 1999 it had increased to 5.1 million.

The emergency physicians have appealed for a national standard of care. They report:

> The triage protocols used by every hospital in Canada ensure that the truly ill or those in need of urgent care will always be moved to the head of the line. Given the overcrowding situation behind-the-scenes in emergency departments, doctors and nurses must sometimes resort to seeing patients in the waiting room and administering treatment and tests (e.g. blood tests) there. Very few Canadians are at risk of being overlooked, even in a busy emergency department. Still, overcrowding definitely has an impact on patient care and operational efficiency.

■ ■ ■

Modern medical science has made extraordinary advances in the treatment of chronic disease and the ability to comfort patients. However, there is still no absolute cure for many diseases that are a consequence of an aging population. People are living long enough to get cancer, Alzheimer's, arthritis, and heart disease. Spending billions of dollars to research these diseases has achieved more for the advancement of human science than it has benefited individual patients.

The most tantalizing of all medical challenges, in the eyes of bio-chemical scientists, is AIDS. The disease demonstrates all of the properties that it one day may be conquered by a penicillin-like discovery, an injection that will kill whatever has neutralized the immune system, and let the healthy components of the blood go back to work.

The last item on the Friedman/Friedland top 10 list, the discovery of DNA, is the anchor point of the scientific revolution in genetics. We have embarked on a new era in medical history that anticipates many exciting, yet ethically-troubling opportunities. Genetic and genome research, advancing with the benefits of computer technology, represents the most dominant thrust of today's science worldwide. Listening to some of the more enthusiastic scientific reports, one can almost imagine the day when we go into a human tune-up shop for a genetic cocktail that will flush out the bad and regenerate the good, and, if that fails, plug in a new part.

Social planners have not yet been asked to plot the implications of vastly extended lives. It is still taboo to discuss the moral justification for pampering and artificially prolonging the lives of aging western citizens who are no longer productive or contribute significantly to society, while millions of impoverished people continue to die elsewhere from malnutrition and preventable — if not curable — diseases.

The curse of the cures

Sir Alexander Fleming, and other medical pioneers of the period 1850 to 1950, had no idea that they would be the architects of a miracle-pill society. Successes were so frequent and amazing that society came to expect that the doctor could fix anything, and if it could not be cured today, one would just have to wait awhile. This was great news for the medical charities, which started pounding out promotions such as "Cancer Can Be Beaten" even though the credibility gap between the promise of that statement and the reality was disturbingly broad. Millions of dollars poured in. Universities and laboratories used the same theme in their campaigns to attract funding for new research. No problem. We believed. And so did the politicians. Research continued and the cure for [fill in the blank] was just around the corner.

In at least one way, however, this chronic optimism had a negative impact: people assumed less responsibility for their own health. For pre-1950 generations, survival was often the only motivation behind any action or decision. They lived through world wars, the Great Depression, plagues, influenza, smallpox, diphtheria, scarlet fever, rheumatic fever, whooping cough, and polio. Fitness was assured by the rigors of hard physical labor and food was nutritious and simple. But, by the time a basic standard of living became guaranteed to most Canadians during the 1950s and 1960s, who worried about smoking, drinking, or eating too much? If these indulgences created a problem, the doctor could fix it. Miracles could be produced on demand. This became the cultural expectation.

But if our health slips, we have the drug companies and media to remind us that "every itch has a remedy." Billions of dollars worth of commercial bombast, punctuates news reportage about usually insignificant — but entertaining — research and new treatments. If you don't think you have anything wrong with you, pay attention to the media and they will soon remind you of something, but — lucky for you — they also promise a CURE! There is a pill for every ill, and a potion for every emotion.

Those who suggest that the Canadian Medical Association, the American Medical Association and far too many medical doctors are pompous and self-important, bathing in the inherited — but unearned — aura of Pasteur, Banting, Jenner, and Fleming, should not be too hard on them. We created the monster of assigned perfection.

Society expects doctors to be infallible and many people seem genuinely surprised whenever they are not.

"Doctors. Just because a bunch of whiners complain about 23,000 deaths a year caused by Canadian acute care hospitals, no one is blaming you. Those hospitals are just accident prone!"

3.
Adverse Events

A hospital is like a war. You should try your best to stay out of it. And if you get into it you should take along as many allies as possible and get out as soon as you can. For the amount of money the average hospital stay costs, you could spend an equal length of time at just about any resort in the world, transportation included. And unless your condition required emergency treatment, your health might be better off if you spent the time and money at the resort, too. For the hospital is the Temple of the Church of Modern Medicine, and thus one of the most dangerous places on earth.

— ROBERT MENDELSOHN, MD

Serious traffic accidents, particularly if there is an injury or loss of life, can paralyze whole freeways for several hours. Thousands of cars and commercial vehicles sit and wait, spewing carbon monoxide. People miss appointments, airline flights, and delay-caused business losses accumulate. Hospital, patient, and doctor schedules fly asunder. Everyone must wait while police, emergency crews, and expert accident investigators gather the evidence they need to determine the who, what, why, where, when, and how of the tragic event. Accuracy is thought to be far more important than either the cost or inconvenience caused to thousands of other citizens. It is important to be precise in the assignment of responsibility and, if facts dictate, blame. In order to do that, the investigation must take place right away, before evidence disappears.

In Canada each year, about 3,000 people lose their lives in highway accidents. Unfortunately, this great toll is a minor statistic compared to the tragic mistakes made within the health care system of the country. The "adverse events" study released in May, 2004, by the Canadian Institutes of Health Research (CIHR) and the Canadian Institute for

Health Information (CIHI) reported that as many as 23,750 deaths occur each year in Canadian acute care hospitals due to error, clearly preventable mistakes, most often due to surgery, infection, and drug reactions.

A truly alarming aspect of these numbers is that all of the data came from medical charts, and not from any independent assessment of the circumstances. In other words, those who committed the mistakes and their associates were the only sources of evidence. A similar American study stated bluntly, "Only 5-20 percent of iatrogenic events (medically caused) are ever reported." If all this is not sufficiently chilling, the Canadian study analyzed only a representative sample of acute care hospitals, and based its findings on 2.5 million admissions each year. Of these, 7.5 percent (185,000 admissions) suffered an adverse event, which extended their stay in hospital or resulted in death. In addition to the human carnage, the financial waste is staggering.

Acute care hospitals represent only one slice of the total health business. Procedures performed in clinics, diagnostic centres, physicians' offices, nursing homes, psychiatric institutions, and an array of other health centres, were not included in the study, and represent a far bigger area of concern. No one has the slightest idea how many iatrogenic errors might be uncovered if the entire field of medicine were to be studied, particularly if the same forensic intensity were applied that is accorded highway accidents and crime scenes. A controversial American paper entitled *Death by Medicine* (Null et al.) assembled all of the data from respected research agencies covering the full gamut of health care, including senior citizens' homes. The paper concluded that adverse events currently cause 783,000 deaths per year. All official U.S. sources admit to 100,000 deaths per year as a result of medical mistakes and over 100,000 as a result of drug interactions.

What is most shocking is that this epidemic surprises no one who works within the health system. Managers of the best long-term care facilities now routinely perform thorough examinations of their residents before they go to acute care hospitals. It is standard practice to count any bruises, wounds, or abrasions before they depart. One executive of a multiprovincial long-term care corporation said in an interview that patients invariably have "more wounds on their body" after a hospital visit than before they went. Regular complaints seem to do little to improve the situation. These minor cuts and bruises may be the result of careless handling in hospitals or even self-injury as a result of insufficient monitoring. But they do demonstrate indifference and a system that too often regards patients as merchandise, something to process and accommodate.

Following the May release of the Canadian report, media scrambled to interview doctors and hospital administrators across the country. The interviewees made all the right noises about it being a "wake up call," and the "need to be more vigilant," and so on, but there was not the slightest sense of surprise, shame, or embarrassment. The indifference was overwhelming: "Germs go with the territory," some said. "It's because government doesn't provide sufficient funding," was heard in some quarters.

It is not unreasonable to estimate that mistakes within the entire Canadian health system may be inadvertently or negligently killing 50,000 people a year or more, rivaling heart disease and cancer as the greatest threats to life. No one knows the exact number, because the formal adverse events investigation focused only on a narrow slice of total medical-pharmacological care in the country. If documented American numbers can be used as a guide, 50,000 may be conservative. This compares to 3,000 deaths due to car accidents and about 500 as a result of crime. Yet, despite this high fatality rate, iatrogenic errors receive the least investigative attention of any other cause of death. The reason for this is that the evidence and motivation required for a thorough investigation must come from the same culture as the one that made the errors in the first place.

Only in the relatively rare instances of formal inquests or malpractice actions is there any independent investigation of cause, and then only a considerable time after the event. In these instances, the investigators are dependent upon the formal records maintained by those who, in all likelihood, were party to the misadventure.

Medical nightmares

Among the first to sound the alarm in Canada was Penticton, B.C., coroner Susan B. McIver, whose 2001 book *Medical Nightmares: The Human Face of Errors*, estimated 10,000 Canadians die as a result of medical errors in hospitals. She argued that medical errors usually result not from one person's recklessness, but from communication breakdowns, fragmented care, inadequate supervision of medical staff, and the fact that when family members raise concerns, they are too often ignored.

The Kansas-born McIver, who has a PhD in entomology, was a professor at the University of Toronto for 17 years with appointments to the Faculty of Medicine. Her book lets patients tell their own stories, a sad litany of confusion, inefficiency, tunnel vision by doctors, and outright incompetence. Exhaustively outlining 33 different case histories, Dr. McIver dramatically personalized what the health system attempts to write off as an institutional quality control statistic.

The most important part of her title is the phrase "The Human Face of Errors." Publicity about the all too frequent medical horror show portrays the "inadvertent and unfortunate" as being the result of a third-party conspiracy of extraterrestrial spirits. The reality is that every case represents the legislatively enshrined responsibility of one doctor in a relationship with one patient. No matter whose blunder it was that resulted in tragedy, one doctor is responsible, and if that physician's patient was hurt by other caregivers or technical failures, it is the absolute duty of that doctor to become the patient's advocate. The doctor should take the view that he or she has been victimized along with the patient, and fight like hell to find out the truth, hold the perpetrators to account, and seek justice.

What becomes obvious when researching incidents of medical error is that the interests of patients come dead last — and the word "dead" is all too appropriate. "Shoddy medical care has been shrouded in secrecy," Dr. McIver said. Doctors, medical associations, the lawyers they hire, hospitals, and an impenetrable wall of health bureaucrats who passionately "see no evil," conspire to protect the perpetrators of all but the gravest and most obvious calamities. Self-regulation and self-policing, the prerogative of the medical establishment, is used to systemically suffocate thorough investigations.

The CIHI-CIHR study

In May 2004, the Canadian Institutes of Health Research (CIHR) and the Canadian Institute for Health Information (CIHI) published their study called *Adverse Events in Canadian Hospitals*. The report received intense media coverage, which focused on the same startling statistics in story after story — medical errors are responsible for as many as 23,750 deaths in Canadian acute care hospitals every year. Since media stories require the distillation of large volumes of text and data into relatively few words, the process ensures that statistics emerge out of context. Therefore, the highly credentialed people who conducted the investigation would view excerpts from their text and the use of numbers without context, as misleading. This important effort is worthy of a closer examination.

In 2002, Dr. John Millar, CIHR vice-president of research made the following remarks as he announced the beginning of the study:

> We have very limited reliable data on adverse events in Canadian hospitals and there are no systems in place to routinely collect data that are necessary for ongoing monitoring. This study will provide us with baseline data on the extent of this problem in Canada. . . . We are hopeful that the study's results will provide the impetus for action to seriously address the quality of care. . . . There is an urgent need to develop indicators, data definitions, standards and systems to collect data on adverse events (which should also include near misses, hospital-acquired infections and the adverse effects of drugs).

The adverse events study was led by Dr. Ross Baker, Associate Professor, Health Policy, Management and Evaluation at the University of Toronto and Dr. Peter Norton, Professor and Head of the Department of Family Medicine at the University of Calgary. Seven universities participated.

Highlights of the Report

- an "adverse event" is defined as an unintended injury or complication resulting in death, disability or prolonged hospital stay caused by health care management rather than the patient's underlying condition.
- 3,745 adult patient charts — not including pediatric, obstetric or psychiatric admissions — were randomly selected from 20 acute care hospitals across five provinces (B.C., Alberta, Ontario, Quebec and Nova Scotia).
- the overall rate of adverse events in the year 2000 was 7.5 per 100 patient admissions (185,000 out of 2.5 million medical and surgical admissions).
- the majority of adverse events resulted in temporary disability or prolonged hospital stay.
- five percent of patients (9,250) who experienced adverse events were judged to have a permanent disability.
- adverse events were associated with death in 1.6 percent of patients admitted to acute care hospitals (40,000).
- surgical care accounted for the largest number of adverse events.

- expert reviewers considered 37 percent of adverse events (70,000) to be "highly preventable."

- most patients recovered from adverse events within six months, but between 9,250 and 23,750 people across the country died, possibly as a result of the event.

- teaching hospitals had a higher rate of adverse events than other hospitals. The authors concluded that patients with more complex illnesses may be treated in teaching hospitals and that the complexity of care in teaching hospitals means patients may be attended by several providers, increasing the potential for adverse events relating to communication and co-ordination of care.

Upon release of the study, Baker said, "The good news is, this study gives hospitals a clearer picture of the scope and nature of this issue and will help them to determine why these problems are occurring and to develop strategies to address them." Norton added: "It would be a mistake to focus on the performance of individual health care providers when interpreting these findings. We recommend that hospitals and health providers focus on system-wide changes — such as ensuring that medications don't look or sound alike — to reduce the number and likelihood of adverse events."

However, the true bottom line is far worse than anything contained in this report. The CIHI-CIHR study focused on a narrow segment of medical care, which did not include pediatric, obstetric, or psychiatric admissions. Research from other jurisdictions demonstrates that only a fraction of iatrogenic errors are ever reported in the first place and no detached professional investigator would have much confidence in records kept only by those involved in the situation. They would be skeptical about potential omissions and the "spin" given negative incidents on medical charts.

Another world

Among the impressions Canadians often have after spending time in the central cores of major American urban centres, is how frequent and cacophonous are the sirens. It's as if some kind of bizarre musical score had been written for that moment's urban tapestry. Because we watch so much American film in theatres and on television, we naturally assume that this must be a reflection of crime and violence.

Not so. The noise is often the sound of competition among local hospitals, many of them private for-profit hospitals. Ambulances play a role in acquiring business. Anecdotal evidence suggests that many hospitals encourage their ambulances to look for business. Every city and state is different and almost every one of them has suffered the embarrassment of fights among ambulance drivers at the scene of a tragedy. There have been scandals concerning police officers being paid a commission for directing emergency business to certain hospitals. As a result, each city has developed a system to achieve order out of the mayhem, so it is not quite as wild and woolly as what is described here. Nevertheless, patient prospecting by ambulance attendants at the scene of crimes, fires, and accidents is standard operating procedure and a business gamble. *The New York Times* and many other journals have exposed "steering" by private ambulances, which is a term used to describe bypassing the nearest hospital in order to get the most profitable patients, or dumping uninsured patients elsewhere.

The gamble is this: 45 million Americans, including 20 million working people and 8.5 million children, currently do not have health insurance of any kind. U.S. Medicaid (uninsured poor) and Medicare (handicapped and the elderly) cover large segments of the population with basic services and everybody with good jobs has medical coverage ranging from adequate to the best in the world. The problem for hospitals is the other population of 45 million people who are uninsured. The law in most states obligates hospitals to treat all patients that arrive at their door.

So, when an ambulance arrives at an affluent, often doctor-owned, private hospital, fingers are crossed that it is not one of those folks. The hospital is required to treat and stabilize the patient but, while that is going on, wallets are checked to determine insurance coverage and whether there are a few gold and platinum credit cards. By the time the patient knows where he is, he's either being treated like royalty or, if the condition permits, he's back in the ambulance on the way to a local charity hospital. Everybody in the U.S. can get care at no cost, but the resources at the state, county, and charity hospitals — often the largest in the region — can be hit or miss.

As the world's most affluent nation, the United States invests more per capita in health care than any other country (14 percent of Gross Domestic Product, compared to 10 percent in Canada). Despite enjoying a disproportionately high percentage of top health facilities and professionals, Americans are the only people in the industrialized world who do not benefit from universal health care. Even working families with good health plans live in constant fear of a catastrophic event. Coverage has been progressively cut back by Health Maintenance Organizations (HMOs) as costs have soared for drugs, diagnostic services, hospitals, and health providers, and when a person changes jobs, medical coverage for any chronic ailment diagnosed during the last employment is usually not transferable to the new plan. This means that as workers age and acquire arthritis, diabetes, high blood pressure, chronic back pain, or any one of a long list of common conditions, care for them and their families might be exempted under a new plan. This often forces people to cling desperately to bad jobs, and makes downsizing and the elimination of redundancies more difficult, emotionally and financially, for employers.

Soaring drug prices have, for the first time in years, brought some of that terror back to Canada. Those diagnosed with chronic illnesses requiring the most expensive of drugs could face bankruptcy. A subdued, but persistent tremor is rocking the foundation of all insurance plans, private and public, and drugs have become the top policy priority for government leaders.

National health care is always near the top of the political agenda in U.S. elections, but the American Medical Association, the Health Maintenance Organizations, the major insurers, the hospital corporations, the pharmaceutical companies, and equipment suppliers, eventually purchase whatever decision they wish the politicians to make. There are never any substantive changes. This wealthiest of nations with the most abundant of health resources, is invariably quite a few pegs down the list when the health of its citizens is compared to other countries. The U.S. is far behind in every category and dramatically so when comparisons are drawn between rich and poor, and among ethnic groups. Perhaps the most revealing statistic is in its rate of infant mortality (death within the first year of life): the U.S. ranks 24th among developed countries, just ahead of South Korea, with 6.69 infant deaths per 1,000. Canada is 15th at 4.95. But the damning American statistic is the infant mortality among blacks at a rate of 14 per 1,000, 77th in the world, right with Belarus and Bulgaria.

Death by Medicine

When one studies the tragedies in the U.S. caused by needless surgery or operating room mistakes, pharmaceuticals, and the other misadventures of medicine, it would appear that there is a silver-lining to the lack of equal access to health care for the American poor. Those who cannot afford either drugs or surgery, at least have the benefit of avoiding being either exploited for profit or mishandled. The negative outcomes of vanity medicine such as breast implants, for example, have not been big issues in the ghetto. But there are other dreadful American statistics: studies in 1995 and 1997 concluded that 115,000 people die each year from bedsores; and a year 2000 investigation pegged malnutrition as the cause of 108,000 needless deaths per year. Both statistics involve predominantly the poor and the elderly, indicating a lack of basic nursing and domestic care in the United States which has produced an annual death toll 70 times worse than the World Trade Center catastrophe — and the kind of data one might expect from Third World nations.

These are among the findings in a paper entitled *Death by Medicine*, which is often cited wherever iatrogenesis, adverse health events, and the frailties of medical science are discussed. The most cursory of Internet searches into any of these terms will deliver multiple addresses in which this paper is featured, often a listing within other health professional sites.

The authorship of this classic reference title is a list of nutrition-oriented and orthomolecular physicians and PhDs, led by author, media host, and relentless fitness promoter, Gary Null, PhD, founder of the 30-year-old New York nonprofit organization, the Nutrition Institute of America. Critics of *Death by Medicine* seem to delight in trashing Null's academic credentials and, for entertainment purposes, it is worthwhile for anyone to check two web sites: *www.garynull.com* and *www.quackfiles.com*. The first web site demonstrates Null's talent for self-aggrandizement and his enthusiasm and passion for flagellating the establishment. The second website is a response to Null's criticisms written in an even more inelegant and less credible fashion. The rhetoric on these sites is irrelevant to the key issue. What becomes obvious, however, is that Null et al.'s detractors are unable to attack the content of this paper, so they are assaulting the authors instead.

What makes *Death by Medicine* an astounding document is the meticulous assembly of peer-reviewed literature by distinguished authors with impeccable credentials, under the auspices of Harvard University, the *Journal of the American Medical Association*, the Center for Disease Control, the *New England Journal of Medicine*, the World Health Organization, *Psychiatric Times* and many other prestigious addresses.

This is what *Death by Medicine* claims to be the estimated annual mortality as a result of mistakes by conventional medicine in the U.S.:

- Adverse drug reactions   106,000
- Medical error   98,000
- Bedsores   115,000
- Infection   88,000
- Malnutrition   108,800
- Outpatients   199,000
- Unnecessary procedures   37,136
- Surgery-related   32,000

TOTAL   **783,936**

The authors estimate the annual cost related to the above numbers, both in the creation of the problem and the management of what follows, to be a waste of $US 282 billion per year. In fact, they believe these numbers understate the issue. Despite efforts to write off Null and associates as "health nuts" and zealots, obsessed with bashing the medical establishment, their conclusions get solid support from official agencies, such as health research libraries nation-wide and the National Institutes of Health. Each of these report worrisome statistics involving medical mistakes, hospital deaths, overuse of pharmaceuticals, incorrect prescriptions, fatal interaction of drugs and access delays for emergency cases. While every number is subject to debate, no one doubts the enormity of the problem.

One of the most noted authorities in the world on iatrogenesis is Harvard's Dr. Lucien L. Leape, who is an expert on the subject of truth in reporting medical mistakes. He claims that 5-20 percent are reported and all the others are quickly forgotten. If Leape's calculations were used, the figure of 783,000 annual deaths by error reported in *Death by Medicine* would become closer to one million. During the late 1990s, Leape estimated that 420,000 deaths occurred each year due to iatrogenic errors.

Dr. Leape, a surgeon and former Professor of Surgery at Tufts University, is not as condemnatory as the numbers he researched would indicate. He said the following in a 2001 interview with *Managed Care Magazine*.

Until recently, health leaders didn't know how bad the situation was, and health care was locked into the wrong paradigm for ensuring safety. People seem to think this issue has been around forever, but the first research results were published just 10 years ago. . . . That study showed 3.7 percent of people had an adverse event or injury caused by treatment, nearly two thirds of which were caused by errors. But that was just a single study, so it didn't receive a lot of attention.

Leape cited several celebrated cases: a chemotherapy overdose, a wrong leg amputation, brain surgery on the wrong side of the head . . . .

These cases came out just about the time we started talking about a different way to look at safety. That raises the second point. Until recently, we in health care thought that we had an effective way to ensure safety. The concept was that if you're well-enough trained and careful enough, you won't make mistakes. If you do, we'll punish you and then you'll be more careful the next time.

People had never really questioned that approach. Eventually that was called into question and we said, "Look, industries that are much safer than we are don't do it that way." The concept that errors are always with us but can be minimized by looking at systems rather than just focusing on punishing people who make mistakes was a brand-new idea in health care. That approach has been adopted only in the last six years, so I think we've moved very rapidly, all things considered, during that period.

Many of us think that the punitive mindset is the biggest obstacle that still exists in most health care institutions. It's very hard to overcome. The theory behind a nonpunitive approach is very straightforward: It's inappropriate to punish people for making mistakes because very few are due to misconduct. Errors are almost always caused by systems failures, and those are not under the control of the individual who makes the error. Punishing people is counterproductive, because if you punish people for making errors, they will report only the errors they can't hide. Several studies show that when there is a punitive environment, 95 percent or more of errors do not get reported. We also know that when the system changes, reporting goes up dramatically. We've seen that happen in a number of hospitals. If you're serious about safety, you need to know what's going on, and you're not going to find out what's going on if you punish people. The two cornerstones of safety are, one, creating an environment where it's safe for people to talk about their errors and, two, leadership.

Statistics would indicate that Dr. Leape's forgiving tone and compassion among doctors toward each other is embedded in the medical culture, but so is malpractice. Public Citizen Health Research Group analyzed the data and came to the conclusion that repeat offenders are rarely ever disciplined: "A small percentage of doctors are responsible for the bulk of malpractice in the United States, and better oversight by state medical boards could drastically reduce the damage they cause. . . . about five percent of the doctors in the United States are responsible for half the malpractice." Public Citizen said this meant that 40,118 doctors have paid two or more malpractice awards to patients, were responsible for 51 percent of all reports and paid out nearly $US 21 billion in damages, more than 53 percent of the total damages paid since 1990. An additional 14,293 doctors have paid three or more malpractice awards, totaling $US 11 billion. The study cited 6,000 doctors who had each paid out six or more claims and all of them were still practicing!

"Rather than a random, lottery-like pattern, this distribution very much resembles the pattern of drunk driving recidivism," Public Citizen said. "Negligent doctors are rarely disciplined with loss or suspension of their license for inferior care. Instead, state medical boards focus on more easily documentable offences such as prescription drug violations and fraud convictions or disciplinary action in another state as potential indicators of substandard care."

One Pennsylvania surgeon with 24 separate malpractice claims for incompetently hacking patients, has never been disciplined by the State of Pennsylvania and, in fact, is still performing his dubious services. Every health professional in the area knows this ongoing disaster, but few patients ever get warned before it is too late. During a recent criminal prosecution of a gynecologist in England, it became known that he had practiced in different cities in Canada and the U.K., leaving a trail of devastation, maimed patients and malpractice suits behind him, everywhere he had been.

In each case, the local College of Physicians and Surgeons seemed to be content to send him packing, leading media editorialists and other critics to suggest that they were more worried about the public relations damage than patients. These cases are extreme and - mercifully - rare, but what is true of every hospital is that the professionals who work within them know that the skill levels and success rates vary greatly among doctors and there are some who should be avoided at all cost. Patients are invariably kept in the dark.

The double standard

When there is the slightest hint that any individual health professional, other than a physician — nurse, midwife, physiotherapist, podiatrist, naturopath, dietician, optometrist, pharmacist — has been responsible for a harmful outcome, the medical profession pumps itself up like a Goodyear Blimp with sanctimonious, derogatory judgments. Here is where the Canadian Medical Association, the American Medical Association, and the limitless number of derivative specialized professional organizations attempt to prove how hard they work to protect the public, and why society must give them the powers of a god and the wealth of Midas. The best salvos are saved for chiropractic. This is the profession that poses the greatest threat to their business. Most of the five million Canadians who regularly see a chiropractor had previously been unsatisfied patients of medical doctors, who are consistently unable to successfully treat the neuro-musculoskeletal problems upon which chiropractic education is focused.

The principal battleground chosen by the medical doctors is the subject of neck manipulation, the chiropractic treatment for problems of the upper cervical spine. Millions of patients worldwide have obtained help for whiplash, neck pain, migraine headaches, and ancillary issues stemming from the central nervous system. Some neurologists believe this practice is dangerous and can cause strokes. They suggest that neck manipulation runs the risk of damaging arteries going to the brain, ignoring the fact that chiropractic doctors spend years in training for all the procedures they perform.

Before continuing upon this theme, it should be noted that the most conservative scientific study of chiropractic neck manipulation established that the risk of stroke from the treatment is one out of every 400,000 patients. A study in the October 2, 2001 issue of the *Canadian Medical Association Journal* put this risk at one patient in 5.85 million. Contrast that to the facts presented earlier in this chapter — between four and nine out of every 1,000 patients entering an acute care hospital in Canada will die because of a preventable medical mistake. The risk factor for chiropractic neck manipulation shows that it is safer than taking Aspirin. The risk of stroke caused by birth control pills is one in 24,000. This means the birth control pill is from 16 to 240 times more dangerous than chiropractic neck manipulation.

Other scientific studies have documented the high rate of deaths and disabilities that result from common medical procedures, including a one out of 200 mortality rate for laminectomies and a two in 100 mortality rate for spinal fusions. One out of every 145 cervical neck surgery procedures end in death. And in a study of 1,000 workers' compensation patients who received lumbar fusions, 71 percent of single-operation patients had not returned to work four years after their operation, and 95 percent of multiple-operation patients had not returned to work. They remain disabled.

No one in the chiropractic profession has ever denied the potential risk associated with the procedure and ethics require the patient to be fully informed. Strokes have occurred. There are many risk factors for stroke including blood clotting problems, hypertension, smoking, high cholesterol, use of birth control pills, heart disease, and trauma such as sport injuries or blows to the head from an accident. All carry a greater degree of risk than spinal adjustment. Strokes or stroke-like symptoms are also associated with many normal everyday activities such as cradling a phone between your ear and shoulder during a prolonged conversation, having your hair washed at a beauty salon, dental procedures, painting a ceiling, and turning your head while driving. They can also occur spontaneously in some people for no apparent reason. The physicians' routine approaches are far more threatening. Death as a result of long-term use of nonsteroidal anti-inflammatory drugs (NSAIDs) such as Aspirin, Naproxen, Ibuprofen, or Motrin is one in 1,200 persons. Surgeries for neck and back pain cause 15,600 cases of paralysis or stroke and 700 deaths per million.

Insurers are the ultimate referees of risk. Malpractice insurance premiums for chiropractors in Canada average $1,000 a year, while the medical doctors average about $5,000. Most surgeons, particularly in high risk areas such as cardiology, neurology, obstetrics, and orthopedics, pay $25,000–$90,000 a year each. Rates are cheapest in Quebec where claims are low and are the most expensive in Ontario. The argument is moot since the provinces reimburse the MDs for most of this cost, a benefit awarded no other health professional. This inexplicable subsidy amounts to a free pass in view of the high costs of litigation faced by aggrieved patients. But the premium rates and claims statistics demonstrate to insurance actuaries the source and extent of risk. They must sit back with amusement wondering that physicians have the gall to condemn other health professionals.

Is the concern money or patients?
Based on the evidence, the attack on chiropractic is fraudulent nonsense,

unless the motive is something other than health. Paranoid chiropractors suggest a conspiracy purely based on money, a fear campaign to drive patients away from their profession. If that is the purpose, then the neurologists can pat themselves on the back. In every jurisdiction they seem able to attract as much media attention to chiropractic complaints as is usually reserved for mass murder. The fact that there is one death remotely related to chiropractic care in contrast to thousands on the other side of the equation, seems to be of no concern to gullible reporters.

This brings us to the mystifying case of Lana Dale Lewis, a 45-year-old from Toronto who died of a stroke in 1996. The mystery is why members of the Canadian Stroke Consortium — another physicians' lobby — chose this specific case as the line in the sand? Ms. Lewis was overweight, a heavy smoker and drinker, who suffered from what was described as "uncontrolled hypertension." She had, over the years, been treated with various drugs. There was a history of heart disease in her family. She suffered from severe arteriosclerosis. Her medical doctor was unable to help her manage migraine headaches so she sought the services of a chiropractor. For 18 months she received chiropractic care and consistently reported fewer and less severe headaches, but 17 days after one of these sessions, she died. Her family, encouraged by local medical doctors, blamed the chiropractor.

Nothing much happened until another Canadian case made the news in 1998. For the first time in the 103-year history of chiropractic in Canada, a patient had died as a result of an event during the course of treatment. An artery ruptured and the 20-year-old Saskatchewan patient was rushed to hospital — too late to save her. An inquest heard evidence that this woman ignored her chiropractor's advice, and would routinely give herself neck adjustments. (In order for patients to do this themselves, more physical contortion is required, leading to a less accurate process and a more severe physical jolt than what is administered by professionals.) In the end, the jury determined only that the cause of death was a rupture of the left vertebral artery, but did not address causation. They made a number of useful recommendations for the further study of neck treatments.

One outcome of the Saskatchewan case was the motivation it provided to the Lewis family and those determined to attack chiropractic. This was the case upon which they would build a media circus. They demanded an inquest. Unfortunately, in 2000, the local coroner did not agree. He determined that the facts of the case were self-evident and that an inquest would be a waste. But the Consortium, the family, neurologists, and others continued to lobby the media, public servants, and politicians for an inquest. It was rejected a second time, before finally, in 2002, an inquest was announced by the Chief Coroner of Ontario. Through various stops and starts, often dictated by the schedules of expert witnesses from other countries, it took until January 2004 before a final verdict was announced. The jury of lay people concluded that the death was an accident set in motion by the chiropractic treatment 17 days earlier. This inquest also announced recommendations for the study of neck treatment by all health professions.

It was a pyrrhic victory at best for the critics, including the Canadian Stroke Consortium. Frequently at the centre of anti-chiropractic fervor over the years has been Dr. Murray Katz, a Montreal pediatrician. Katz has traveled the world for more than 25 years lecturing and testifying as an "expert" wherever he feels needed. The regularity of his travels and the inexhaustible availability of his professional time have raised questions about who must be paying the bills. In 1978, his testimony before a New Zealand commission — which concluded in favor of chiropractic — was totally repudiated. The commission said about Katz: "It is disappointing to find that a practicing medical practitioner could think it right to indulge in a deliberate course of lies and deceit of that kind."

In fact, the New Zealand Commission was so appalled by Dr. Katz's performance it devoted an entire chapter to him in their final report presented to Parliament by the Governor General.

> We think the kindest thing to say is that Dr. Katz has become so emotionally involved in his self-appointed role as a 'concerned advocate of consumer rights' that over a period of some years he has allowed his enthusiasm to override his judgment, his sense of reality, and his sense of what is proper. In his evidence in chief he was voluble, and we are satisfied that he found it difficult to distinguish between the role of expert witness and that of an advocate. In cross-examination he tended to be evasive. . . . Having regard to the matters we have specifically mentioned, and to Dr. Katz' general demeanour as a witness as we observed him during the three days of his submissions and evidence, we are abundantly satisfied that it would be quite unsafe to rely on his opinions, or on any of his evidence on matters of fact which were not completely verified from an independent and reliable source.

Although helpful in fanning the fires that led to the Lewis inquest, he was discredited right at the start. Katz acted as the Lewis family's legal agent and attempted to get status before the inquest in that capacity. After this was denied, Coroner Barry McLellan blocked a subsequent attempt by Katz to gain legal standing as an individual, separate from the family. In support of his decision, McLellan referred to earlier behavior by Katz. Katz had warned a specific coroner that there would be dire personal consequences if an inquest was not approved. The coroner said he was upset by Katz's "threatening letter to a public official," and "behavior inconsistent with what the public should expect of an agent of a party with standing." Katz would ultimately express his opinions as a witness in the inquest.

But the key figure for the Canadian Stroke Consortium was its past-Chair, Dr. John Norris, a neurologist from Sunnybrook Health Centre in Toronto. Dr. Norris had a habit of saving his best material for the media, with far more colorful language and alarming statistics than he was able to present at the inquest. Katz and Norris were among 60 doctors — most of them neurologists — whose names were on a study warning about the dangers of neck manipulation. Some of these doctors later protested that they had not endorsed the paper and had not agreed to let their names be used. Contrasting the critics, lawyers representing the chiropractic profession and the Ontario coroner's service brought in a battery of expert witnesses, each of whom had outstanding credentials.

The chief of neurology at St. Michael's Hospital, Dr. Richard Moulton; neurologist Dr. Scott Haldeman of the University of California; pathologist Dr. Michael Pollanen, consultant to the Coroner's Office; and, prominent orthopedic surgeon Dr. Hamilton Hall, all testified that, in their expert opinion based on a review of all the medical evidence, Ms. Lewis died of natural causes completely unrelated to her chiropractic treatment.

But the most devastating contradiction of the critics' case came from internationally-acclaimed epidemiologist Dr. David Sackett, an officer of the Order of Canada and member of the Canadian Medical Hall of Fame. He described Dr. Norris as "incompetent" in scientific research and "irresponsible" with regard to the Canadian Stroke Consortium's work attributing strokes to neck adjustment. Dr. Sackett pointed out that Dr. Norris had publicly misrepresented the Consortium's study and that it was not a prospective study as Norris had claimed, but a series of cases which Dr. Sackett explained are highly prone to bias and "can't begin to address causation." A prospective study researches events that are going to happen, which is a more objective approach, as opposed to what Norris had done, which was to go find events which had already occurred and then make claims on their reporting after the fact. Dr. Sackett characterized Norris's description of the study as "scientifically nonsensical .... he's incompetent as a scientist in the study of causation." Dr. Sackett added: "I think he has contributed nothing of scientific value . . . he has caused enormous confusion."

The quality, accuracy, and intent of the Consortium study were exposed under cross-examination. During the course of his own testimony, Norris was confronted with the remarks he had made to the media. He retracted, under oath, numerous statements about the risk of stroke from adjustment of the neck. In various comments, Norris used words such as "speculation", "sheer guesswork", "way-off", and "irrelevant" to describe the Consortium study. When asked to explain to the jury why he knowingly made public statements for which there was no scientific substantiation, he responded, "I can't explain that to the jury. I'm sorry."

Chiropractors were surprised and disappointed that the jury in the Lewis inquest determined that the treatment had led to the stroke. The inquest, however, had produced an indirect benefit for the profession. The experts testifying at the inquest were of different specialties, but their testimony publicly demonstrated their respect for one another as professionals and their mutual concern for truth and the advancement of patient care. Facts overwhelmed opinion and self-interest. The distinguished medical doctors and scientists who supported the chiropractic arguments stood in sharp contrast to the shabby performance of the detractors.

Yet there was a far more serious downside. The amount of media attention given to chiropractic neck manipulation was grotesquely disproportionate to the issue. Only a rare few complaints had surfaced over a period of many years, but each complaint was inflated into a headlining story by partisan doctors and ill-informed editors. Where was the perspective? Why don't the media report on the documented safety of chiropractic, the negligible malpractice insurance premiums, and the rarity of any complaints in contrast to the official statistics involving physicians, hospitals, and pharmaceuticals? The CTV flagship newsmagazine *W-5* gave the Lewis inquest "second coming of Christ" treatment on at least three separate occasions, but ignored all of the evidence put forward by the experts who spoke on behalf of chiropractic. It was as if the discredited doctors, Katz and Norris, had been writing the scripts. Media reports of the Lewis inquest demonstrated neither restraint nor accuracy, including one egregious Page One headline screaming, "Chiropractors Kill!"

Any negative impact to chiropractors because of this case was of serious concern to them at the time, but it is insignificant in the long-term. The information age is being kind to chiropractic. Good, solid healthy information is being written for an Internet audience and is being shared around the world. As a consequence, the chiropractic profession continues to grow. So much so that panicked medical doctors are quickly trying to learn how to do spinal adjustments and to win legal approval for the therapy — a rather perverse irony in view of their historic opposition to chiropractic. Almost one-third of all visits to health care professionals concern back-related issues, for which physicians traditionally have little training.

The real concern is for patients. How many people have been improperly discouraged from seeking treatment that would get them better faster, without relying on either drugs or surgery? What has the cost been to Workers' Compensation Boards, auto insurers, extended benefit plans, employers, and even medicare billings, because people remained in pain longer and unable to work?

A New Jersey Superior Court decision in recent years has created a new legal concern for all health and insurance plan managers, as well as individual health professionals. The court found an orthopedic surgeon negligent because he did not inform a patient about alternate therapies, in this case chiropractic. The decision became an extension of "informed consent." What it means is that if evidence indicates that superior outcomes are achieved by one treatment or professional over another, the patient must be given that option. It is now anticipated by malpractice and class action lawyers that major damages will be sought against compensation boards and insurance plans that improperly place their clients into the wrong hands or facility.

Postscript

During the summer of 2004, the following story appeared in *Capital News*, a quality newspaper serving the city of Kelowna (regional population 150,000. This is presented precisely as it appeared.

Mom challenges medical system

By Kevin Parnell, *Capital News* contributor

Pam Rankel wasn't going to let it happen again.

Twenty years ago the Kelowna woman lost a son due to complications in childbirth.

Now she was in a fight to save her second born son, Ryan, who up until the age of 16 appeared to be a normal, healthy teenager.

But severe migraine-like headaches as well as nosebleeds were the first indication something was wrong with Ryan.

Rankel's fight would be waged within the conventional medical system.

Twice before, once when Ryan was an infant and once when he was 16, doctors had looked at complete head X-rays and found nothing abnormal.

In fact they missed something that stood out.

Ryan had a rare neck disorder called agenesis of the dens. The dens is a tooth-like piece of bone that holds the first two vertebrae in a person's neck together.

Ryan didn't have one. His neck was being supported by muscle and ligament alone.

The diagnosis was made by a chiropractor. It ultimately saved Ryan's life.

It also outlined a riff between conventional medical doctors and those practicing "alternative" health care.

Chiropractor Dr. Markus Thiel made the diagnosis on Ryan after seeing the young man for variable back pain.

After taking a history, Thiel ordered another round of X-rays. His finding would be nearly immediate.

"Based on my preliminary findings I knew this was going to be something exotic," said Thiel.

"When I saw the X-ray it was one of those times that you take a step back and go 'wow'. It was amazing that he had gone on this far without serious injury.

"His head was hanging off of two ligaments."

For Pam Rankel, finally, it was a diagnosis.

Ryan had been living dangerously, playing sports and all the things young men do.

But he was told to immediately stop everything. It was back to the family doctor and more frustrations for Rankel.

"The first thing my family doctor did was he started cutting down the chiropractor," said Rankel.

"I said, 'My son is very sick and the only reason I'm here is to get a referral to see a neurosurgeon.' They had missed this several times and I needed to see a neurosurgeon."

In a letter to Rankel's family doctor, Thiel wrote that "even the most trivial of trauma could cause significant neurological damage, paralysis or death."

Letter in hand, Rankel got the referral she needed from her family doctor and went to see the neurosurgeon.

"He treated us very poorly," she said. "I was treated like a raving mother hen.

"We waited about two months and when the MRI came back the shit hit the fan.

"The neurosurgeon realized Ryan was very sick and told us they couldn't operate here, they didn't have the capabilities. Right away we were referred to Foothills Medical Centre in Calgary."

Two neurosurgeons in Calgary would operate for seven hours, placing two three-inch long screws in Ryan's neck along with a series of wires designed to act like the dens and support his neck.

The operation was a success but not without its effects.

Ryan has lost over 50 percent of the movement in his neck on each side of his body.

Now 18, he is otherwise healthy, readying to take a welding apprenticeship this fall at Okanagan University College.

While Pam Rankel fought to save her son, she also lost something in the process.

She lost faith in conventional medicine. But she's not bitter. She won't give out names of the doctors involved. She's not suing anybody.

But she wants people to learn from what she went through, learn to take responsibility for their health.

"Through everything I've learned I'm much more aware that I do have choices," she said.

"I think everybody should know they have a choice when it comes to health care. I'm not saying all doctors are bad. I have a new doctor and he's wonderful.

"But I don't have much faith in conventional medicine. I have Dr. Thiel to thank for saving my son's life."

It would be no more appropriate to conclude from this story that one should distrust family physicians and neurologists than it has been for the Canadian Stroke Consortium to seize upon individual chiropractic cases with negative outcomes and imply that they represent the norm. Given recent history, however, it is not hard to imagine what the medical associations would have done, had this Kelowna story been the reverse, with the chiropractor seen as the villain who missed the obvious. The alarm would have sounded with all the usual bluster and bombast.

Patients and their families should never be afraid of a second opinion, particularly if they are dealing with a chronic problem that is not responding to current treatment. If you get the impression that your doctor is guessing, groping around in the dark for a cure that seems to be elusive, you are probably right. Try someone else.

And, if the problem is neuro-musculoskeletal (the spine and the central nervous system), the second opinion should be chiropractic. In fact, for a vast range of injuries, aches, pains and disorders, chiropractic should be the first opinion, because all treatments are non-invasive — no drugs or surgery. Yet if any form of care seems not to be working — including chiropractic — the second opinion is vital. If a doctor's first therapy fails and you sense that he or she is guessing, RUN!

"When there is the slightest hint that any individual health professional, other than a physician — nurse, midwife, physiotherapist, podiatrist, naturopath, dietician, optometrist, pharmacist — has been responsible for a harmful outcome, the medical profession pumps itself up like a Goodyear Blimp with sanctimonious, derogatory judgments. Here is where the Canadian Medical Association, the American Medical Association, and the limitless number of derivative specialized professional organizations attempt to prove how hard they work to protect the public, and why society must give them the powers of a god and the wealth of Midas."

"Oh look. Here's one we haven't tried yet."

4.

Big Pharma

> *. . . if you suffer from erectile dysfunction in the
> industrialized West, Big Pharma is there to help you out
> with Viagra. If you suffer from malaria, diarrhea, or
> measles in Africa, it's likely you will die.*
>
> — JEFFREY ROBINSON

In his 2001 book *Prescription Games*, Jeffrey Robinson portrayed
Africa as a symptom of moral tragedy, the indifference of the pharmaceutical industry and its unholy alliance with the governments, physicians, and health care monopolies of the affluent world. Africa represents
one percent of global drug revenues, despite having 70 percent of the 40
million HIV-infected people worldwide and devastating statistics among
other diseases and disabilities as well. Japan, North America, and
Western Europe represent 80 percent of the drug industry's revenues. As
a result, major drug companies discontinue or decrease production of
products to cure often fatal illnesses, such as measles and malaria, in the
poorest regions.

Until shamed into action by media and western governments at a
2000 conference in South Africa, "Big Pharma," as the major pharmaceutical companies collectively describe themselves, priced effective
AIDS treatments much too expensively for Africa. Impoverished or cor-
ruptly governed nations chose to let people die rather than pay the impossible price. Jeffrey Robinson reported that the first company to yield to
the pressure, lowered the daily cost of its AIDS drug from $US 16.50 to
$US 2, merely a symbolic victory in view of nations where annual health
expenditures per person averaged $US 10. Africa has been a dumping
ground for the drug industry for decades, accused of offloading flawed
or less-than-successful surpluses. There are those who believe that best-
selling author Michael Crichton was not far off the mark with a terrifying plot suggesting that a killer world plague originated with flawed drug

products dumped on Africa. Although HIV (human immunodeficiency virus) existed pre-1970, no one truly knows the origin of the current pandemic. It was given a name, acquired immunodeficiency syndrome (AIDS), during the early 1980s after the first serious North American outbreak in San Francisco.

Big Pharma justifies its need for patent protection and high prices because of the cost of research. They emphasize — with some justification — that new drugs are more economical than the alternative of surgery, hospitalization, and rehabilitation. The public relations machine emphasizes lifesaving miracles, incredible boasts in view of the fact that far more is spent on marketing than research. The National Institute for Health Care Management reports that $US 2.5 billion was spent on mass media advertising in the United States during 2000, part of $US 16 billion of promotional spending. This includes incestuous and ethically questionable investments in doctors, government lobbying, scientific-medical journals, universities, research labs, and professional congresses. Research by Public Citizen Health Research Group, a US non-profit organization, concluded that the drug industry spent a record $US 108.6 million in 2003 on federal lobbying activities and hired 824 individual lobbyists.

World drug revenues approached $US 500 billion during 2003 ($20 billion in Canada). One major company spent more money advertising one arthritis drug in 2000 than was spent advertising Pepsi-Cola. Led by the spectacular sales of Viagra, Pfizer alone achieved sales of $US 32 billion in 2001. The profit potential of a new "blockbuster" drug is measured by the pharmaceutical industry the same way energy traders regard oil reserves — by how long profits can be drawn from one well.

Robinson writes:

> To understand how blockbusters shape the industry, you have to realize that not every therapeutic category lends itself to blockbuster potential. Blockbusters are harvested out of chronic illnesses, as opposed to acute illnesses, because the real money is in drugs that must be taken every day for years and not in one-pill miracles. You also need very large disease populations located in countries where sufferers have the money to pay for expensive drugs. Chief among the categories that meet those criteria are cancer, hypertension, psychiatric disorders, osteoporosis, rheumatoid arthritis, and thrombosis. Also included are almost anything that alleviates constant pain and treatments that lower cholesterol. Added in are lifestyle medications, the drugs people take because they

want to, which includes diet drugs, sexual enhancers — Viagra, launched in sixty countries in its first year, is the prime example — and stuff that grows hair.

The pharmaceutical industry pays $US 20 million a year to the American Medical Association to obtain detailed professional information about each member. Other purchased data includes the doctor prescription records from pharmacies, particularly those incorporated into the large retail food and merchandise chains. The industry claims that private information about individual patients is protected, but data of individual doctors' prescription choices and patterns of specific drug sales in different communities are extremely valuable, and help to refine marketing strategies.

Good information is now freely available over the Internet. Among the excellent web sites are those of Public Citizen, *www.citizen.org*, and another founded by concerned health professionals, *www.nofreelunch.org*. The latter site urges hospital employees and others to order from them, and asks them to wear proudly, in hospitals and health care environments, colorful pins bearing a bright red "X" and the message: "Say No to Drug Reps." The "no free lunch" people describe themselves as follows:

> We are health care providers — physicians, pharmacists, nurses, dentists, among others — who believe that pharmaceutical promotion should not guide clinical practice, and that overzealous promotional practices can lead to bad patient care. It is our goal to encourage health care practitioners to provide high quality care based on unbiased evidence rather than on biased pharmaceutical promotion.

Among the U.S. drug industry's fiercest critics is Dr. Jay Cohen of San Diego, a psychiatrist, psychopharmacologist, university professor, and best selling author of *Over Dose: The Case Against The Drug Companies* (2001). Dr. Cohen's articles have appeared in scores of publications, from *Newsweek* to prestigious scientific journals. His web site, *www.medicationsense.com*, also has valuable information. He points out that 3.3 billion prescriptions were filled in the U.S. during 2002, an astonishing number that works out to 12 for every man, woman, and child in America. Without any appreciable difference in the rate of illness or disease, or changes in public health, the number of prescriptions grew by 32 percent in just one four-year period. Drug prices have soared and pharmaceutical companies have achieved profits that vastly exceed any other area of the economy. Dr. Cohen adds:

> I'm not anti-medication. Medications do a great deal of good, but we must ask, what is the goal of the drug industry? To simply sell as many drugs as possible? Yet, medications aren't like other commodities. Prescription drugs aren't the same as cars, cosmetics, or CD players. Drugs have direct, powerful effects on human systems. Some of these effects are negative, and taking multiple drugs — as 25 percent of Americans do — increases the risks exponentially. Psychologically, the growing attitude that drugs are the answer for every ache and angst is destructive for individuals and societies. . . . Prescription medications are vitally important for treating medical conditions, but they are also the #4 leading cause of death, cause more than 1 million hospitalizations annually, and are a major cause of disability and drug dependency. Overuse of medications is rampant.

Links between the health establishment, educational institutions and politicians have been subjected to severe scrutiny in recent years, and have become a sensitive topic. Although cosmetic efforts are made at distancing themselves from drug companies, these agencies and individuals have become more dependent than ever upon drug patronage. Professional organizations constantly redefine ethical standards and the kind of gifts and bonuses thought to be appropriate and what would be considered excessive. Some governments, such as the United Kingdom, pass laws to ensure that gifts to doctors are small.

Robinson's book identifies prominent doctors and agencies who are among the ethics police of the profession. One of these is Dr. Drummond Rennie, west coast editor of the *Journal of the American Medical Association*, who consistently watches for conflict of interest and secrecy. He is most concerned that drug company funding of research, institutions and authors be openly declared. Robinson quotes Dr. Eric Rose, a faculty member of the University of Washington School of Medicine who has researched doctor relationships with the pharmaceutical industry: "What patients should be worried about is not how many trinkets are on the doctor's desk, but the source of that doctor's information. I think a very legitimate question for a patient to ask a doctor is how do you keep up with new developments in medicine? There's nothing wrong with asking that and I don't think any doc should demur to answer that. Hopefully, the answer will involve peer-reviewed literature and other scientifically sound sources of information. If a doc says, 'Sure I see drugs reps and I read all these magazines that come to my house even though I never subscribe to them, and look at all the neat stuff they give me,' then you might want to reconsider your relationship with that doctor."

A Harvard study on this topic was revealing. In it, 68 percent of doctors said that drug company marketing was only "minimally influential" in their prescription choices for patients but that 62 percent said scientific papers were very important. However, when these same physicians were quizzed about specific drugs, 50-70 percent of responses related to drugs that had only been advertised, not the subjects of scientific papers.

Can there be any more dramatic example of the pharmaceutical industry's ownership of the medical profession than the 2004 offer by the Province of Ontario of $50 million to its MDs as an incentive to cut annual prescription costs by $200 million? Health Minister George Smitherman promised that if doctors could achieve this cost saving with a more prudent approach to prescribing drugs for their patients — particularly for seniors — the province would kick back $50 million to doctors. "There is no bribe here," the minister said, "I think we have an opportunity to influence policy by incenting and rewarding appropriate behavior and I think this is what's at play here." What the government is really saying, is that the Ontario medical profession is hopelessly irresponsible, unethical, and completely in the grasp of the pharmaceutical industry. Obviously, certain that quality patient care is not a priority of doctors, the minister hopes that money talks.

It seems not to have penetrated the thought processes of Ontario cabinet ministers that over-prescription is a matter of professional irresponsibility requiring severe discipline, and possibly even criminal negligence charges in the case of misconduct resulting in death or disability. If the College of Physicians and Surgeons of Ontario cannot control its members, and wrestle them free from the clutches of Big Pharma, its authority should be revoked.

The *Canadian Medical Association Journal* reported in 2002 about efforts by the Pharmaceutical Research and Manufacturers of America (PhRMA) — the drug companies' lobby — to set standards for its member companies, allegedly "to ensure that all interactions between physicians and detailers (sales reps of drug companies) must be focused on information." In this voluntary guide, tickets to sporting events and Broadway plays, free music CDs, rounds of golf, or expensive dinners are forbidden, while pizza lunches or other modest meals are acceptable as long as the gatherings also deliver benefits to patients and cost under $100. The code also spells the end of free travel to medical conferences (except for speakers) and of payment for the professional time of attendees.

There are potential fines through professional medical Colleges in both Canada and the United States for violations of the rules, and the manufacturers set fines as well for breaches of codes of conduct. However, the definition of "violation" is questionable. There are virtually zero prosecutions in either Canada or the United States. Drug money is ubiquitous at all events and within most projects. What must be emphasized is the word "voluntary" in most codes of ethics. But times are changing, as indicated by this 2004 report in the *New York Review of Books*:

> The industry is also being hit with a tidal wave of government investigations and civil and criminal lawsuits. The litany of charges includes illegally overcharging Medicaid and Medicare, paying kickbacks to doctors, engaging in anti-competitive practices, colluding with generic companies to keep generic drugs off the market, illegally promoting drugs for unapproved uses, engaging in misleading direct-to-consumer advertising, and, of course, covering up evidence. Some of the settlements have been huge. TAP Pharmaceuticals, for instance, paid $US 875 million to settle civil and criminal charges of Medicaid and Medicare fraud in the marketing of its prostate cancer drug, Lupron. All of these efforts could be summed up as increasingly desperate marketing and patent games, activities that always skirted the edge of legality but now are sometimes well on the other side.

Big Pharma and the manufacturers of technological equipment have historically been generous travel agents. Bureaucrats, facility designers, and administrators have opportunities to inspect factories and neighboring geography, Germany being among the more favored destinations. For doctors, seminars and congresses prevail, often cloaked in the guise of CMEs (Continuing Medical Education). Although conscientious physicians and health professionals, and their patients, benefit greatly from the legitimate use of CMEs, they are too often merely phony excuses for travel payola. Academic institutions and professional accreditation bodies lay down strict rules about which events will earn professional credits. That being said, the more glamorous the event, the more doctors will attend. Robinson said that one planned drug company junket to the

Bahamas signed up 300 doctors, but when embarrassing public questions forced the host drug company to a change of venue to its own corporate offices, two-thirds cancelled.

VIOXX and other recalls

When Merck and Company (Merck Frosst in Canada) withdrew VIOXX worldwide in 2004, shocking shareholders, physicians, and patients, we heard little about the university labs and medical journals that had been part of Merck's heavy investment in the product.

Every time a drug is withdrawn or recalled, questions are asked about the financial arrangements between the manufacturer, the scientists and research agencies involved, as well as articles in so-called peer-reviewed journals. The usual question is whether scientific standards might have been pinched, ever so slightly, by researchers, universities, private labs and publications eager for the money? In many instances, the criticism is that research was not focused properly on the real issues. It was technically valid, but it was just not asking the right questions. Did the company ignore or misinterpret research less supportive of the desired outcome?

VIOXX, also known as CEOXX in some countries, had been prescribed for the relief of arthritic and other acute pain. It was withdrawn after studies demonstrated a significantly increased risk to patients of cardiovascular events, including strokes and heart attacks. Trials which commenced in 2000 involved 2,600 patients. Conclusive results concerned those who used the drug for 18 months or more, but Merck claimed that evidence did not indicate increased risk for those whose usage was of less duration. VIOXX, with annual sales of $US 2.5 billion worldwide, was used by 84 million patients since it was introduced in 1999. It had been the 10th best selling drug in Canada with sales of $200 million in 2003.

VIOXX has been associated with an increased risk of serious, adverse cardiovascular complications, including heart attack, stroke, angina pectoris, atrial fibrillation, bradycardia, hematoma, irregular heartbeat, palpitation, premature ventricular contraction, tachycardia, venous insufficiency, cerebrovascular accident, congestive heart failure, deep venous thrombosis, pulmonary embolism, transient ischemic attack, and unstable angina.

A Canadian dimension to this story is that warnings issued to Americans were not given to physicians, pharmacists, or patients in

Canada. United States Federal Communications Commission advertising regulations required Merck to include in its advertisements for Vioxx that "Heart attacks and other serious cardiovascular events, such as blood clots have been reported in patients taking VIOXX." No such warning was ever given to Canadians.

Merck, globally, has been flooded with litigation. Lawyer Jim Poyner, who has filed a class action suit in British Columbia, said, "It is simply not good enough in the health field to say 'oops, we're sorry,' and then carry on as if it is business as usual...the essential point in an action like this is the phrase that they 'knew or ought to have known' the dangers to patients. The evidence is clear that Merck knew something was wrong as early as 2000 and failed to inform Canadians, not even the cautionary warning given to Americans."

Once again, the issue begs the question, "Why were Canadian doctors failing to inform their patients of risks long after public American advertising added the cautionary words?" Merck will have to defend in court why it failed to give Canadians the same warning as Americans, but does that excuse Canadian physicians? Surely their professional information must have carried these advisories? Failing that, they must have seen the warnings in American television ads. Or, is it simply more evidence that the only education doctors get about drugs is from the industry salespeople?

Recalls are commonplace in the drug field, although few are as dramatic as the Thalidomide recall of the 1950s. First introduced in the 1950s as a sedative, Thalidomide was prescribed for nausea and insomnia in pregnant women because it was deemed to be so safe. It turned out to be a terrible tragedy. Many children, whose mothers used the drug in their first trimester of pregnancy, were born with serious deformities. The drug today, marketed under the brand name Thalomid, has found many useful applications, including the treatment of leprosy, neuritis, and some cancers.

Until recently, hormone replacement therapy drugs (HRTs) were almost universally prescribed to ease symptoms among menopausal women until alarming bodies of evidence began to demonstrate the increased risk of several cancers, blood clotting, and other problems. Other important recalls in recent years have included Baycol, a cholesterol-lowering agent (Bayer); Propulsid, used for heartburn and gastric problems (Janssen); and Lotronex, prescribed for irritable bowel syndrome (Glaxo Wellcome). Each of these drugs were found to cause serious consequences — including death in some cases. Those interested in reviewing the long list of pharmaceutical misadventures should visit the web site of the United States Food and Drug Administration. (*www.fda.gov*).

Pharmaceutical companies can suffer staggering losses due to drug failures. The costs of recalls and litigation can put even a big drug company out of business. This is usually disguised by the word "merger." But Big Pharma blames regulators for the high cost of drugs, claiming that it can cost more than $500 million to get a new drug to market. These statements have been thoroughly trashed by Merrill Goozner, former chief economics correspondent for the *Chicago Tribune*. In a recent article, he debunked a comment by a Big Pharma CEO of this alleged $500 million cost:

> Every independent study that's ever looked at the sources of medical innovation has concluded that research funded by the public sector — not the private sector — is chiefly responsible for a majority of the medically significant advances that have led to new treatments of disease. Moreover, the drug industry's expense for bringing those advances from lab to market is well below the $500-million claim. If one discounts the research clearly aimed at marketing and producing drugs whose contribution to public health does not exceed that of drugs already on the market, the assertion collapses on its face.

Merrill Goozner's 2004 book published by the University of California (Berkeley), *The $800 Million Pill: The Truth behind the Cost of New Drugs*, is an eye-opener.

No amount of research could ever anticipate the infinite complexities among a human population. Everyone's genetic composition and environmental circumstances are different. As it is, it takes many years and awesome amounts of research and testing to get one new drug to market. The benefit to humankind of many of these achievements has been extraordinary, and worth a calculated risk. The ultimate test for all pharmaceuticals comes after the public release, when millions of personal stories add to the body of knowledge. But the key word is "calculated." This is why so many distinguished people within the health field are extremely worried today about Big Pharma's investments in doctors, scientists, medical conventions, universities, research labs, health industry decision-makers, and politicians. The fear is that greed — corporate, institutional, and personal — has corrupted the science and that the preponderance of evidence about drug risks is being ignored.

Canada's march to Pharmacare

The focus of most health debates in Canada today is the increasing cost of pharmaceuticals for chronic conditions. Sales of drugs in Canada totaled $22 billion in 2004, more than the $16 billion paid to physicians. Drug costs have more than doubled since 2000 and, as in the American experience, there would appear to be no measurable changes in the state of public health to rationalize such a cost explosion.

The pharmaceutical industry must be salivating at the prospect of the Canadian government sponsorship of universal Pharmacare. The drug companies would find Canada an easy target for their marketing strategies: Canadian bureaucrats, doctors, and patients drive the market, and none of them have any personal stake in minimizing costs. Big Pharma is expert at compromising politicians and public officials through lobbying, political donations, and promotions. Big Pharma can influence doctors through professional advertising, research grants, conference travel, universities, laboratories, and in-hospital promotions. And, increasingly, Big Pharma's Direct to Consumer Advertising (DTCA) hypes wonder drugs and urges patients to inquire about them in the doctor's office. Among the sales phrases is "banana in a bunch," a situation where several drugs could treat a condition, but one stands out because either the patient asked for it, or the doctor's bias is in favor of the supplier. Technically, DTCA advertising is still illegal in Canada but the Canadian market is overwhelmed by signals from the U.S. where it is legal. And, despite the VIOXX story and other recalls, Canadian media managers are lobbying to be able to afflict their audiences with this questionable source of revenue.

The commission led by former Saskatchewan Premier Roy Romanow and the Senate of Canada inquiry led by Senator Michael Kirby advocated substantial federal participation in Pharmacare. In recent meetings, provincial premiers and health ministers have also called for a federally supported drug program. This is an example of history repeating itself. Significant variations in hospital insurance from province to province encouraged federal intervention to level the playing field in 1957. That proved to be an incomplete measure because families could still go bankrupt in one province, because they couldn't afford the doctor bills, but could obtain complete coverage if they lived somewhere else in Canada. Federal medicare ultimately included both hospitals and physicians in 1968. Today, the loudest cries concern pharmaceuticals and the affordability of drugs for long-term chronic conditions. Once again, there is fear that some families could be bankrupted by this need.

What Canadian industry?

Several major nations manage proprietary drugs under compulsory licensing. A government may choose to honor a patent from another country, issue its own patents, or override all of the patents and license a manufacturer to produce the product for the domestic market. Drug companies owning the patent could choose to obtain a license in that country and do the manufacturing and marketing, or obtain a royalty on sales from whomever is granted the license. Canada was among these nations until 1987. In 1984 a major government commission into pharmaceuticals declared Canada's home grown system of free market forces, but compulsory licensing, "the best in the world," ensuring that Canadians had access to both the best of science and fair pricing.

And then came Prime Minister Brian Mulroney, consistently a supporter of corporate agendas. He gave   the pharmaceutical industry unprecedented support. Big Pharma applied lobbying pressure and financial generosity to politicians and their parties. It became a free trade issue with heavy pressure from Washington. And, since most of the multinational drug companies were headquartered in Quebec, that province climbed aboard the Big Pharma lobby. Beginning in 1987 and finishing the job in 1993, compulsory licensing was completely eliminated.

The information blitz of the industry pointed out that each new drug took up to 10 years and $500 million to get to market, and the industry needed secure patent protection to continue research and recapture the investment. They boasted how the end of compulsory licensing would mean more jobs for Canadians and more research in Canadian institutions. Supporters of compulsory licensing argued that a professional process existed to determine fair market price, assessing all of the proprietary rights and values, and that a free market for pharmaceuticals would only duplicate an obscene situation in the United States, where the sky is the limit on prices without any consumer or government opportunity to assess a fair market return on a product monopoly. Once a Valium, Prozac, or Viagra is established, an era of patent protection stretching 20 years into the future shelters prices over which no one has any control.

By 1987, Canada had become one of the most formidable and dependable generic drug manufacturers in the world, led by Apotex and Novopharm. To obtain a license for a generic, it cannot be an exact copy of the original, but it must achieve the same results. Therefore, the basic drug chemistry is the same, but the coatings, shape, and style might be different. The average cost to get a new product approved and to market is between $1 and 2 million, although there are often fierce legal battles with the holders of the original patents. Drug companies are notorious for "evergreening" their valuable products, surrounding them with a forest of patents on every conceivable ingredient of the drug, and obtaining these subsidiary patents in different years, hoping to delay the eventual expiry of their protection.

Barry Sherman, the founder of Apotex and a leader of the global generic drug business, was incensed by Ottawa's concessions to the multinationals. He told Jeffrey Robinson in *Prescription Games* (2001):

> Merck and others spend money doing research in Canadian hospitals because it's cheap, but it's for the benefit of Merck worldwide. If there's anything discovered, it leaves the country without payment, it's exploited abroad, and then those products come back into the country at very high prices. Meanwhile, they deduct any research money spent in Canada from Canadian income as if it were an expense to earn money in Canada, which it isn't. Anyway, it's subsidized by the tax-payers because the companies get tax benefits for doing research in Canada. If the research is being done in Canada for the benefit of for-eign companies, it should not be deductible for Canadian tax purposes. In addition to paying ten times what we should for drugs, we're paying for half the research on them too. Is this good for Canada? It's insane.
>
> . . . .They take in $9 billion in Canada. Well, the average industry creates 10,000 jobs for each billion in sales, so there should be 90,000 jobs. But there are only 15,000 jobs. And nobody seems to care. If you look at our figures, Apotex is by far the largest employer in the indus-try in Canada. We have 3,500 employees, Merck has 900. But Merck takes twice as much money as we do out of the health-care system. Our prices are low and we make everything in Canada. Our jobs per dollar are several times what theirs are and nobody seems to notice or care. I figured I should be a national hero for what I do, but I'm not. If any-thing, I'm a villain.

Canada's generic drug industry took a beating as a result of the Mulroney legislation, but there has been little of the promised growth from the multinational companies. The world brands will point to Canada's meteoric rise in biotechnology, but today's superstars were either non-existent or unknown just a few years ago, and, while many of them benefit from international partnerships, investments and research funding, most of them are refreshingly Canadian. Names such as QLT,

Biovail, Angiotech, Adherex, Nexia Biotechnologies, Forbes Medi-Tech, MDS Proteomics and ID Biomedical dominate the business press. Corporate spin-offs radiating from great research facilities at the University of Toronto, the University of British Columbia, McGill, and other campuses are generating world excitement. Montreal and Toronto are stronger than ever within this industry, but the collective represented by the Ottawa Life Sciences Council and the Vancouver-based companies are coming on strong. In fact, Vancouver now leads the country in the achievement of finance for biomedical industry development. Most of these new corporate entities and all of the universities would credit the multinational pharmacological companies for their participation, but, from Canada's point of view, the bottom line today is that they need us as much as we need them.

The core issue behind the protection of patent monopolies in Canada is the absence of sensible explanations for their pricing policies. This has become a political crisis in the United States. Because of our strong legacy of quality generic manufacturers and more government control on pharmaceutical purchasing (directing economical product choices where available), our prices remain much lower than in the U.S. There has been an explosion of Internet drug sales from Canadian sites into American markets where the prices for specific products are much higher. There are daily bus tours of visitors from south of the border — particularly senior citizens — who stock up on drugs while in Canada. This does not demonstrate the wisdom of the Canadian market, but rather the exploitation that goes on in the U.S.

The generic drug industry was baffled by a 2004 report of the Vancouver-based Fraser Institute, claiming that Canadians were being overcharged $810 million per year for generic drugs. The researchers claimed to have found lower prices in the U.S. markets than what Canadians were paying. Industry spokespersons were quick to ridicule the report, asking why the Fraser Institute was focusing on 10 percent of the entire Canadian drug industry, rather than the 90 percent operated by Big Pharma. They also demonstrated that "there is no U.S. price." Prices vary dramatically from region to region, depending upon local competition and multifaceted purchasing contracts.

Canada could learn a lesson from Australia, where government-sponsored coverage is better, but the average annual drug cost per family is half what it is here. That is because of the national drug purchasing monopoly run by government, called the Pharmaceutical Benefits Scheme (PBS). About 90 percent of all prescription drugs sold in

Australia are under the PBS program, and manufactured under compulsory license much as it used to be in Canada. Brand products are patent
protected but PBS negotiates what it considers to be fair pricing and,
wherever possible, approves the least expensive option, often generics.
The remaining 10 percent of drugs not covered by the government face
no price restriction other than free market forces.

Beware of the quicksand!

Once again, the politicians and planners define the need in "billions" of
dollars and then argue over who should pay. There seems to be no concern at all about cost-benefit analysis or the alarming volume of statistics
now available about the mistakes and abuses of prescription drugs. The
House of Commons Standing Committee on Health studied the pharmaceutical issues and, in 2004, came down with a set of recommendations
to improve the testing of drugs before being released to the market. The
committee recommended that Health Canada undertake a comprehensive
study of the adverse effects issue and it advocated a crackdown on Direct
To Consumer Advertising of prescription drugs.

Much more investigation is necessary. Without detailed study,
Pharmacare will merely strengthen existing extravagant, mistake-ridden
monopolies, further enriching the physicians who write the prescriptions,
and slamming the door on all of the other health professionals who see
drugs and surgery as a last resort.

Consider all of these factors:

- If medicare stopped excluding registered health professionals
  who promote drug-free therapies, the competitive environment
  would benefit the consumer. The issue is patient choice of legal,
  regulated health care providers.

- Government policies support and reward mismanagement.
  There is no personal accountability for poor performance or
  most mistakes, even the lethal ones. The system is dominated
  by politicians, bureaucrats, hospital administrators, and
  physicians, all of whom are on the public payroll, directly or
  indirectly.

- Every study indicates that drugs are either over-prescribed or
  incorrectly prescribed. Surely this disastrous situation should be
  addressed before facilitating far more of the same at taxpayer

expense? Surveys have shown that 70 percent of patients believe they have, on occasion, been given an improper prescription.

- The 2004 Canadian acute care hospital study determined that 7.5 percent of the 2.5 million patients admitted were victims of "adverse events" and that as many as 23,000 may have died because of mistakes. The problem of adverse drug reactions was second only to surgery as the cause of these mistakes. If the same error rate is assumed for drugs prescribed in physicians' offices, the problem must surely be epidemic.

- There are over 2.2 million adverse drug reactions a year in the U.S., resulting in over 100,000 deaths.

- Quebec is different. The Quebec government has given its resident Big Pharma companies a guarantee unequaled in the world. The government will continue to buy their products — presumably at their prices — long after generics would be available elsewhere in Canada. Should all Canadian taxpayers subsidize the parochial industrial incentives of one province?

- Dependence on prescribed tranquillizers rose by 290 percent between 1962 and 1975, a period in which per capita consumption of liquor rose by only 23 percent and the estimated consumption of illegal opiates by 50 percent.

- In 1973, the entire drug industry spent an average of $US 4,500 on each practicing physician for advertising and promotion. The 2003 figure was estimated to be about $US 25,000 per physician.

- Big Pharma gave out $US 7.2 billion worth of free samples to doctors in the U.S. during 2003. It is estimated that there is one Big Pharma sales representative for every nine MDs, a remarkable statistic in view of the vast numbers of physicians in administrative, teaching, research, and non-drug involved specialties.

- Studies have demonstrated that 50 percent or more of prescribed drugs are most likely useless. In their 1989 book *Follies & Fallacies in Medicine*, Petr Skrabanek PhD and James McCormick MD said that 35 percent of drugs prescribed for specific illnesses have no effect, and that placebos usually work just as well. These authors suggest that the "10-minute" medical visit guarantees a high rate of needless or incorrect prescriptions.

- The most cost-effective drugs are most frequently neither the best known nor the cheapest. The proper drug for a condition, even if expensive, may save the expense of more costly hospital and surgical treatments.

- Several inferior drugs outsell their competitors for similar conditions, simply because there is more advertising and promotion.

- U.S. doctors prescribe about twice as many antibiotics as do doctors in the United Kingdom and they commonly prescribe antibiotics even when bacteria are not likely to be present. European doctors, however, tend to prescribe antibiotics only if they know that an infection is caused by bacteria and is also serious. Antibiotic drug resistance, caused by overuse, has seriously undermined the effectiveness of antibiotics, leaving humankind more vulnerable to new strains of bacteria.

- In a 2002 report, Dr. John Conly, Professor of Medicine and Microbiology with the Centre for Antimicrobial Resistance at the University of Calgary, said, "Canada reportedly spends at least $659 million dollars a year for the more than 25 million prescriptions of oral anti-infective drugs. This makes antibiotics the third highest drug usage category in the health system. Unfortunately, studies indicate that over 50 percent of the oral antibiotics prescribed are unnecessary."

- Joe Graedon, pharmacologist and author of the best-selling books *The People's Pharmacy*, says, "There is no such thing as a safe drug. Each medication is a double-edged sword, with a good side and a bad side. Successful treatment is a careful balance between the beneficial and harmful effects. Unfortunately, just the opposite is often the case."

Canada should retain expert and independent financial and biomedical consultants to analyze world drug prices and try to determine what is best for the Canadian market. The analysis must include a comprehensive examination of all relationships among pharmaceutical companies, medical doctors, research scientists, universities, and government decision makers, including gifts, advertising, promotional travel, and incentives. Tax auditors should be part of this process.

Among the groups advocating more thought with respect to drug policy is the Canadian Health Coalition, which consists of organizations representing unions, seniors, women, students, consumers, and health care professionals. The coalition has taken strong positions against privatization of health services, and it has also appeared before the House of Commons Standing Committee on Health recommending an independent public inquiry into the pharmaceutical industry in Canada.

Areas suggested by the coalition for investigation include:

- the integrity of clinical research and commercialization of health research;
- the pricing and profitability levels in the industry and its impact on medicare;
- the abuse of patent protection measures and its impact on access to essential medicines and the sustainability of medicare;
- the costs and benefits of pharmaceutical research and development;
- the integrity of the federal regulatory process and cost-recovery;
- the lack of independent scientific research capacity at Health Canada;
- the lack of post-market surveillance and adverse drug reactions; and
- the effects of promotion, marketing, advertising, and prescribing practices.

"I told you I would get my best team together in
your case . . . . I would like you to meet my
business manager, my insurance
agent, my lawyer, ..."

5.
Defensive Medicine

There is still another reason why the modern physician is estranged from his own judgment. To put it in the words of a doctor who remains skilled in examining his patients and in evaluating their histories: "Everyone who has a headache wants and expects a CAT scan." He went on to say that roughly six out of every ten CAT scans he orders are unnecessary, with no basis in the clinical evidence and the patient's reported experience and sensations. Why are they done? As a protection against malpractice suits. Which is to say, as medical practice has moved into the stage of total reliance on machine-generated information, so have the patients. Put simply, if a patient does not obtain relief from a doctor who has failed to use all the available technological resources, including drugs, the doctor is deemed vulnerable to the charge of incompetence. The situation is compounded by the fact that the personal relationship between doctor and patient now, in contrast to a century ago, has become so arid that the patient is not restrained by intimacy or empathy from appealing to the courts. Moreover, doctors are reimbursed by medical-insurance agencies on the basis of what they do, not on the amount of time they spend with patients. Non-technological medicine is time-consuming. It is more profitable to do a CAT scan on a patient with a headache than to spend time getting information about his or her experiences and sensations.

— NEIL POSTMAN, PHD in *Technopoly*

There are debates as to whether the modern buzz about "defensive medicine" is a genuine health risk of this era or merely a façade to justify more profitable, but risk-free, and intellectually lazy practices within health care. The term means that foremost in the physician's mind are the consequences of error, not the potentially best treatment for the patient. It leads to overtesting, often at great expense. Among those bandying around this phrase have been no lesser personages than United States President George W. Bush and prominent trial lawyer Johnny Cochrane, who died in 2005. It is unlikely that either of them spent too much time contemplating the sociological and intellectual components of the issue - with them, it seems all about money.

Dr. Neil Postman, who died in 2003, was one of those philosophers who defined a generation. A protégé of the famous Canadian media thinker Marshall McLuhan, Postman was a prolific writer and lecturer, the Chair of the Department of Culture and Communication and Professor of Media Ecology at New York University. Among his focuses was how a reliance on technology was eroding the character and independence of humankind. His book *Technopoly* is required reading at universities around the world.

The healing arts used to be a matter of expert judgment. Physicians would hear what the patient had to say, probe a bit, observe, and then attempt to define the problem and propose solutions. Gradually, diagnostic equipment and the chemical analysis of blood, urine, saliva, and tissue have evolved to provide a wealth of data. Ideally, this is to merely assist the professional in the diagnostic process, and in determining an appropriate course of treatment. These tests are often extremely expensive and profitable to every agency and professional involved.

Essentially, the medical profession has surrendered much of its subjective judgment — the expertise that brings us to them in the first place — and replaced it with technical processes done elsewhere by others, with primary assessment achieved automatically by computers and technicians. Once problems are red flagged, the next referral is often to more focused testing and doctors who specialize in the specific area. This is what seems to be turning the general practitioner into an order taker and business broker, raising serious economic questions as to whether there is a purpose for them at all.

Postman, in *Technopoly*, is convinced American professionals place profit for themselves and the system as a higher priority than caring for patients:

Although the U.S. and England have equivalent life-expectancy rates, American doctors perform six times as many cardiac bypass operations per capita as English doctors do. American doctors perform more diagnostic tests than doctors do in France, Germany, or England. An American woman has two to three times the chance of having a hysterectomy as her counterpart in Europe; 60 percent of the hysterectomies performed in America are done on women under the age of forty-four. American doctors do more prostate surgery per capita than do doctors anywhere in Europe, and the United States leads the industrialized world in the rate of Caesarean-section operations — 50 to 200 percent higher than in most other countries. When American doctors decide to forgo surgery in favor of treatment by drugs, they give higher dosages than doctors elsewhere. They prescribe about twice as many antibiotics as do doctors in the United Kingdom and commonly prescribe antibiotics when bacteria are likely to be present, whereas European doctors tend to prescribe antibiotics only if they know that the infection is caused by bacteria and is also serious. American doctors use far more X-rays per patient than do doctors in other countries. In one review of the extent of X-ray use, a radiologist discovered cases in which fifty to one hundred X-rays had been taken of a single patient when five would have been sufficient. Other surveys have shown that, for almost one-third of the patients, the X-ray could have been omitted or deferred on the basis of available clinical data.

Although the "defensive medicine" issue is essentially an American debate, negotiators on behalf of Canadian doctors were quick to seize upon this as yet another excuse for dramatically rising costs, overuse of drugs, and far heavier utilization of labs and other diagnostic tools. The logic seems to be that the "good" doctors (all but a handful, in the profession's opinion) are prevented from doing their work intelligently, economically, and courageously, because lawyers and the courts make such a fuss about the "bad luck" (mistakes, tragedy, malpractice) encountered by hospitals and "poor" doctors (hardly any). As a postscript to the "hardly any," it can be said that this represents a documented five percent in the U.S. (40,000) and the only accurate use of the phrase "hardly any" is that "hardly any" are ever disciplined and removed from practice. One can assume that the worrisome Canadian equivalent would be 3,000 dangerous doctors. So how did this American situation evolve?

Whitey's insurance company

The late San Francisco icon Melvin Belli is credited with changing the legal world with respect to fair compensation for poor people and aver-age-income families. In Belli's early career, only the affluent and power-ful would ever consider seeking anything but pennies in compensation for medically-inflicted tragedies. He and a few other courageous American lawyers started using the jury system in an attempt to change the world. They underwrote the costs of the actions themselves, living like paupers for years, and suffering the abuse of the legal establishment. They were called "ambulance chasers."

Their success would not have been possible in Canada and the United Kingdom, where juries were unavailable for this type of civil lit-igation and judges tended to evolve from a smug establishment, usually favoring the rich and powerful. The practice of law also had firm rules about contingency fees (lawyers pay all costs, work for free, but then take a percentage of final settlements), but Belli thundered into the head-lines with an astonishing legacy of success.

After decades of standing the American medical industry on its ear — the doctors and the rich folks who always lined up on their side — Belli and his generation of trial lawyers rarely had to take a case to court. The vast majority were settled, and continue to be resolved, along fair guidelines set by precedent. In later years, these pioneers also evolved the class action suit, seeking legal redress for thousands of people simul-taneously. Asbestos poisoning of workers, environmental disasters in major industry, cigarette manufacturers, pharmaceutical horror stories, breast implants and many other class action cases have generated yet another multi-billion legal industry. Out of this culture, propelled by injustice and anger — has come a financial nightmare for the medical profession. Much is heard about ridiculously large jury awards in American civil actions, but this is highly misleading. Most of the extrav-agant amounts are reduced to appropriate levels on appeal.

In a Canadian interview 25 years ago, Belli was asked if he had the option of choosing the best place to try a malpractice case, where would that be? He did not hesitate for a moment. "Detroit," he said. Asked why, he replied, "Because, in Detroit, I can always get an all-black jury and they hate whitey's insurance company." When the interviewer ques-tioned whether that was either proper or justice, the famous lawyer said: "Justice is not my problem. My job is to get the best possible result for my client. I have never forgotten that when I was a young lawyer the pet dog of an affluent American was considered more valuable in the courts than the life of a poor black man."

Today, through most of the United States, malpractice insurance for surgical specialties such as obstetrics-gynecology, anesthesiology, neurosurgery, and orthopedics is over $US 100,000 a year, and many pay $US 200,000 or more. The average doctor's annual premium is $US 30,000. But the major war is political. President Bush is campaigning for a nation-wide cap of $US 250,000 for the punitive side of malpractice cases, a limit which began in California in 1975 and which has since spread to 19 states. There is no limit on actual damages — proof that the malpractice cost individuals, their business and their families specific amounts of money. But the problem there, which incenses civil rights advocates, is that the worth of poor, unemployed people and their families is thought to be zero, while the bone idle relatives of wealthy business people, often neurotic, useless progeny, are thought to be worth fortunes because they might inherit something some day.

For the election campaign, President Bush adopted the arguments of the American Medical Association and all the health industries. He has claimed that "defensive medicine," the super cautious, test-dominated approach of some doctors who fear lawsuits, is costing between $US 28 billion and $US 108 billion a year (the AMA says it is between $US 60 billion and $US 108 billion). President Bush doesn't like lawyers. "A lot of times, these lawyers will sue everybody in sight in order to try to get something," he said. "In cases where more than one person is responsible for a patient's injuries, we need to assign blame fairly. . . . there are too many lawsuits filed against doctors and hospitals without merit." The President was particularly concerned about what he describes as "junk" lawsuits. "It costs money to fight off a junk lawsuit, and oftentimes, in order to avoid litigation and oftentimes to cut their costs, docs, and therefore the companies that insure them, just settle."

It should be noted that total U.S. health spending in 2002 was about $US 1.6 trillion, a 125 percent increase since 1987. Malpractice premiums increased by 76 percent during the same period. The total U.S. annual premium income to insurance companies was $US 9.6 billion in 2002, significantly less than one percent of health costs. The average malpractice claim in 1984 was $US 185,000. By 2003, that had risen to $US 291,000. Malpractice payouts totaled $US 4.5 billion in 2003. The combined cost of premiums and claims was still less than 1 percent of health spending. Pharmaceutical spending has doubled in five years. Doctors' incomes have grown faster than malpractice insurance premiums.

Once again, President Bush's research appears to be spoon fed from vested interests — and clearly wrong. Ironically, during the 2004 election campaign, the vice-presidential opponent was Senator John Edwards, who made his fortune as a trial lawyer, often handling personal injury, malpractice, and class action cases. Responding to Bush's bombast, Edwards said: "Senator Kerry and I are going to stand with families and kids, as we always have and as we believe is important for the president and the vice president to do, instead of being on the side of insurance companies and big drug companies. . . standing against seriously injured children and families. We do need to protect doctors from growing malpractice premiums, but we need to ask the hard question why premiums are going up. The truth is the insurance industry has done poorly in the market and is simply passing those costs on to doctors and patients."

Trial lawyer Johnny Cochrane argued that supporters of the $US 250,000 cap aim only to protect special interest groups, providers, practitioners, and suppliers. "One of the most often repeated myths about malpractice suits today is that frivolous cases are clogging up the courts and juries are awarding huge payouts to undeserving injured people; people believe those are the reasons insurance rates keep rising," says a Cochrane colleague, Jeffery Mitchell. "In fact, as noted in a study done by the Harvard Medical Practice Study Groups, for every eight potential medical malpractice claims, only one is likely to ever be filed. Liability insurers do not settle frivolous cases, and judges do not entertain those cases in a court of law. Insurers are aware that if they ever begin to settle frivolous cases, their credibility within the industry will be destroyed, and judges realize that entertaining frivolous cases will clog up already overloaded dockets and encourage more unreasonably grounded litigation.

Consumer advocate Ralph Nader had strong words about Bush:

> He ignores the medical malpractice epidemic that Harvard physicians estimate takes 80,000 lives a year just in hospitals (not emergency rooms, clinics or physician offices). This preventable violence exceeds the combined fatality toll of motor vehicle crashes and AIDS patients. He ignores the unwillingness of most medical societies, including the American Medical Association, to demand that state licensing boards investigate and discipline the small percentage of physicians who repeatedly account for the mayhem. These dangerous doctors practice dangerous medicine and escape the 'responsibility' that Mr. Bush always talks about when he discusses welfare mothers and teachers. He ignores the economic costs of this malpractice epidemic, estimated by Harvard physicians over ten years ago to cost our people $60 billion a year.

The health industry regularly protests that juries, composed of lay-men who act on emotion, not reason, are responsible for huge settle-ments. Cochrane disputed this: "According to Jury Verdict Research, in the year 2000, health care providers won approximately 62 percent of the cases that were tried by a jury. That means that the patients only pre-vailed in approximately 38 percent of all the jury trial cases in this coun-try. . . . In cases involving the allegation of misdiagnosis in a medical malpractice case, patients only won 37 percent of the jury trials against the defendant health care providers. These lopsided statistics demon-strate that the jury system in this country is not using sympathy to give runaway verdicts to patients of medical malpractice."

The AMA claims that the average jury verdict in the United States is now $US 1 million, but *U.S. News and World Report* magazine calcu-lated that the actual average amount per case of initiated litigation is $US 295,000, since the vast majority get settled before getting to a jury deci-sion. It seems apparent that the only agencies campaigning to minimize public access to the courts are those who profit most substantially from the health care system. Insurance premiums are rising faster in the 19 states which have a cap than those which do not, and the number of cases reaching the courts in the United States are going down, not up.

Canadian Medical Protective Association (CMPA)

Founded in 1901 and incorporated by an Act of Parliament in 1913, the Canadian Medical Protective Association is, effectively, the self-insur-ance safety net for Canadian physicians. It is owned and funded by its 62,000 members, including 95 percent of the doctors licensed to practice in Canada. In many respects, it is one of the most outstanding agencies of its kind in the health world, a valuable source of information and a cooperative that pays equal attention to the interests of its membership at large, as it does to the actuarial science necessary in any insurance pro-gram. Therefore, the dues paid by members reflect the risk factors asso-ciated with claims experience in the region where they work, and also their particular area of medical practice. There are about 300 different categories for the payment of dues, essentially about 100 job descriptions divided into three regions: Quebec, where claims tend to be low; Ontario, which has the most litigation and highest damages; and, the rest of the country. The minimum CMPA fee is about $500 for a member who prac-tices outside of the country and doesn't treat patients, to a high of $90,000 for an Ontario surgeon in obstetrics and gynecology. The national average fee is about $5,000. Quebec doctors, who have the lowest rates of litigation and claims, pay substantially less than elsewhere. One medical journal described Ontario as "The Texas of Canada."

The work of CMPA is explained in detail on the web site *www.cmpa.org*. The fee structure and relationship with its members are transparent, a rarity in the health field, where vested interests are usually propelled by secret agendas, special privilege, and sometimes questionable if not corrupt political lobbies and associations. The association defines itself as "a mutual defense organization, not an insurance company." It has $2 billion in reserve, which earns income to keep down dues, and regularly warns members that "this fund should be considered as already spent, as it provides for the costs of future judgments, settlements, legal expenses and administration for claims related to all the medical care given in the past as well as in the current year."

Malpractice premiums in Canada were insignificant until the 1980s, but following on the heels of American experience and the costs of substantial class action suits in that country, doctors here began to panic. They protested to their provincial governments that they did not have the ability to pass on these rising costs to their patients, since the rates were set by provincial negotiation. Fee-for-service physicians protested that salaried doctors in government, educational environments, and hospitals, along with all hospital employees were indemnified for malpractice risk, so why should they have to assume this burden? One after the other, the provinces set up reimbursement schemes, to the point, today, where most Canadian doctors get the lion's share of their malpractice premiums back. But CMPA is concerned today by the inconsistencies from province to province, in how the matter is managed. The CMPA states:

> The current approach to provincial/territorial reimbursement of CMPA fees is unsatisfactory in several respects. First, the level of reimbursement is subject to periodic negotiations between the provinces/territories and the provincial/territorial medical associations or, in the case of Quebec, the (health care) federations. There is an element of uncertainty in the minds of practitioners whether they will be subject to personal medico-legal or financial risk as these negotiations recur on a cyclical basis. This uncertainty in turn may impair all patient access to medical services, especially to high-risk care. While the CMPA's fees are now set on a regional basis, reimbursement programs are negotiated on a provincial/territorial basis. Physicians who provide medical services in more than one province may not be eligible for reimbursement

of CMPA fees in such circumstances. For example, a physician in the currently lower cost region of Quebec may not be eligible for reimbursement of the higher fee payable if he or she provides services in the higher cost region of New Brunswick. We have been made aware of cases in which physicians have simply stopped providing care in other regions for this reason alone. Again, patient access to medical services may be put at significant risk.

This is how malpractice premiums have become part of the government-physician bartering process in Canada. What is completely astounding is that no one has stood back a pace and considered what this means in terms of physician performance and accountability. By assuring the reimbursement of most, if not all, of the malpractice premiums, government has exempted the MDs from responsibility for their own actions. Instead of calculating specific costs of doing business, considering the CMPA dues in the same light as rising rent, staff costs, and other overhead, during the annual negotiation of fees, governments have accepted this cost directly. This bizarre safety net, diluting the consequences of malpractice, is rationalized to a gullible public as necessary to maintain an adequate supply of physicians, particularly in the high risk specialties.

Government versus the victims of medicine

Patients and their lawyers suing medical doctors soon become incensed that they are, in terms of costs, really suing the government. The CMPA is a tireless litigant with a track record of fighting everything, even the most trivial and basic issues. The $2 billion reserve of funds provides a foundation few opponents can match. A strategy to aggressively pursue cases proceeds with the knowledge that a high percentage of actions can be made to go away simply as a result of time, manufactured complexity, expense and, sometimes, even the death of the complainant during the interim. Malpractice is a Mount Everest for plaintiffs anyway, because doctors must be found to testify against colleagues. Records become stale-dated and often prepared by those involved in the incidents, if not dishonestly, then certainly designed to put the best possible face on a bad situation. Only 5-20 percent of such incidents ever get reported, so the plaintiffs often are faced with the task of reconstructing history, burdened by all of the associated costs. Expert witnesses — particularly doctors — require compensation for both research and testimony. The fees are exorbitant.

What makes this so odd is that "adverse events" are costing the health system fortunes. The CIHI/CIHR study shows that 7.5 percent of patients are made ill, not better, as a result of their hospital experience. Therefore, investments by government in protecting the perpetrators encourage this expensive and tragic behavior, while any assistance given to those seeking satisfactory redress would motivate more careful and, hopefully, better performance by the system. But we have precisely the reverse in Canada.

Since the taxpayers and their provincial governments are, indirectly, paying the dues for the country's doctors, it essentially means that injured patients and their families are fighting the government. Doctors and hospitals get a free ride with respect to costs associated with their own incompetence. This is in the face of Canadian statistics about hospital and medical-caused adverse events that are epidemic. But the perpetrators of these personal tragedies can sleep comfortably with the knowledge that the taxpayers will purchase for them the finest legal defense team available, spare no expense. No other health care providers, unless they are indemnified as staff of hospitals and public agencies, enjoy such protection. All other health professionals are on their own: naturopaths, dieticians, chiropractors, podiatrists, dentists, acupuncturists, physiotherapists, massage therapists and others. Only the most expensive, most protected, most powerful, least self-sufficient and most accident prone enjoy the benefit of government absolution from cost, if not responsibility.

During 2002, the CMPA opened 15,100 new files and closed 17,000. A "file" could be anything from an inquiry to a threatened action. Of the pending files, 1,225 new actions commenced and during the course of the year, 372 cases were settled out of court and 843 claims were abandoned. Of those that went to trial, 22 were won by the plaintiffs and 89 by the CMPA on behalf of their member physician defendants. Contrast this with five years earlier, when there were 11,738 new files opened and 10,194 closed, a big difference. But the actual litigation numbers were almost identical: 332 cases settled in 1998 and 824 abandoned. Plaintiffs won 21 of those that went to trial and the defendants won 86. The total cost of litigation, settlements and damages paid by CMPA during 2002 was just over $200 million.

This works out to one fifth of one percent of total health care in Canada, described in the words of one plaintiff's lawyer, "a monumental tempest in a teapot." Furthermore, the success rate of CMPA in the face of solid statistical evidence of medical misadventure, demonstrates conclusively that Canadians are not being adequately protected and in the event of difficulty, they are not being fairly compensated either. The fact that their government defends only the accused and the system, but not the victims, is a prime case in point.

Other issues

- Canadian doctors have become extremely nervous about treating patients from other countries, most notably the U.S. They are frightened by AMA statistics about $US 1 million jury settlements. CMPA has affirmed that it will defend its member doctors only if actions are launched in Canada, but not "in circumstances where the care could reasonably be provided outside of Canada," or where the doctor solicited or advertised in the foreign jurisdiction to attract patients. It will "generally" help doctors who treat non-resident patients in emergency circumstances, providing the patient is asked to sign a waiver stating that they would sue only in Canada.

- CMPA has warned doctors taking part in the brisk cross-border Internet pharmaceutical business that they are on their own. Media and U.S. investigative agencies have taken a dim view of phony prescriptions signed by some Canadian MDs to assist in this cross-border traffic. If they have physically diagnosed the patient and then subsequently written a prescription, there would be no ethical concern in either country, but since these doctors are prospecting for business in the U.S., it would be their personal responsibility to purchase malpractice insurance for this work.

- Actions involving sports stars in the affluent major leagues, where diagnostic and treatment mistakes could potentially cost multiple millions of dollars in lost income for athletes and their teams, creates a potential risk never anticipated in CMPA planning. Therefore, doctors dealing with professional sports injuries have been told to negotiate indemnification from the teams or to purchase additional insurance protection from private sources.

"That **Desperotex** recall was just bad luck! . . . . This new one, **Precortex**, is a good story for you — a big bounce for the stock market, more money for us to dominate university labs . . . . a terrific generator for doctors and pharmacists . . . . win, win I say ! "

6.
The Cheerleaders

Propaganda is to a democracy what the bludgeon is to a totalitarian state.

— NOAM CHOMSKY, PHD in *Media Control*

The so-called "perp walk" has been among the more entertaining spectacles in world media, as agents of the United States Federal Bureau of Investigation, the U.S. Marshall's Service, the U.S. Treasury, County Sheriffs, and local police marched a steady parade of millionaires and billionaires in handcuffs in front of television cameras and waiting reporters. We have watched Kenneth Lay and Andrew Fastow of Enron; Bernie Ebbers and Scott Sullivan of WorldCom; John Rigas and his two sons of Adelphia Communications; Martha Stewart's pal Samuel Waksal of ImClone; and many other former members of the global corporate elite parade ignominiously to the courthouse and jail, where they resided for at least a few hours.

Through it all, media headlines have screamed about the billions of dollars bilked from investors, life savings vacuumed out of society by unbridled greed and fraud, pension plans bulldozed into dust, and the security of millions of people thrown into question. Sanctimonious media commentators searched for adverbs and adjectives sufficiently powerful to emphasize how awful it all was and how contemptible these people are.

The media circus of righteous indignation begged just one question: who made these people famous in the first place?

Who put them on the covers of magazines and in the lead slots of television documentary programs as poster people for new age wealth, prime examples of how everyone could make a fortune in America? Who indeed? How could you fault a pension manager for putting a disproportionate amount of fund assets into one of these big ventures, after all of the major media organs — *Forbes*, *Time*, *The Wall Street Journal*,

Newsweek, 60 Minutes, NBC Dateline etc. — had previously treated these shameless crooks as geniuses and heroes? Didn't any of these journals smell a rat? Why did they all so giddily publish corporate press releases as fact? Whatever happened to investigative journalism?

Third World Traveller (*www.thirdworldtraveller.com*), a web site analyzing media, posted this observation attributed to a former agent of the Soviet Union who spent five years in America:

> I have the greatest admiration for your propaganda. Propaganda in the West is carried out by experts who have had the best training in the world — in the field of advertising — and have mastered the techniques with exceptional proficiency ... Yours are subtle and persuasive; ours are crude and obvious ... I think that the fundamental difference between our worlds, with respect to propaganda, is quite simple. You tend to believe yours ... and we tend to disbelieve ours.

Modern media — classy, but?

We are the best-informed society in human history. The sheer volume of radio, television, and print media of all descriptions catering to every conceivable human interest and backed up by libraries, great universities, museums, and other repositories of information should ensure that truth prevails. If traditional media were not enough, then the explosion in Internet use has filled in every crack in the system. In western society, at least, it takes discipline and effort to remain uninformed, the conscientious avoidance of facts and stimuli.

News reporters today are far better educated than they ever were in the past and they report to sophisticated editors. A generation or two ago, most newsrooms were dominated by self-educated, but aggressive and determined people. University degrees and the products of the establishment were sprinkled among them, but the star reporters were usually individuals with outstanding street smarts who did their research in police stations, city council chambers, legislatures, and war zones. Within their respective specialties, journalists who covered the arts, sports, health, the sciences, and business had also climbed an apprenticeship ladder. By the time any of them reached an editor's desk, it was just about impossible to fool them. They had acquired a healthy degree of skepticism.

The media culture was adversarial. Reporters and editors felt they represented the middle and lower working classes. They were champions of the underdog. A reporter's greatest joy was found in exposing fraud and corruption. That's what Pulitzer Prizes were all about. It was said about that era that a successful reporter lived like a millionaire, but never became one. That is untrue today. The superstars of journalism — particularly in television — make millions, work little, and spend more time in make-up than they do on the street where news happens.

An even more profound change has occurred in corporate media ownership. Media critics suggest that a symbiotic relationship exists among wealthy media owners, their friends, and the multi-billion dollar advertising industry that ultimately corrupts the news. Most of these conspiracy theories about the manipulation of information are clearly ridiculous. Although reporters and editors are often hired and shaped to fit a media organ's editorial stance, their domain is so far below those lofty ownership perches, it is a separate world. Those who produce the news remain quite independent. The more serious modern change is the replacement of proactive and issue-driven ownership by impersonal corporate processes. At one time, just about every newspaper, magazine, radio station, and television outlet was the enterprise of an individual owner and manager, each of whom had a meaningful stake in the communities they served. Lord Beaverbrook, Roy Thomson, William Paley, Joseph Pulitzer, and William Randolph Hearst had a reason for being in media. What they produced often had a strong political point of view and journalists were fired if their stories did not conform. But rocking the boat was the name of the game. Business success depended upon readership and there was always lots of competition. The top story of the day made the bucks. In any community, it is easy to trace the roots of each historic media organ and discover a founder who had a stake in the local area, was motivated to improve the society, and was held to account by each and every friend. Whatever excesses were perpetrated by the autocrats of the past, at least they cared about the specific communities their media organs served. Few of today's top media executives could pass even the most basic public affairs quiz about the market areas covered by their holdings.

Leonard Asper, who succeeded his late father Izzy as Chief Executive Officer of CanWest Global Communications, is typical of today's executives. A major concern for him is the ban by the Canadian government on Direct to Consumer Advertising (DCTA) of pharmaceuticals. At a 2004 broadcasting convention, Asper protested that Canadians get these ads over American signals, so why should Canadian broadcasters be denied the income? In Canada, Big Pharma is restricted to the traditional practice of influencing doctors, hospitals, and other government and institutional decision makers. "It's a big advertising category and it will get to be a bigger one as the baby boomers age," Asper said.

Under Canadian law, prescription drugs cannot be advertised through mass media. Professional opinion has it that no good can come from patients pestering doctors and pharmacists to acquire whatever drug was advertised to them during last night's soap opera. Canadian broadcasters have won some prominent politicians over to their side, including cabinet ministers, but the House of Commons committee dealing with the issue remains determinedly opposed. Senator John Kerry made DCTA an election issue in the U.S. He views it as one of the major pharmaceutical problems in the United States, contributing not only to soaring costs, but also to the adverse events death statistics.

Once again, it begs the question: where is media leadership on this subject of public interest?

Today's media is run by conglomerates. Owners measure their success by merging multiple entities and eliminating layers of duplicated infrastructure. It has nothing at all to do with the quality of the product at the consumer level. Underlings — salaried gnomes — worry about those things. Accountants and tax experts descend upon media corporations like an airborne regiment. If spending $10 million to attract a blonde bombshell to read the evening news will generate $20 million in advertising sales, go for it fast. Quality, probative news reporting is expensive and an infuriatingly slow route to success. By the time the news team gets the local nightly show up to number one in the city's ratings, the ownership of the station may change three times. With each change, platoons of former insiders fly off with their bonus money and windfall profits. In their wake is usually left increased debt, required to help finance the takeover, which must be serviced from existing operations. Invariably that means cuts of local staff and programming.

In this age of corporate media ownership, effective competition in many areas of the news business has been eliminated, particularly in print news. Few cities today are able to sustain more than one major newspaper company. In local markets, most radio and television stations depend upon print for most of their news. They get their stories from wire services, which are almost completely gleaned from daily newspapers — the phrase in radio is "rip and read." Television cares about little other than pictures and entertainment. Therefore, when there is no newspaper competition in a city, the quality of all media takes a downward turn.

Investigative journalism is time-consuming, expensive, and wasteful to owners in the quick buck era.

Thus, we have the paradox of modern media in western society. We have better educated and well paid professionals operating within corporate systems. Through the sheer volume of media, the availability of information has never been better. Our media are largely honest, although frequently lazy and afraid of lawsuits. Few media companies are major risk takers. Media are often condemned for being too negative, but that is nonsense, a reflection of a largely positive society. "News" means whatever is unique. In a "positive" society, the unique is "negative." The late American Senator Daniel Patrick Moynihan once said, "If you go to a country and read nothing but good news in the newspaper, you can be assured that all of the good people are in jail."

Television can be spectacular in terms of delivering us right to the scene of major news. When there is a natural disaster, a war, or a major spectacle of any kind, the best television coverage makes all other journalism a quaint anachronism by comparison. We are there. We can see. We can hear. Later, we can turn to all media to benefit from skilled, expert commentators to help us interpret. Unfortunately, on a day-to-day basis, television news is as empty as a *Road Runner* cartoon, a formulaic collection of predictable political comments, accidents, crime, sex, health, and show biz, a snippet of everything to bake the daily pie.

Robert MacNeil, author and former executive editor and co-anchor of the *MacNeil-Lehrer Newshour* on PBS said, "The idea is to keep everything brief, not to strain the attention of anyone but instead to provide constant stimulation through variety, novelty, action, and movement. You are required to pay attention to no concept, no character, and no problem for more than a few seconds at a time.... bite-sized is best, that complexity must be avoided, that nuances are dispensable, that qualifications impede the simple message, that visual stimulation is a substitute for thought, and that verbal precision is an anachronism."

Neil Postman once wrote:

Whereas we expect books and even other media (such as film) to maintain a consistency of tone and a continuity of content, we have no such expectation of television, and especially television news. We have become so accustomed to its discontinuities that we are no longer struck dumb, as any sane person would be, by a newscaster who having just reported that a nuclear war is inevitable goes on to say that he will be right back after this word from Burger King; who says, in other

words, "Now . . . this." One can hardly overestimate the damage that
such juxtapositions do to our sense of the world as a serious place. The
damage is especially massive to youthful viewers who depend so much
on television for their clues as to how to respond to the world. In watch-
ing television news, they, more than any other segment of the audience,
are drawn into an epistemology based on the assumption that all reports
of cruelty and death are greatly exaggerated and, in any case, not to be
taken seriously or responded to sanely.

Media and health

If the Enrons and WorldCom frauds came as a complete shock and surprise to media, how does one explain how Canadian media missed the
fact that up to 23,000 people a year were dying in acute care hospitals as
a result of medical mistakes? Remember that the data from the 2004
CIHR/CIHI study represented only a small slice of total medical care; it
excluded pediatrics, obstetrics, and psychiatry; the study consisted of
records kept at the time of incidents by the people who were party to the
problem; and, American studies show that only 5-20 percent of adverse
incidents ever get reported. So, what is the real annual death toll in
Canada as a result of medically-caused problems? 50,000? Worse? How
big is it in each community? In each hospital?

How could Canadian media not notice that the number of iatrogenic
deaths in hospitals was many times greater than, for example, the number of deaths that occurred on our highways? The first clue might have
been the American reports on the same subject published during the early
1990s. Since Canadian media missed that train, one might have thought
they would have noticed the 2002 announcement by the Canadian
Institutes of Health Research and the Canadian Institute of Health
Information that "adverse events" was going to be a major study.
Couldn't at least one editor have said maybe we could beat them to the
punch and see how many locals might be saved before the official agencies finish their work?

Finally, when the report was published in 2004, the road map was
there for any media outlet in any community and, like faithful puppies,
they went to hospital administrators and doctors for comment. Whatever
they said was good enough for the media: a pledge to try harder, the
impression that all this was news, vague discussions about how it was a
matter of definition and the problem was NEVER caused by the individuals quoted. It was caused by "hospitals" — not people.

With all the public evidence emerging in both Canada and the U.S., leading up to the government-sponsored investigation, it was shameful that reporters had not been assigned in every community to investigate local hospitals. And, in fact, there has been very little media enterprise since. Almost daily now, we hear of hospitals that have become disease factories, but media seems content to interview victims and health apologists, and look no further. What they never do is hold a specific doctor, who placed the patient in jeopardy, responsible for the bad treatment.

Editors and reporters who grab onto issues like dogs on a bone are virtually non-existent today. There are few causes viewed to be so important that a team of journalists is assigned to stay on the job until a logical conclusion is reached. Would a new "Watergate" command the kind of resources *The Washington Post* and other agencies devoted to the early 1970s' American scandal? How many "Watergates" go by undetected these days in modern democracies, because of lazy and irresponsible media? Government and corporate spin doctors know that the attention span of media is limited; they jump into the bunker, convinced that most public relations crises will pass in 48 hours. Surely, the tens of thousands of unnecessary deaths and disabilities that occur within the Canadian medical system are worthy of consistent and aggressive coverage.

Apparently not.

National television networks are obsessed with making sure some sensational health story is included in every newscast. The business sections of newspapers are full of the latest announcements from biomedical companies, each one hinting more effusively than the other that four million mice from now they might have the next Prozac. Stocks prices increase on cue. The popular press seems entirely fixated by the entertainment aspects of health and the public's fascination with aches, pains, and remedies. Readership surveys have taught business media that the stock market is where it's at. Readers are far less interested in the substance of news than they are in share prices. Even Big Pharma, despite its multi-billion dollar investment in advertising and promotion, has a hard time getting the same attention in the business pages as the sexy new start-up companies that create the stock market sizzle.

There may be fewer than 100 medical discoveries in history that were so profound they demonstrably changed the world. Most modern media organs announce more than a 100 new medical discoveries each month. They are seduced by news releases issued by researchers desperate to obtain capital for their work. Private companies, universities, and foundations need support, whether it is for grant applications or investment capital. Therefore, publicity is the key. News releases are issued — hopefully honest and with only forgivable degrees of exaggeration — and media are approached to publish the stories. Most often, the possibility of a medical breakthrough may require years before human testing can take place, and years more before publication in peer-reviewed journals and formal government approval. But media audiences cannot be acquired by saying a "breakthrough" may be 10 years away. That's okay in the fine print at the tail end of news item, but advance promotion of a story sticks to the word "breakthrough" and anything else to suggest an impending miracle. At least every person suffering from that ailment and their families will watch or read the story.

Many media agencies now have physicians on staff or on a permanent retainer. These doctors, invariably have unimpressive professional resumes, but are usually good communicators. They are presented as authorities on topics so vastly beyond their own personal education, experience, and knowledge, the editors might just as well ask the building janitor to comment. Unfortunately, instead of being impartial analysts, these doctors become public relations representatives of the medical establishment, entrenching bias. This reinforces everything that is wrong with the management of health care today. The "gatekeeper" in health is whomever makes the primary contact with the patient, usually a general practitioner, who becomes a broker for other specialists and services. Planting a "gatekeeper" within media strengthens, promotes and protects the monopoly and fundraising imperatives of medical associations, universities, biomedical companies, and hospital-related industries. They tend to "filter-out" any health topic that may not fit the medical association agenda.

Peer-reviewed journals

If the most important publications in health such as the *British Medical Journal*, the *Journal of the American Medical Association*, the *New England Journal of Medicine* and the *Canadian Medical Association Journal* had been exposed for journalistic incompetence as was the case of mainstream media with respect to the unpredicted collapse of Enron, WorldCom, and Adelphia, heads would have rolled. There would have been a rebellion of physicians and biological scientists around the world, who would have demanded answers: "How could the peer-review committees of these journals have been so negligent?"

Each of these distinguished publications has been, individually and collectively, dealing with a crisis of their own. The encroachment by pharmaceutical companies on both research agencies and researchers gradually compromised the integrity of far too many important articles. It was not just that the author was on the payroll of a drug company, it had become so pervasive that even the laboratory and university at which the scientist worked had become dependent upon this industry money. In fact, just about every time some calamitous failure hit the headlines about adverse reactions to drugs, it was possible to trace the history to an article in one of the quality publications, where the wonder drug was shamelessly promoted. The problem continues to this day, but the journals are all trying to improve the controls over content.

Ethicists worldwide, many of them on the staff of peer-reviewed journals, focused most heavily upon disclosure. The principal concern is the funding of the research and the researcher, direct or indirect. It is not good enough to cite a "foundation" or a "university," which frequently have been used to hide the real source — Big Pharma. The editors concentrate on content, to restrain some of the more enthusiastic preliminary boasts, particularly if the financing has less than purely scientific motives. These journals respect their readers. The feeling is that if disclosure is complete, the readers can attach their own level of credibility and due diligence to the content. Mainstream media could learn much from these editors.

Nancy versus Goliath

One Canadian story became a symbol of this entire issue. The story sadly placed two of our most accomplished citizens on opposite sides of the issue, with institutions such as The Hospital for Sick Children (Sick Kids) and the University of Toronto in the middle. Medical doctor and scientist Dr. Nancy Olivieri, who worked for Toronto's Hospital for Sick Children, had made extraordinary strides researching a rare blood disorder called thalassaemia, and her work had been published in important journals. In 1993, Dr. Olivieri, the hospital, and the university applied for, and were subsequently granted, funding from the generic drug giant Apotex to continue the work. The new drug's research label was "L1."

By 1998, Dr. Olivieri was growing increasingly anxious about patient side effects from L1 and reported this to her stakeholders, including Apotex. She asked permission to stop the tests and to warn her patients and the public. Enter, one of the most successful Canadians of a generation, billionaire Dr. Bernard (Barry) Sherman, an aeronautical

118

engineering graduate of the Massachusetts Institute of Technology, who took over a small family generic drug business early in his career, and who went on to create Apotex, the largest pharmaceutical company in Canada.

Apotex and Dr. Sherman reminded Dr. Olivieri that she had signed a confidentiality agreement upon receiving the funding. Apotex lawyers advised both Sick Kids and the University of this fact and they threatened to sue both institutions, in addition to Dr. Olivieri, if the agreement was violated. Dr. Olivieri suffered enormous pressure from her colleagues, the hospital, and the university, all of whom seemed to put their own interests ahead of either their distinguished doctor or her patients. Finally, she ignored them all and went public. Apotex sued, and one of the greatest debates in the history of medical research erupted world-wide.

In matters this grave there can be no winner except the public and future business and research ethics. Dr. Olivieri suffered greatly. She made a serious mistake at the outset by signing the confidentiality agreement. Her peers concluded this was a matter of inexperience on both sides of the contract. Sherman and Apotex were made to look like inconsiderate villains. An independent committee of inquiry into the matter concluded that neither the university nor the hospital offered Dr. Olivieri appropriate support. The matter was resolved out of court.

The bottom line was simple. No obligation can possibly override a physician's primary responsibility to the patient. Doctors may face penalties for other contractual failures related to the same issue, but they have no choice over the propriety of informing patients. The case has done wonders for those within medicine and science who have been fighting for years to attain full disclosure of all secret agreements, funding, and special interests.

This story was, in fact, a triumph for Canadian media. It was approached with diligence, determination, intelligence, and sensitivity. Most media paid equal attention to all four parties: Olivieri, Apotex, Sick Kids and U of T. Each was given an opportunity to have their say and when, at various stages, lawyers put the muzzle on their clients, reporters dutifully explained this to the public without the all too frequent tendency to imply that something evil was hiding behind the curtain. There were a few obvious exceptions, but most of the media coverage was highly professional. And interesting. And it was extremely beneficial to the public who had an opportunity to learn about a major dilemma of modern science.

An important part of the story was Apotex's usual role as defined by the international pharmaceutical giants — the big generic drug company-villain allegedly doing no research, but waiting to prey on another drug manufacturer's patents. The Olivieri case was a demonstration of the reverse. Big Pharma did its best on the sidelines to maximize the discomfort of Apotex, the precocious Canadian upstart. Apotex has over 90 full-time scientists, a significant percentage of whom are engaged in original research, not just $1-million conversions of patented drugs that may have cost $300 million or more to develop. The company also finances foundations and universities for research elsewhere. Barry Sherman is one of Canada's most generous philanthropists.

Medical congresses and the media

There is a wealth of literature about Big Pharma money improperly benefiting physicians by sponsoring travel, courses, recreational pursuits, and individual pleasures. When is the last time an investigative story about this appeared in your local newspaper or broadcast outlets? Have local reporters ever probed the issue? The most glaring examples of Big Pharma largesse can be found at major medical conventions and, most notably, world congresses. These occur with some regularity in the larger cities of Canada. Despite published ethical standards and rules of conduct, it is not at all unusual for pharmaceutical companies to block hundreds of hotel rooms, charter harbor cruises, and buy gift packs of tickets to local attractions in host cities, well in advance of these conventions. Pharmaceutical companies openly sponsor medical conventions, but how can the rest of it be explained?

If a big drug company has booked hundreds of hotel rooms in a city, usually the prime locations for the Congress delegates, but only sends two corporate representatives, who sleeps in the rooms? Who goes on the harbor cruises or to the entertainment attractions? What's the *quid pro quo*? It is permissible for drug companies to finance the travel of "speakers," but not a lot of investigation goes into how the definition of the word "speaker" is applied. The congresses themselves are usually quite circumspect about identifying the corporate sponsors of specific lectures.

Uncovering these questionable practices requires only elementary journalistic investigation. Every hotel manager, sales person, front desk employee, tourist co-ordinator, and airline employee has experienced the ubiquitous involvement of drug companies in medical conventions. Convention management requires a cast of thousands, most with only small tasks to perform, but they all have seen this story in action. The reason one hears little about this dark side of medicine is that the questions are rarely asked. Reporters show up, dutifully accept the press releases about the latest alleged miracles and scientific breakthroughs, and happily go away, rarely examining the commercial relationships between the sellers of chemicals and the medical professionals. More meaningful stories are thought to be too much work, and, as long as no one else in media is doing it, the public will be none the wiser. It is also a mystery why the Canada Customs and Revenue Agency never seems to put these drug-financed events under the microscope.

Have they no shame?

Whenever you turn on the television news and see desperate patients attached to respiratory equipment or IV bottles, protesting long waits for medical care, you can be certain that someone is in the midst of negotiations with the government: doctors, nurses, technicians, staff, or one of the many derivative groups under those headings. It is the suffering patient — never the financial interest of the practitioner — that is front and centre in the news story.

"SEE THESE SICK PEOPLE? GIVE ME MORE MONEY AND THEY WILL GET BETTER." This is the underlying caption to the heart-wrenching images. There seems to be no shame at all in using patients to assist in negotiations, and the media never fail to get suckered into participating in the campaigns. There are always waiting lists and there will always be people who cannot get the surgery or treatment they and their doctors think is appropriate, precisely when they think they need it. There will always be people unhappy with the health care they are receiving.

How do you suppose the media finds these aggrieved patients? Without doubt, media get many unsolicited calls from angry citizens with respect to health care and many of the stories are precisely as they appear. But when you see similar stories in all local media at the same time, it is certain that some employee group is cranking up the rhetoric. Amidst labor negotiations, the most eager audience is the media, ever watchful for any stories involving blood and government criticism. These clusters of stories magically disappear from news prominence immediately upon the conclusion of any negotiation.

'There may be fewer than 100 medical discoveries in history that were so profound
they demonstrably changed the world.
Most modern media organs announce
more than a 100 new medical discoveries
each month. They are seduced by news
releases issued by researchers desperate
to obtain capital for their work. Private
companies, universities, and foundations need support, whether it is for
grant applications or investment capital.
Therefore, publicity is the key."

7.
The Red Herring

Hospitals budget on the basis of an annual lump sum, and from then on view the patient as someone who is using up the hospital's money. They don't really know what any procedure costs. There is too much bureaucracy and too much overhead that has nothing to do with patient care. . . It is normal for me to come out of a lengthy surgical procedure and see three or four unionized employees leisurely waiting — who knows how long — to go in and clean up the operating room. Competition is good for everybody, because now we know exactly what everything should cost. In the public system there is overt rationing of health services and you are forced to take whatever they decide to give you.

— BRIAN DAY, MD, a Vancouver orthopedic surgeon

In Canadian medicine, the irrepressible official fantasy is our so-called equal, free, and universally accessible medicare. It is certainly not free. There is no equality. And universal access depends on where you live and what ails you. The term "accessible" applies almost exclusively to medical doctors and hospitals. There is almost no access to the other licensed and regulated health professionals who, within their own specialty, are far more able and less expensive. For many people, "accessible" simply means a place in the queue, rather than quality, efficient, and timely care. The main issue should be patient health. Not dollars. Not policy. Not federal-provincial wrangling or turf wars among health providers. At the patient-care level our results are embarrassingly poor by any international comparison.

There is another preposterous notion, passionately opposed by all officialdom. It argues that the right of an individual to purchase whatever health services they desire within Canada, entirely at their own expense, would not lead to two-tiered health care. Inequality already exists, but without dramatic improvements in management and productivity in the public system, this would inevitably escalate today's problem into an intolerable class society.

The standard definition for the idiom "red herring" is "any diversion intended to distract attention from the main issue." David Wilton's wonderful web site *www.wordorigins.org* explains the roots of the phrase.

> This term for deliberate misdirection comes from hunting. Poachers would interpose themselves between the prey and the hunting party and drag a red herring across the trail to mislead the dogs. This would give them the opportunity to bag the prey themselves. . . .a red herring was chosen because dog trainers often used the pungent fish to create a trail when training their hounds. The dogs, upon encountering the herring scent, would follow that trail as it was the one they had been trained with.

Those who "bag the prey" in the health care field in Canada are the politicians, medical associations, health unions, senior bureaucrats, and hospital administrators. Everything about today's health system concerns power, monopolies, restrictive business practices, and elitism. The outrageously dishonest medicare debate allows the ultimate beneficiaries of the status quo to bellow from the rafters that they are defending the public. They and the limitless list of consultants, inquiries, task forces, and meetings — none of which ever treat a patient — consume vast resources that would be better spent on care. These are the self-appointed, and handsomely well paid, Lancelots out to savage the heathens of free enterprise.

The secondary "elite" are those with outstanding extended health benefit plans, which include — what a surprise! — everybody in the public sector, but a rapidly eroding number of people in the private sector. The "elite" under the Canadian system are those who are paid by government. Politicians head the list. Most government employees not only have unbeatable coverage today, the benefits are extended to them and their spouses until they die. Their benefits are usually portable, from one government job to another. "Rationalizations" in the private sector, along with mergers and acquisitions, usually terminate former plans. Federal politicians also benefit from VIP care at National Defense Department facilities in Ottawa.

We are becoming a society in which the non-government sector "serves" the servants. The ultimate mercenaries, in a philosophical sense, are politicians seeking votes, who use health care issues in search of approval and, ultimately, power. Public sector unions dominate the Canadian Labour Congress today. The national health debate is almost exclusively conducted by people on the public payroll and the principal beneficiaries of the system. Look at the names: Canadian Medical Association, provincial medical associations, health unions, politicians, university professors, and hired consultants. When public hearings are held, Chambers of Commerce, citizens' organizations, corporate representatives, and many "non-covered" health professions show up to present briefs, but they are merely humored with a polite, patronizing reception. Their views, and those of the vast majority of expert health economists in Canada, are ignored. Those who live, work, eat, and sleep in the trough determine the debate and dictate the policy.

The principal inequality lies in the phrase "extended health benefits." Many private sector health plans have been trashed by the economy in recent years. Each time federal or provincial governments apply limits or restrictions in coverage, it ultimately just transfers the health problem and associated costs to patients and, frequently, their employers. Private insurers who provide extended benefits either have to increase their premiums to fill the void, or keep the dominos from falling by also eliminating items or capping coverage. The benefits area is a private sector minefield today. The workforce has been progressively splintered into smaller and smaller units at the same time that corporate ownership has, paradoxically, been consolidated into ever-larger entities. Every time an employee changes jobs these days, they move into a new benefits situation, likely with more items eliminated. Any "pre-existing conditions" at the time of the new job start (any illness encountered by themselves or their dependants), get axed from the list.

There is an essential logic missing in many of today's coverage decisions. Each time a specific item is removed from universal coverage, the size of the covered base is reduced. The patient may still be protected by their private extended benefits plan or that of an employer, but whoever pays the premium for the plan will now be doing so on a smaller group, possibly just a group of one, if the patient pays directly. Therefore, any time the national plan covers all Canadians, the insurance rate becomes pennies by comparison to dollars. It must be emphasized, when governments or insurers cut a covered item, the patient's health issue does not go away.

Private diagnostic and surgery clinics have prospered from treating medicare-exempt services. Workers' compensation boards, the Royal Canadian Mounted Police, Veterans Affairs, members of the armed forces, federal prisoners, and other so-called "vital" institutions can legally queue-jump. No waiting for Magnetic Resonance Imaging (MRI), CT scans, and treatment procedures, the thought being that there is either a public service need or obligation to expedite treatment for these people.

Medicare, supposedly, opposes "for-profit" health care. Every one of the 60,000 medical doctors is a "for-profit" business, including the considerable number who are on salary. But what a business! Government ensures that there will be no competition and that the product is free to customers. There will never be a bad debt. All that is necessary is to coerce them into the medical lobster trap. (It easy to understand why those doctors who opted out of medicare failed as a private business and came scrambling back to the public system.) There are hundreds of thousands of other caregivers, including pharmacists, dentists, chiropractors, nurses, naturopaths, dieticians, technicians, physical and psychological therapists, and optometrists — an infinite list of specialties — who are also "for profit" either through salary or fee-for-service. What, pray tell, is the difference between a business group creating a clinic to sell a service and procedure at a competitive price, and an individual fee-for-service office charging for a consultation? In fact, many teams of physicians and specialists have come together under different types of clinics, community health centres, and group practices either on salary or fee-for-service arrangements.

Provincial governments in Canada shelter officially approved monopolies from competition. Optometrists, the most appropriate, most accessible and economical gatekeepers with respect to eye care, are experiencing rapidly deteriorating coverage under provincial medical plans. Patients now must either pay the optometrists personally, wait months for a "free" ophthalmologist (more expensive to the system), or surrender to an ill-trained clerk in an eyeglass store. Chiropractors should be the preferred initial consultant for anyone with most neuro-musculoskeletal problems. Every victim of whiplash and back pain should be examined by a chiropractor, but patient coverage under medicare is being progressively reduced or eliminated. Every reputable study ever done shows quicker recovery from these injuries through treatment from doctors of chiropractic than by going to medical doctors, who are not adequately trained to treat these conditions. Patients are effectively bribed by the word "free" to seek more expensive, inadequate, and inappropriate care, inevitably leading to a panoply of needless pharmaceuticals and — too often — surgery. We shelter and enrich incompetence, adding to patient suffering, time lost from work and high public cost. Every study shows that there are fewer drugs prescribed, there is less surgery, and results are better if a less expensive nurse practitioner is part of a care package, yet public policy has assisted the medical associations in suffocating the evolution of this competitive threat.

A national disgrace that has received far too little public analysis is the salary levels attained by health administrators. In most provinces, the managers of the largest hospitals have earned three, four, and five times the income of the Deputy Minister of Health, the top official in the field in any province. For what? The economic mismanagement of hospitals by any analysis has been scandalous. Health administrator salaries — $300,000 to $500,000 a year and more — soared between 1980 and 2000, a scandal largely perpetrated by the executive search industry. These recruiters told governments that they would have to pay top dollars to get "the best," whatever that was. The other standard practice was to compare a hospital to similar-sized private sector corporations. This could not possibly be an adequate comparison. Private sector leaders are accountable in terms of product development, customer service, the bottom line, and shareholder value. There has never been a similar analysis of hospitals and there has rarely been much accountability.

The Canadian hospital field has been overwhelmed by duplication of expensive equipment within communities, poor labor relations, $100-million computerization boondoggles, and white elephant new buildings that should never have been built. Despite hundreds of millions of dollars of extra funding, there is never any measurable benefit in terms of improved diagnostics, patient volume, numbers of procedures performed, reduced waiting list times, or results per dollar spent. The recent, terrifying statistics of adverse events in hospitals — deaths and serious illness due to mistakes and mismanagement — demonstrates how poorly that industry has been led through all of the years that the executive search industry was hyping the high salaries. These placement firms profited handsomely from each recruitment and, incredibly, they continue to recycle the same people all over the country.

A feature of this hospital administrator racket has been the so-called "wrongful dismissal" business. The head-hunters designed contracts that ensured these hospital executives find getting fired just as rewarding as working. Dozens of top-paid hospital and health executives in Canada have been ignominiously fired within the first three years of employment, departing with substantial golden handshakes. And, magically, the same executive search company that inflicted them upon one hospital, often has been able to plant them somewhere else, usually in a different province.

The top 10 myths

Brian Lee Crowley, PhD, prepared an assessment titled *Ten Myths About Canadian Medicare* in 2003 for the Winnipeg-based Frontier Centre for Public Policy. Dr. Crowley, a constitutional advisor to former Manitoba Premier Howard Pawley, and more recently a member of Alberta's Mazankowski Committee on Health Care Reform, is the founding president of the Atlantic Institute for Market Studies in Halifax.

Here are the " Ten Myths."

1. **Canada has the best health care system in the world.** Not even close. Canada's health care system placed 30th in an international ranking done by the World Health Organization in 2000.

2. **The Canadian public loves medicare.** Various polls show that a majority of Canadians support substantial reforms to the system. By using a flawed process riddled with conflicts of interest and unprofessional methods, the Romanow Commission made it look like citizens were against experimenting with major reforms.

3. **Canadian medicare is sustainable.** The system has huge unfunded liabilities, rising costs and declining services. These are most visibly seen in crumbling infrastructure, loss of access to the latest technology, falling numbers of medical professionals and lengthening queues.

4. **The single-payer model, Canadian-style, keeps costs under control.** The appearance of better cost control is due more to the fact that it was introduced during a time when Canada's economy was growing faster than the American one. Canadian costs are rising at the same rate but from a lower base - which is why they appear lower.

5. **More cash is the solution to medicare's problems.** The recommended extra infusion of taxes by the Romanow

Commission would merely postpone the day of reckoning. Inflation within the system eats up the new spending in two years.

6. **Under medicare, people get the health care services that they need.** Pharmaceuticals, dentistry, home care, chiropractics in most provinces and other services are not covered by medicare. While services may be free at the point of consumption, people are required to queue in occasionally life-threatening waiting lists for access to scarce medical resources.

7. **"Free" health care empowers the poor.** With "free" health care, users are not powerful customers who must be satisfied. The system can provide shoddy service, but because it is free the individual is totally disempowered. The more educated, and connected middle class can use their networks to get better service than the poor. The inarticulate, the poor and the most vulnerable have much more limited ability to circumvent these systems.

8. **Canadian medicare is fairer because no one gets better care than anyone else.** Workers compensation recipients, the RCMP and military, those with political connections, the famous, and those able to buy service at private facilities in Canada and the U.S. get better care than those lined up in the "free" public system.

9. **Medicare-type spending is the best way to improve health.** Rising health budgets are cannibalizing scarce public dollars that could improve health outcomes like education, roads, environmental and water protection. Higher taxes, 8 to 10 percent of GDP higher than the U.S., slow economic growth and lower wealth levels, which ironically correlate closely with better health.

10. **Medicare is an economic competitive advantage for business.** There is no advantage in terms of a lower production cost to manufacturers. Canadians pay for their system with higher income taxes. American workers pay for higher health premiums with lower wages and salaries.

The world scene

The Vancouver-based Fraser Institute documented in 2002 that Canada spends more on health care than any other industrialized country providing universal access, yet winds up near the bottom of the heap in quality of service. Defenders of medicare invariably point to the same two bogeymen: the United States with 45 million uninsured and a private-sector dominated system favoring the wealthy, and England, with two-tier care. The difference in facilities and service in the U.K. between National Health and the private system has been notoriously stark.

But the Fraser Institute looked at all of the industrialized affluent nations. Every country but the United States has universal, publicly-funded, health care coverage. Seven indicators of access to health care and outcomes from the health care process were examined: four related to access to high technology equipment, and three related to health outcomes. Many of the countries examined produce superior outcomes in health care and at a lower cost than Canada. The authors of the report, Fraser Institute director Michael Walker, PhD and health economist Nadeem Esmail pointed out that governments continue to spend more and more money without making any appreciable impact on quality of care, access and waiting times for treatment, available technology, and facilities. In fact, in most instances, the service is deteriorating, relative to other countries. "You would have expected to find that if they spend more money then at least you would get an increase in supply of services," Dr. Walker said. "We find that the provinces spend more money and nothing comes out the other end."

Esmail presented a series of comparisons between Canada and other countries, demonstrating that all of the leaders have universal access to health care, but also some form of user-pay or two-tiered system. Concerning access to care, Esmail revealed these comparisons, showing how Canada compared to universal access countries:

- 17th of 20 countries for access to physicians
- 18th of 23 countries for access to MRI machines
- 17th of 22 countries for access to CT scanners
- 8th of 22 countries for access to radiation therapy machines
- 13th of 14 countries for access to Lithotripters

The Fraser Institute is a business think tank and its findings are invariably branded by a right-wing bias. The critics of this report failed to address the issues, but focused, instead, on the Fraser Institute itself. The facts and the arguments went unchallenged. The report pointed out that all countries except Canada have a mix of private and public care, and that the real issue is to compare patient services. How does a citizen of France or Belgium or Japan or wherever, with a specific problem, get cared for, compared to the care in Canada? This is where our system fails. "The models that produce superior results than Canada all have user fees. They encourage appropriate use of health care services with some small cost-sharing component," Esmail reported. "They have alternate comprehensive private insurance systems of some form and they have private hospitals.

The hip replacement

Canadian health officials spend a great deal of their time comparing our service to the worst in the developed world, not the best. We hear infinite detail about inequality in the health care provided in the United States and the United Kingdom. They say little about all of the countries of Western Europe, Scandinavia, Japan, Singapore, Australia, the two dozen or so in the world with universal access and outcomes significantly better than ours.

The attention paid to hip replacement surgery in global health debates, relative to its actual priority in life-and-death decisions, is likely absurd, but the subject has become a useful benchmark for assessing the quality of national health care. It does not have a high priority in Canada because the basic condition is not life threatening. It principally involves an elderly, economically non-productive group of patients, so no employer, insurer, or compensation board is clamoring for rapid attention. The arthritic pain is excruciating and mobility can be near zero. Many of these patients pop 20 pills a day, and most of those bills are paid by government.

If a patient resides in just about any country of the industrialized world, except Britain, New Zealand, and the uninsured population of the United States, the necessary surgery would take place within days. Immediate treatment is widely available, even from universal access systems such as we have in Canada. Total hip replacement is usually a $US 40,000 procedure in the U.S., involving up to four days in hospital. Post-op rehabilitation can be expensive as well. Partial hip surgery is usually half that. These procedures usually range in cost from $10,000 to

$20,000 in Canada, but the cost analysis in Canadian hospitals is never market-based and always questionable. Canadian patients spend up to a week in hospital.

In Canada, the average wait from general practitioner diagnosis to surgery is 32 weeks. What makes hip replacement such an interesting focal point for analysis, is that the procedure is now routinely successful. Chronic pain ends abruptly. Failing to act swiftly needlessly adds to the cost of care. The procedure will be performed after additional months of costly drugs, extra physiotherapy, expensive walkers, wheelchairs, and other supports and multiple doctor visits. In fact, care workers say that a high percentage of these patients are overstressed and anxious. They have many falls. Broken bones, expensive repairs, and treatment become the inevitable consequence.

Many patients have the benefit of not just basic medicare and the supplementary services for seniors, they also have extended benefits through private and public sector retirement packages. This means extra care workers and therapists, who can minimize the downside of any condition, and educate the patient in the best means of self-management. The paucity of care available to those without extended coverage presents a dramatically different picture. One wonders if the politicians ever talk to homecare nurses and therapists? Frequently, because there is little or no home care, seniors fall and break hips, for which they will become hospitalized at great expense, one of the economic insanities in our system! Each year, Canada repairs hundreds of hips that should have previously been replaced, and finances the victim's care resulting from this negligence. We have thousands of seniors in expensive hospital and nursing home beds simply because they need help getting to and from the bathroom, or they need professional help to become self-sufficient within their own homes.

Our inability to effectively deal with the backlog of patients needing hip replacements has spawned an important export industry. Many affluent Canadians have sought VIP care in the U.S. But a global evacuation of dollars has also evolved. Our ethnically diverse and world-wise population has connections and information sources everywhere. Patients are flying to Hong Kong, Singapore, South Africa, Malaysia, Thailand, Cuba, Israel, and other nations for immediate, inexpensive and high quality surgical procedures. India promotes this business with the slogan, "First World Treatment at Third World Prices." Patients can get a total hip replacement for $US 4,500 plus travel costs. People find funds for cruises, new cars, cottages, yachts, and other pleasures. Does it surprise anybody that someone incapacitated by heart disease or in agony from arthritic pain, would rather make a small investment now than wait several months? Why do we make refugees of so many people?

The growth of private diagnostic and treatment facilities in Canada has been dramatic, including MRI machines and surgery centres. The private facilities tend to be more modern, more elaborate, and better equipped than the public hospitals, for the specific range of services they offer. Their business includes non-Canadians, contracted work for compensation boards, and other medicare-exempt clients, professional sports teams, and, increasingly, contracted procedures with the public system to reduce waiting lists in hospitals.

The extent of private diagnostic and surgical procedures permitted varies from province to province. Quebec probably leads the parade. Privatization is not an entirely new phenomenon. Shouldice Hospital in Toronto, a hernia specialty centre, has been treating public and private patients for 55 years. A contract price for each procedure is paid by the Ontario Health Insurance Plan, a good deal for everybody: fast, expert work, outstanding outcomes, patient satisfaction, and more cost effective than the public hospitals. Clinics are prevented, in most cases, from providing local residents surgical procedures that are covered by the *Canada Health Act*, but they can treat all out-of-province Canadian customers. Diagnostic centres are not only free to compete for cash business from any walk-in client, including locals, public hospitals have started to compete for this trade. There is a brisk private sector business coast to coast in MRI and CT scans, ultrasound, gastroenterology, and colonoscopies. Professional and even amateur athletes cannot wait for the slow-moving public queue in order to get needed diagnostics.

What has now generated disgust among the investors in these private centres is the public hospital competition. Non-emergency services at public hospitals are motivated with civil service enthusiasm, which means a 9 to 5 work schedule, and the active avoidance of work on any holiday, throughout the summer, and between Christmas and New Year's. This leaves radiology, operating rooms, and other diagnostic services unattended for many hours each day and many days of the year. Hospitals have started providing direct commercial services to sports teams and other clients, renting the facilities to achieve income. The private-sector complaint, of course, is that the facilities have been built and equipped by tax dollars and they are only ever idle because of immensely bad management. The system is either overbuilt or under-utilized. Government cannot have it both ways.

There is a long list of services, not covered by medical plans, that have always been free for private contracting in Canada. The principal areas of legal private surgery are for cosmetic purposes (plastic surgery) and some dermatological procedures. Private clinics do most eye surgeries — for covered procedures and private contracts — including laser techniques. Everyone who has investigated the expansion of private services concludes that officialdom is turning a blind eye to many practices that violate the rules. Quebec is notorious for taking federal money while ignoring the letter of the law. But there are rarely any prosecutions. One of the reasons is that the number of politicians and VIPs who have jumped the queue, usually with fees paid by their private insurers, would lead to political embarrassment.

This has created some amusing anecdotes. There was the opposition question in 2004 to newly elected Prime Minister Paul Martin, asking him about reports that he had "paid" for a private MRI scan. The question was taken under advisement. Days later an aide issued a formal statement that "Mr. Martin has never paid for an MRI scan." Does anyone seriously doubt whether Mr. Martin enjoys executive health benefits from Canada Steamship Lines and that this multinational company's insurer would not make instantly available any Canadian or American service he wished?

During the 2000 federal election, Canadian Alliance Party leader Stockwell Day was the only leader to advocate the restructuring of health care, to permit what was happening anyway, the limited purchase of private, for-profit health care. He was also the only leader that had never used anything but the public system. Jean Chretien, Joe Clark, Gilles Duceppe, and Alexa McDonough had all, at one time or another, bypassed the public system to obtain quick private services. But Day was trampled as an enemy of medicare, and our seriously ill health system continued to disintegrate, irrespective of how much money was being spent.

Many patients have been faced with a puzzling dilemma in the offices of medical specialists, most notably surgeons, ophthalmologists and dermatologists. They discover that their doctor works both sides of the fence: the so-called "free" medicare service, as well as the for-purchase commercial services. These doctors divide their booking calendar into two: competitive direct sales to consumers, and the usual medicare practice. The dilemma that is now routinely presented to the patient is this: "I can schedule you for 90-days down the road under the medical plan, or I have an opening at 3 p.m. tomorrow if you pay me directly." In some specialties, such as dermatology, many useful and recommended procedures are not covered by medicare. It is, therefore, not controversial that these doctors have a direct billing practice on the side, but there are many gray areas leading to the suspicion that the physician's interpretation of coverage is whatever is most profitable that day. Another complaint is that when cash is involved, waiting lists disappear.

VIP health and the Mayo Clinic

There is no other brand in the health-care world to rival the name "Mayo." Over 100 years ago in the small town of Rochester, Minnesota, Dr. Charlie and Dr. Will Mayo envisaged a new kind of health care in which a team of doctors would thoroughly analyze the patient before proceeding with any remedy. The accurate diagnosis of an illness was the most important step in its treatment. They and the associates they assembled took whatever time was necessary to thoroughly examine the patient. Only then was a course of treatment proposed.

Today's Mayo Clinic is a $US 5 billion annual operation with assets totaling $US 6 billion. It is a multifaceted business with centres in Rochester, New York; Jacksonville, Florida; and Scottsdale, Arizona. These are full-service hospitals offering every treatment from the mundane to the most sophisticated procedures, including transplants. There are 50,000 employees that serve 500,000 patients each year. Mayo spends over $US 350 million in research annually, with funding from multiple sources, including government. But the core product of the Mayo Clinic brand respects the vision of its founders. Unique among the famous treatment centres, Mayo is all about health and not just treatment. Mayo Clinic books, diets, and counseling are respected elements of public education. Their web sites provide an outstanding source of free public information about most conditions and diseases.

The Mayo Clinic diagnostic package is legendary within corporate boardrooms, and there are many imitators in the U.S. and around the world, some of which seem confused about whether they are a five star resort and spa, or a healing centre. You are nobody in corporate America, if you are not required to go to the Mayo Clinic, or an equivalent facility, for a "complete workup." Companies place extremely large life insurance policies on key executives; but before they do, they need to know the risk. For these firms, the executive medical assessment and many follow-up treatment services are often a gift from the large medical insurance companies. They pamper the executives, company directors, and often their spouses and families, in order to win the true corporate bonanza: health insurance for the whole company, often tens of thousands of employees, each of whom contribute to their own benefits plan. Unions and their employees rarely know that their monthly premiums achieve major league bonuses for the corporate elite. But the ordinary employee does not get sent to the Mayo Clinic.

The basic diagnostic package of the Mayo Clinic is delivered with a panache that only Americans can achieve. From the point of arrival at the clinic, the patient is treated as a VIP: private room, luxury surroundings, an army of attendants, and a food menu to rival the best hotel, as long as what is ordered does not conflict with the immediate schedule of tests. Body samples are extracted and dispatched for laboratory analysis. Every kind of scanning technology known to man is employed. About 20 different doctors — all specialists — will analyze results according to the bodily parts with which their specialty is concerned. The basic package is just a one-day affair, but other options are usually discussed at the time of the appointment. Often, the patient can be sold a 2- to 3-day diagnostic package. The examination costs begin at about $US 5,000 and often run to $US 25,000. Within VIP medicine in the U.S., there really is no price list. The clientele is uniformly affluent and egocentric. Each wants to be convinced they are getting the best. Many arrive with a shopping list of aches and irritations that need attention. A major American magazine reported in August 2004, about a rich Arab who flew to the U.S. demanding the best possible care for a heart bypass operation, and the services of a specific surgeon. The surgeon was paid $US 1 million, in addition to equally inflated hospital charges. There's nothing new about this. In 1996, Sheik Zayed bin Sultan al-Nahayan, president of the United Arab Emirates, checked into the Mayo Clinic for neck surgery. He brought an entourage of 140 people and stayed five weeks.

Often, pure show biz can escalate medical centre profits. Canadian hospitals think (but never really know, as each hospital has a different guess) that coronary bypass surgery costs around $30,000. The average Blue Cross payment in the U.S. ranges from $US 75,000 to $85,000. Many wealthy Canadians opt to pay the U.S. price. They may choose the renowned Texas Heart Institute in Houston, established by transplant pioneer Dr. Denton Cooley, or any of a number of VIP imitators. The fees may be $US 150,000 or more, but surgery begins with a limousine at the airport. The patient and spouse are escorted to a five star hotel near the hospital, where they are housed in a suite. This becomes home for the spouse and there is never a bill — for anything. Once the medical conveyor belt starts, the patient base is a beautifully decorated private room, with many attendants. The most famous surgeon at the hospital will likely pay the patient a visit, part of the conjuring act. Surgery will be performed by someone else. The patient and spouse return to Canada convinced that they have purchased the best surgery to be had in the world. It only cost them $200,000 more than if they had stayed at home. Canadian medical procedures don't come with limo rides, hotel suites, or complimentary Godiva chocolates.

Canadian health care is so top heavy with administrators and paper pushing it is almost impossible to subdivide annual hospital budgets into specific procedures. Oddly, the private for-profit surgical centres have no difficulty doing this. They let the market establish the prices. There is a good understanding through their insurers what the rates are in the U.S. Few Canadian cities are far from American hospitals, where sales efforts have always been successfully made to attract Canadian business. Some provinces, including Ontario, experimented in the past by giving patients a statement of what their hospital visit or procedure cost the system, clearly indicating that it was not a bill. Wholesale confusion erupted. The accuracy of the statements was questioned. Many patients didn't understand the purpose of the statement. They were afraid it was a bill. The prices were often so low that Americans and other visitors rushed to the hospitals waving their credit cards, hoping to purchase the cheap medical services. Typical U.S. prices for basic procedures would shock Canadians: $US 15,000 for a Caesarean section or $US 10,000 for a natural delivery; $US 8,500 to treat basic pneumonia with little hospitalization; and $US 11,000 to fix a broken leg.

The front line of the privatization debate in Canada focuses on services the overtaxed public system should be providing in an expeditious and competent fashion. But we cannot expect a growing "for-profit" sector not to specialize and narrowly focus on the most profitable services and patients. Private sector competition, unless careful planning takes place, will inexorably keep Canada moving toward limousine medicine.

What has generated the privatization mania today has not been the free enterprise sector but, rather, gross mismanagement and restrictive trade practices in the public sector. The monopoly serving only the interests of medical doctors, hospital administrators, and bureaucrats has created a demand so extraordinary that Canada has become a private sector bonanza. People are desperate. And desperate people become eager customers.

Supreme Court decision may change medicare forever

A Supreme Court of Canada decision in June, 2005, should have a dramatic impact on the future of health care in the country. The case overturned two Quebec court decisions that supported the province's prohibition of private purchase of health services covered by medicare. One of the core comments of Senator Michael Kirby's Senate of Canada inquiry into health care was to the effect that a right of citizenship should be reasonably fast attention for medical problems. If the public system is unable to deliver care, the medical plan should be obligated to purchase this service privately. While it is difficult to fault the logic of making reasonable and prompt access to health services a right of citizenship, the fear is that surgeons and specialists would devote less time and effort to the public system, adding to waiting lists, while profiting more greatly by performing the same work at for-profit clinics.

That is what the Supreme Court of Canada case was all about. George Zeliotis is an elderly man who had to wait months in excruciating pain for a hip replacement through the public health-care system. He and his family physician, Jacques Chaoulli, sued the Province of Quebec. Ultimately, the Quebec Court of Appeal rejected the challenge to the provincial law on the basis that a private system would threaten the integrity of the public one.

Montreal lawyer Bruce Johnston, who argued the case in the Supreme Court of Canada, said in a Global Television interview that Canadians' right to receive private health care is being violated as waiting lists for certain procedures grow longer. "It's a matter of choice whether you send your children to public or private schools. It should be the same with health care," said Johnston. He argued that patients have a constitutional right to pay privately for certain services, such as hip surgery. He further maintains that this will not undermine public health care because more resources would be available.

Many intervenors presented briefs, including the British Columbia Medical Association opposing the proposition and Vancouver surgeon Dr. Brian Day in support. According to one medical ·commentator, "If successful, the court challenge will end a state-enforced, self-regulated monopoly in the delivery of health services." But there are strong contrary views. Colleen Flood, a law professor at the University of Toronto, appearing on the same Global TV show, said: "The publicly funded health-care system is the one that ensures justice for the most people."

"Cut, freeze and squeeze"

Private sector medical services are like bulls crashing against the gate of their pens at a rodeo. The business potential is enormous, entirely created by hopelessly bad management of the public system. The business opportunity is a product of demand. The demand flows from the inability of the public system to provide competent, efficient service.

There were two fatal flaws in Canada's medicare, both of them pointed out from day one by the country's health economists. The first fundamental flaw was the monopoly gifted to medical doctors and hospitals; the second flaw was the unlimited access provided patients. Lack of competition in any field is certain to result in economic disaster, intellectual laziness, inefficiencies, and a decline in quality. Exceptions to this principle are rare in any field of human enterprise.

It was never Emmett Hall's intent to squeeze out all of the other health professionals. In fact, his emphasis was always on insuring the patient and necessary health services, deliberately leaving the door open for the inclusion of all legislated and regulated care providers. This would have been the competition to not only keep physicians honest and motivated, but to help them focus on the skills and knowledge that is theirs and theirs alone.

Led by the Dean of all Canadian health economists, Dr. Bob Evans of the University of British Columbia, a steady parade of them warned government that we have permitted doctors to manufacture whatever demand they needed to achieve their income targets. This, they all predicted — Evans, Stoddart, Barer, Manga, and others — would generate over-prescription of drugs, needless surgery, and demands for ever more hospitals, services and support facilities.

Not only did Canada refuse to apply limits on the supply side, nothing was put in place to encourage responsible patient behavior. The only developed country in the world with universal access to health care that doesn't insist upon a modest user charge per visit, is Canada. Other nations rebate these charges to seniors and the poor through tax and refund processes, but the user fee discourages over-utilization. It is not as if we do not assess fees. It varies from province to province, but all Canadians, or their work-related insurers, pay monthly fees for the medical plan (except for beneficiaries of social programs). It would have been better if these monthly charges were lowered and per visit fees were assessed. When other countries imposed minor fees, doctor visits dropped significantly, along with drug sales, surgery, and hospitalization, and there was a measurable positive impact upon public health.

University of Ottawa health economist Dr. Pran Manga, who was instrumental in the evolution of the *Canada Health Act*, takes the criticism a step further. "As individuals we expect the health care system to 'repair' us when we become ill, and to protect the environment in which we live. Yet, at the same time, we want the freedom to behave irresponsibly in how we manage our own personal and community health." About our system of paying doctors' fees, Manga has consistently emphasized for 25 years in notable reports, many of them prepared for Health Canada, "the fee-for-service method generates powerful economic incentives for over-servicing of patients." In practice, this means unnecessary visits and referrals as well as too many drug prescriptions, lab tests, surgical procedures, and days spent in hospital.

By 1990, the health system had begun to collapse. Overspending on health was impoverishing every other department of government. Ottawa, deep in debt with annual deficits out of control, began a series of dramatic cuts in exchange payments to the provinces. In each provincial capital, health-care costs soared beyond 30 percent of provincial budgets with no ceiling in sight (the range is 40-48 percent of provincial spending today). Neither federal nor provincial authorities had the political courage to address the key weakness: budgets were generated by hospitals, doctors, and patients, none of whom were ever held to account for their own behavior.

Instead, Manga reported, provincial government cost containment was of the "cut, freeze, and squeeze" variety. Services were delisted. Hospitals were closed. The number of covered items has been consistently reduced. But the accountants who wielded the axes seemed to think that if they removed an item from the medical plan, the problem would go away. Unfortunately, the illness of the patient remains, and often deteriorates as a result of neglect or inadequate treatment. Costs escalate, because medical care often leads to physiotherapy, drugs, and surgery. Some patients seek help through their extended benefits plans, unfairly impacting upon their employers and the premiums paid for coverage. Private insurers are forced to either raise premiums or also cut their covered items. But when patients are not treated, they fail to be productive at work or school. Some just get sicker, requiring more expensive remedies later. The business of "cut, freeze and squeeze" has created today's demand for private health services. As the cliché goes, the chickens have come home to roost.

In the vacuum of political courage, solutions appear difficult. The private sector would have a hard time competing for anything but the

most exotic or most vanity-oriented services if governments took decisive corrective action. This would break down the medical monopoly,
encouraging all health professions. Implementing measures to make
everybody more responsible in how they utilized the system and an
emergency program at public hospitals to eradicate waiting lists within a
12-month period, by contracting with private surgical clinics where necessary at fair prices, would lessen the demand. In fact, the private clinics
should be part of the permanent matrix. They should be allowed to bid
on the public sector business on a package-price basis, and only succeed
if they deliver a better product for less money. How could they compete
with a high quality, expeditious, and free public sector, except by offering obvious luxuries such as extra nurses, better food, more elegant
rooms? These frills are not what the *Canada Health Act* is all about, and
who cares if some people want to spend their own money for unnecessary extras?

An article by Robert Chernomas in the October 2004 *Bulletin of the
Canadian Association of University Teachers*, suggests that the private
sector might have a hard time competing in Canada, if the public system
was operating as it should. Chernomas wrote:

> In 1999, a *New England Journal of Medicine* article revealed that no
> peer-reviewed study has ever found that for-profit hospitals are less
> expensive than non-profit hospitals. On the contrary, those studies have
> found that for-profit hospitals are three to 11 percent more expensive
> than the non-profit hospitals. The facts show non-profits spend more on
> administration, marketing, executive salaries and dividends to share-
> holders.

When critics of privatization suggest that we are risking a two-tier
health system, they base their comments upon today's reality in Canada,
a false crisis created by flawed governance, and what they see in
England. National Health in the U.K. has been starved for funds since the
1970s. Poor public services created the demand for the upper tier.
England was spending just 6.5 percent of GDP on health. It has been
much improved by the current government, now approaching 8 percent
of GDP. Canada spends 10 percent of GDP.

What makes the arguments of those who propose complete freedom
to buy whatever services the market offers so compelling, is that they
provide hard evidence, while the defenders of Canada's medicare
respond in political clichés. They offer no studies to contradict statistics

of improved health outcomes for everybody, rich and poor, in just about every other universal access country of the world. Instead, we hear nothing but the kind of blather Roy Romanow put forward about the alleged glories of our system.

"Universal access" must always mean equal opportunity for the same level of health care, delivered by the same health professionals in the same facilities, except for clearly optional services. Only the force of law can maintain that in the current Canadian environment. The best way to curtail privatization is to develop a fiscally sound health program, with demonstrably improved patient outcomes, from coast to coast.

Canada has usually been masterful in finding a middle ground. The government could take some basic steps to make medical doctors compete on the basis of quality and open the door to more for-profit services. For example, they could encourage competition from community health clinics, co-operative health practices, nurse practitioners, chiropractors, optometrists and others — all under medicare. They could provide incentives to encourage more responsible patient behavior (possibly co-payment for those who could afford it). They could take determined steps to reduce backlogs and demand.

If the public system was operating optimally, it is unlikely that we would end up with a big "for-profit" patient care industry. It is extremely hard to compete with "free" or minimal costs. We could end up with the best of both worlds, a health industry similar to what exists in education, which has a niche market of private schools enhancing the public system.

The single insurer

Senator Michael Kirby and noted heart surgeon Dr. Wilbert Keon prepared a report for the Montreal-based Institute for Research on Public Policy, which emphasized not the word "medicare," but rather the value of a single national insurer. This was released in September 2004. They demonstrated that we have negated the value of such strength by creating monopolies on both sides of the equation: payment and delivery of service. A strong central purchaser should be able to command the best deals for all needs. The report said:

> The debate about competition in health care is marked by confusion over the difference between the funding of health care and the delivery of health care services. The advantages of equity and cost-effectiveness associated with having a single public insurer do not apply to the deliv-

ery of health care. It is this lack of a clear distinction between funding and delivery in the public debate on health care that has led to the impression that because the single public/government insurer is good, private delivery must be bad. In fact, as we have seen, delivery has been almost entirely in the hands of the private sector (independent doctors et al.) since the founding of Medicare. Thus, to claim that the private delivery of health services threatens the integrity of the single public insurer is manifestly false, given the actual structure of Canada's publicly funded health care system.

They emphasized the need for more competition.

. . .the Canadian health care system precludes competition among sellers of health care services. The resulting monopoly occurs at two levels: health care professionals and hospitals. Health care professionals hold monopoly power because they are the sole providers in their respective areas of expertise (doctors, nurses and so on). Hospitals hold monopoly power because they do not compete for patients on the basis of either price or quality of service. The result of this structure is an imbalance of bargaining power between governments, as funders, and groups of providers. The imbalance stems from two facts. First, health care is an essential service, and governments (and the public) greatly fear strikes in the health care sector. Second, work rules — who does what and under what conditions — are virtually never part of collective bargaining, as they are in other industries. The excessive power wielded by associations of health care providers has enabled them to win pay increases that have surpassed those achieved in other industries. These increases were secured with virtually no consideration for increases in productivity or variations in the quality of services delivered by different providers. We do not suggest that reform should be accomplished on the backs of those who deliver health care services. Rather, what concerns us is the structure of a system in which truly essential work (health care) is performed by groups of workers whose monopoly position is not effectively counterbalanced in the course of collective bargaining.

Repeatedly in the report, Kirby and Keon emphasized the need for other health professionals to be able to compete within the range of their expertise with medical doctors. Nurse practitioners were cited most strongly, but the message was clear: "Scope-of-practice rules must be

revised to allow all categories of health care professionals to practice to
the full extent of their capacities.

These revisions would:

- make better use of limited human resources throughout the
  health care system,

- create stronger incentives among the different health care
  professions to compete for contracts to provide various health
  services,

- foster greater productivity in all health care professions,

- ensure, from a patient's perspective, that health care is delivered
  by the most appropriately qualified health care provider,

- enhance collaboration and multidisciplinary approaches, which
  are essential, and,

- assist in the reform of primary care and other forms of
  health care."

Just as Mr. Justice Emmett Hall suggested in 1964, a theme that has
been consistently advocated by leading health economists for decades,
common sense that gets lost within the self-serving processes dominated
by doctors and their captive bureaucrats.

Yes, Minister!

Dr. Brian Day — an orthopedic surgeon — was among British
Columbia's medical stars long before he became a prominent name in
national media debates. In 1996, he and 45 other physicians established
the Cambie Surgical Centre. Recently expanded, it now represents a $10
million investment. Many of the surgeons and consulting physicians are
also on the Faculty of the University of British Columbia School of
Medicine. They have a foot in each camp, public and private. Located
just a few hundred yards from the gigantic Vancouver General Hospital,
it seems like another world: modern, immaculately clean, relaxed,
friendly, and obviously efficient. It has six operating rooms, including
dental surgery, and 182 staff members. On the floor where a small number of inpatients have private rooms, there are gleaming hardwood
floors. Not a scratch to be seen anywhere. "Luxury" is not the right word.
There is no sense of unnecessary embellishments, but the atmosphere
exudes quality, cleanliness, and healing.

Dr. Day, who is the Chief Executive Officer, is proud of the mini-malized overhead. The tight corner into which the administration and accounting are squeezed would be considered a shoe box by any self-respecting civil servant, worthy only of bottom tier clerks. The CEO/sur-geon is proud of one extravagance, developed in partnership with an American high technology firm: fully digitized and satellite-linked audio-video services in all operating rooms and the boardroom. Anything happening of medical, business, or scientific interest anywhere in the world, can be beamed into the in-house closed circuit network. Conversely, anything taking place within the Cambie Surgery Centre can be broadcast worldwide. On a more routine basis, the boardroom is used for the instruction of surgeons and medical students.

Day's entry into the private world of medicine was a product of frus-tration. In essence, he simply got angry about the overstaffing in public institutions, the long waits for treatments and bad business practices. He cites the all too typical cases of injured Americans — such as a rich skier hurt on the Whistler slopes — getting billed a mere few hundred dollars for services that would cost thousands, just across the border. "Most of these people who are able to travel have first class insurance. Treatment costs them nothing. If they went to a hospital in Blaine or Bellingham, their insurer would get billed $US 5,000. Vancouver General might charge $1,000 or less. He relates a 1997 story involving an orthopedic surgical procedure that he alone in Canada was able to perform. A local police officer needed this surgery and Dr. Day offered to do it at his then-new surgical centre for $3,500. Worried about setting a bad precedent, the public officials declined. Eventually, they found a surgeon to do it in San Francisco. The final cost was $25,000.

Brian Day never set out to become a media figure, but he has found himself repeatedly thrust into the middle of public debates. He has made presentations at major inquiries, including the Romanow Commission. He delights in showing visitors an encounter he had on a CBC news show hosted by Peter Mansbridge. The host had Roy Romanow on as a guest, and invited Dr. Day to participate. Day confronted Romanow with a comment that he has regularly made to media: "We have a system in which you can buy private health care or insurance for your dog, cat, or pig, but not for your loved ones. . . if Canadians have the right to spend money on tobacco, gambling, or even pornography, why should we pre-vent them from spending their after-tax dollars on the health care of themselves and their loved ones?"

Romanow set off on a lugubrious reply in which he:

1. advised that he knew and respected Dr. Day.
2. said that Brian Day was a very good doctor.
3. advised the audience that Dr. Day had presented his arguments to the Inquiry and that they were very good arguments indeed.
4. acknowledged that this went right to the core of the issue . . . .

At this point, Peter Mansbridge was forced to end the interview. Time was up.

Following the video of this encounter, Dr. Day then runs a video of a segment from the British television classic, the *Yes, Minister* series. In this episode, the Hon. James Hacker is on a BBC Radio show, and he is delivered a tough question. Hacker's response is as follows:

> Please let me finish. Because we must be absolutely clear about this. And I want to be quite frank with you. The plain fact of the matter is, that, at the end of the day, it is the right — nay, the duty —of the elected government, in the House of Commons, to ensure that government policy, the policies on which we were elected and for which we have a mandate, the policies for which the people voted. . . .are the policies which, finally, when the national cake has been divided up — and, may I remind you, we as a nation don't have unlimited wealth, you know, we can't pay ourselves more than we've earned — are the policies... er, what was the question again?

Brian Day thinks Hacker's comments are an excellent précis of the politicians' input to the Canadian health care debate.

"A national disgrace that has received far too little public analysis is the salary levels attained by health administrators. In most provinces, the managers of the largest hospitals have earned three, four, and five times the income of the Deputy Minister of Health, the top official in the field in any province. For what? The economic mismanagement of hospitals by any analysis has been scandalous."

"Now let's see if I have this straight. You are the only person to see patients. You decide when there is a need for a specialist, an MD, a dietician or maybe even a chiropractor."

"And I make far more home and hospital visits, check on our patient's recovery than doctors do."

"What do doctors do?"

"Mostly government relations, fee negotiations. It's exhausting really."

8.
The Nurse Practitioner

In 1971 and 1972 . . . a landmark Canadian study of nurse practitioners looked at a family practice in Burlington, Ontario. Two family doctors were swamped and hadn't accepted new patients for two years. They believed that two of their office nurses could, with appropriate additional education, take on additional responsibilities and allow them to start accepting new patients again. The nurse practitioners took care of 67 percent of patient visits for two years, and all measurements showed the patients in the nurse practitioner group were as healthy and satisfied with their care as the patients who saw the doctors. Perhaps most notably, the practice was able to expand its coverage dramatically and provide health services to almost 1,000 new families.

— CANADIAN HEALTH SERVICES RESEARCH FOUNDATION

Results of this physician-inspired evolution of patient care, parallel-ing the first nurse practitioner university program in Canada at Hamilton's McMaster University, were so startling a healthy buzz whipped through not just the nursing profession, but health care from coast to coast in the country.

No one was surprised. The most accomplished of Registered Nurses (RNs), either through extensive on-the-job experience and training or increasingly prominent formal academic credentials, had always per-formed services far beyond anything cited in their actual job descrip-tions. The Burlington study, the McMaster program, and an evolving curriculum at the University of Montreal — all 1971 initiatives — inspired the federal government to launch a study led by Professor Thomas J. Boudreau of the University of Sherbrooke. In those early days of Canada's medicare, the Boudreau Report became an unreserved endorsement of a new "team" approach to health care, with nurse practitioners at the core of it all.

In a sense, the new thinking was merely a formalization of autonomous skills and responsibilities senior nurses had been using since the time of Florence Nightingale. In the absence of anyone else in emergency situations, in public or in hospitals, they would do whatever was necessary and within their considerable realm of competence. As trust grew in responsible physician-nurse relationships, doctors invariably delegated tough jobs, technically outside the mandate of RNs and in some cases of irresponsibility, the only physician role was to bill for their personal services, while the nurses did the work.

One of the most outstanding reviews of the nurse practitioner issue was a lengthy 1993 discussion paper prepared by Judith Haines, an RN, complete with a list of authorities for each of the claims she made. This resource is still used today by just about everyone who studies the issue. She described a 1976 survey of 3,000 nurses:

> ... described the frequency with which they performed each of 33 selected activities identified in the literature as belonging to the expanded role (nurse practitioner, family practice nurse, etc). They also described whether they received formal, informal or no instruction to perform these activities. According to the research report, there was no clear differentiation between the 55.7 percent who perceived themselves to be functioning in an expanded role and those who did not as reflected in the type and frequency of performance of the 33 activities. An outstanding feature of the data on the frequency of selected activities was ... the infrequency with which teaching and counseling are performed by all respondents. Of the 1,772 nurses who perceived their role to be expanded, 55 percent listed additional activities — to a total of 595 — that had traditionally rested within the domain of other disciplines, others that had not been identified with any one member of the health team, and some that had not been performed previously.

Several categories of nursing specialties had evolved over the years, bringing both stature and more tangible rewards to surgical, emergency care, intensive care, ambulatory care, pediatric and many other nursing roles. The most defined of these were Registered Psychiatric Nurses (RPN) who established their own criteria for employment and, in most jurisdictions, their own legislation and regulatory college. Although definition of the nurse practitioner role would prove difficult in the years ahead, no one doubted that a higher-credentialed nurse could relieve medical doctors of a great deal of primary patient care. The pioneers wanted to focus far more upon health than illness, and prevention and convalescence than the treatment and procedure-oriented demands upon physicians. This multidisciplinary approach including dieticians, physiotherapists, occupational therapists and others, as needed, was seen as an outstanding way to leverage the assets of everyone in the system, allowing each to concentrate upon their most valuable skills.

McMaster and the University of Montreal were followed quickly by Dalhousie University in Halifax, which had begun pioneering work in midwifery and outpost nursing education as early as 1967. Soon after, programs directed at services for the Canadian north were developed at the universities of Alberta, Manitoba, Western Ontario, McGill and Sherbrooke. Other nurse practitioner programs began later at the University of British Columbia, the University of Saskatchewan and Memorial University of Newfoundland. Memorial, propelled by the urgency of serving populations in remote outports, many of whom had little or no access to an MD, soon became a leader in both the education of nurses and the practical application of nurse practitioner services. It was thought that thousands of these professionals would be at work before the decade of the 1970s was complete.

Yet by 1993 — 20 years later — there were fewer than 250 accredited nurse practitioners in Canada. So what bomb landed in the middle of the planners' and educators' tea party? Nurses and medical journals have created libraries full of reports to ever-so-politely describe the temporary death of a magnificent idea. This bomb can be simply put in one blunt phrase: the concept created a collision with medical doctors' power base and bank accounts.

During the boom years of the 1960s and 1970s, there was a genuine shortage of physicians in Canada. Although medical schools were growing as fast as they could, aggressive immigration policies encouraged the importation of as many doctors, particularly specialists, as possible. Nurse practitioners were seen in those days as an efficient, cost-effective way to ease the burden. But a recession hit in the early 1980s and, suddenly, it was perceived that we had a surplus of physicians. The first of several national studies by professors Morris Barer, PhD of the University of British Columbia and Greg Stoddart, PhD of McMaster, sounded a warning that there were too many doctors in the country. In their important 1991 report, they recommended a deliberate policy of rationalizing the growth of the profession, including an across-the-board reduction of 10 percent in medical school enrollments. Many MDs grew insecure about their financial future and the increasingly competitive health care environment.

In a 1984 editorial called "The nurse practitioner revisited: Slow death of a good idea", published in *The New England Journal of Medicine*, Dr. Walter Spitzer of McGill University advanced this view on the demise of the nurse practitioner movement:

> In Canada, the economic imperatives of a physician surplus in the context of universal health insurance, coupled with the inevitable political pressures brought to bear by an older and somewhat threatened medical profession, have killed the nurse-practitioner movement.

Michael Rachlis, MD, and Carol Kushner addressed the issue in a 1989 report titled *Second Opinion: What's Wrong with Canada's Health-Care System and How to Fix It*:

> During the 1960s and 1970s, government tried to expand the role for nurses by launching training programs for a new profession: nurse practitioner. It was expected that this additional training would make it easy for nurses to become the first line of contact for patients seeking primary care. But it didn't happen that way; the oversupply of doctors got in the way and today there's little support for nurse practitioners.

All of the university programs fell by the wayside, one after another, although some courses were rolled into Schools of Nursing, all of which continued to offer advanced programs. Even during the most worrisome days of doctor shortages, there was never anything but an oversupply in the most affluent and comfortable places to live. The nurse practitioner movement remained alive because of the Canadian frontiers, the Yukon, the Northwest Territories, the northern outreaches of the provinces, Labrador and the outports of Newfoundland.

Aside from the self-serving turf wars within the health professions, with physicians always the first to feed at the trough, there have been genuine issues. During the early years, definition was a challenge. The University of Colorado is credited with leading this modern advanced nurse evolution, but the American motivation came largely as a result of the extraordinary number of talented nurses, paramedics and medical technicians developed during the Viet Nam war. Various descriptions of "physician's assistants" emerged on the job market and each of them had valuable talent, ability, and experience that could ease the pressure on physicians. But who should set the standards and establish professional criteria and regulation?

Within the nursing profession, some of the most accomplished, skilled, and experienced performers had little in the way of formal education. Some of those with a trail of degrees after their names had little experience. It was generally agreed that a superior category of nurse could do more: preliminary patient diagnosis, referral to a general practitioner or medical specialist as appropriate and even prescribing a limited range of the most common drugs. But what credentials are necessary for licensing? Where do they work? If they work for physicians, as in the Burlington study, who pays them? There was no way for the doctors to recoup the investment and there was no category for nurse practitioner billing to the medical plan. They would fit into community health centres, home care or hospitals, but whose budget would their wages come from and how can value be measured for the additional expense? How much should they be paid? If they are to be entrepreneurs soliciting business on their own, would physicians oppose the competition? And even if this were possible, how could a few pioneers explain to the public who and what they are, what they do and how they are paid? Medical plans would have to be amended to provide a new category for billing. These questions and many more made the fledgling nurse practitioner movement an easy target, effortlessly suffocated by an inexhaustible number of petty studies and bureaucratic processes.

Fast forward to 2004. In the face of this history, and the near-death experience in 1990, the pioneers forged ahead. Legislation has been passed across Canada and the final two provinces will have it in place soon. There were 600 nurse practitioners licensed under their own professional designation by 2003 and it is expected that the numbers will not merely grow during the next five years, they will explode. The projection is that there will be 10,000 of them in Canada by 2010.

What is a "nurse practitioner?"

There are several variants from jurisdiction to jurisdiction in everything from the name to the areas of practice. "Nurse Practitioner" is used in some legislation while other Legislatures choose "Advanced Practice Nurse." In all instances, a Master's degree or equivalent is required for certification, along with impressive on-the-job experience. Defining the role, words such as "diagnosis" become major debating points, apparently threatening to MDs. Nurse practitioners — to avoid conflict with doctors — have learned to use the word "prognosticator," which, from a patient perspective, is precisely the same thing. Prescribing a basic list of necessary drugs, including antibiotics, goes with the territory in most locales, but doctors in some regions, jealously guarding their monopoly, maintain a supervisory role, which means they get a few dollars on every prescription, despite adding little or no value to the transaction.

Forcing a supremely well-educated and experienced health professional, such as a typical nurse practitioner with at least Master's degree qualification, to scare and confuse a patient with the title "prognosticator" is symbolic of the monopolistic brutality of the medical profession. Think about it. You arrive at a clinic and expect to visit a doctor. You should be advised that your first meeting is with an "advanced practice nurse" or a "nurse practitioner" who will do the preliminary examination. The best professionals will have available either in a clinic brochure or through a web site address, basic biographical data showing excellent credentials. The patient gets put at ease. In most cases, the Nurse Practitioner can resolve whatever brought them to the clinic or make a referral to a general practitioner, a medical specialist, or whomever the most appropriate health care provider may be. If, however, you arrive at the same clinic, expecting to see a doctor, and the receptionist tells you that you are getting a "prognosticator" instead, what might you think? The following definition from the American Academy of Nurse Practitioners summarizes a more comprehensive role than what is envisaged for Canada, once Ottawa and the provinces standardize professional criteria.

> Nurse practitioners are primary care providers who practice in ambulatory, acute and long term care settings. According to their practice specialty these providers provide nursing and medical services to individuals, families and groups. In addition to diagnosing and managing acute episodic and chronic illnesses, nurse practitioners emphasize health promotion and disease prevention. Services include — but are not limited to — ordering, conducting, supervising, and interpreting diagnostic and laboratory tests, and prescription of pharmacologic agents and non-pharmacologic therapies. Teaching and counseling individuals, families and groups are a major part of nurse practitioner practice. Nurse practitioners practice autonomously and in collaboration with health care professionals and other individuals to diagnose, treat and manage the patient's health problems. They serve as health care researchers, interdisciplinary consultants and patient advocates.

In her 1993 discussion paper, Judith Haines quoted Dorothy Kergin, former director of the McMaster University School of Nursing, who was instrumental in setting up the family nurse practitioner program there in 1971. Kergin described the nurse practitioner as:

> ... a nurse in an expanded role, oriented to the provision of primary health care as a member of a team of health professionals relating with families on a long-term basis and who, through a combination of special education and experience beyond a baccalaureate degree or a diploma, is qualified to fulfill the expectations of this role.

By 1993, the Nurse Practitioners' Association of Ontario, defined the profession in the following way:

> ... a registered nurse who, through special education or job experience, has expanded her/his scope of practice. She has a commitment to primary health care for individuals of all ages and families in the community. Focusing on health rather than illness, she utilizes the nursing process of assessment, planning, implementation and evaluation. She engages in problem solving, teaching and counseling with the client and her approach to care supports and promotes the maintenance of a healthy lifestyle. The nurse practitioner works in collaboration with other health professionals. She is committed to client advocacy.

The results of nurse practitioner work are nothing short of phenomenal. Beginning with the Burlington, Ontario, experiment, and flowing through every other measurable situation, it becomes evident that drug prescriptions are significantly reduced, patient outcomes are improved, and the morale among all participants seems better (physicians, nurses, related caregivers and patients). The focus of practice takes on a more holistic approach to health, nutrition, and lifestyles, including more patient responsibility toward their own health.

A report in the *Canadian Medical Association Journal* in 1976 by a distinguished team of doctors chronicled a 10 percent reduction in the use of prescription drugs when patients were under the care of nurse practitioners. One would have thought that might have served as an eye-opener for health planners. A 10 percent saving in that department today would mean $2 billion per year nationally. To this day, physicians and regulators in some provinces are concerned about nurses prescribing drugs. In a year 2000 article, also in the CMA *Journal,* Debbie

Phillipchuk, a practice consultant with the Alberta Association of Registered Nurses, said: "Nurses don't want to be doctors. Nurses want to prescribe within the roles they have. . .RNs take very seriously the responsibility of prescribing and they feel there must be real restrictions on when and why."

The administrative issues of "where do they work" and "how do we pay them" remain the most vexing. The answer is easy if the geography is a place avoided by physicians. They draw a salary and work in government clinics. Ontario has long had the most sophisticated network of Community Health Centres and that is where most of today's nurse practitioners work. Their average 2004 salary was about $85,000 a year, a significant increment above the top RNs in hospitals. Unfortunately, the Community Health Centres in Ontario and elsewhere in the country are perpetually starved for funds, suffering from every government freeze that comes along.

Here are some of the challenges:

- Most nurse practitioners would prefer to work on a salaried basis, but the evolution of the profession would be far easier if the medical plans established a fee schedule for their occasional use. In this way, they would have the choice of being entrepreneurs or part of other health care teams, including physician practices who could directly bill for their specific services.

- Neither the public nor family physicians understand the role of nurse practitioners. Physicians have tended to view the extended practice nurses as competition, a threat to both their fee base and patient loyalty.

- There is no mechanism anywhere to reimburse facilities or employers who make occasional use of their work.

- There is a cap in most jurisdictions on the development of the new Community Health Centres (CHCs) and Health Services Organizations (HSOs).

- Only Alberta, Newfoundland and Ontario have established authority for nurse practitioners to prescribe a limited number of drugs. It is pointless to consider the profession in a primary care role if an expensive rubber stamp is also required by a doctor.

- Federal authorities are preparing a new *Controlled Drugs and Substances Act* which may include authorization for nurse practitioners to prescribe controlled drugs. But approval of the regulated profession's area of practice would still be provincial. Defining the scope of the practice and obtaining the right to diagnose minor illness has been a key issue in defining the profession.

- The regulated minimum drug list may be a barrier to involvement in rehabilitative care, because it does not allow for independent renewal of medications for stable chronic conditions.

- There is need for national guidelines defining the scope of the profession. Key definitions include when physicians must be consulted, but also the latitude nurse practitioners have in terms of recommending other health professionals.

- Physicians in under-serviced areas of the country have indicated an interest in sharing the burden with nurse practitioners, but governments usually cannot seem to find a way to pay them. An Ontario report demonstrates significant unemployment by fully-qualified nurse practitioners who reside in areas that are desperately short of physician services.

A martyr to the cause

Unfortunately, a common medical response to the nurse practitioner in the early days was patronizing: amusement in the first instance followed by an attempt to downplay the services into the usual subservient role. Finally, when it appeared to be a genuine threat to both authority and income, there was outright opposition.

The medical profession was about to meet a Don Quixote from northern Alberta who launched an attack that was eventually rebuffed in the Alberta Supreme Court, but by the time she was finished, windmills were spinning from coast to coast in Canada, with the arrogance, insensitivity and just plain stupidity of the doctors' public relations posture, available for all to see.

In 1991, a pugnacious nurse — one of the pioneer nurse practitioners in the country — took them all on. Joyce Atcheson, an exceptional nurse with advanced degrees from McMaster University and the University of Alberta, worked in Fort McMurray and set herself up as an independent contractor, associated with a family health clinic consisting of five physicians. She was advanced $25 an hour and the clinic billed for her services under the Alberta government plan. Every three months her case load was reviewed and she was paid 60 percent of the Alberta Health Care billings made for her work by the clinic, presumably less the advances she received. Prior to the Fort McMurray work, Atcheson spent three years serving the frontiers of northern Alberta, including the communities of Fox Lake, Assumption and Garden River. In the last case, she was the only health-care professional in a community of 380 people. A doctor flew in for three or four hours every two weeks.

A complaint was received by the Alberta College of Physicians and Surgeons. This body ordered the doctors — with whom she had contracted — to cease and desist. Atcheson was told that she could be charged with practicing medicine without a license. Subsequent media thrashing of the college made it clear that only threatened medical doctors had complained. Patients were happy, as if that ever has anything to do with the governance of health care in Canada (i.e. who gets the money).

Atcheson testified that while under contract to the clinic, she routinely conducted physical examinations, took blood pressure, did vaginal and breast examinations and assessed patients' conditions. She would also make recommendations for medication; but, prescriptions were signed by the doctors. She consulted the doctors whenever she felt it necessary. She never worked without at least one doctor present in the clinic. At the end of each day, a supervising doctor reviewed her cases. She protested at the trial that nobody was concerned when she provided the same services to aboriginal people and in the far north where there were no doctors, but the complaint arose only when she worked with five physicians.

The intervention of the college terminated her income and Joyce Atcheson sued for $50,000 lost income and $25,000 punitive damages. She ultimately lost, but the black eye she delivered to the medical profession cost them an incalculable value in credibility. While Joyce Atcheson became a hero in the eyes of visionary health planners from coast to coast, the medical profession was once again seen to be desperately clinging to every penny of income and every lever of control over health care in the country. The judge who ruled against her was sympathetic and took pains to explain that the college decision was purely on a matter of billing regulations as they existed at the time, and her lost income was an unfortunate consequence, not intent.

But the *Edmonton Journal* reported that when asked at trial if she was not really practicing medicine rather than nursing, Atcheson responded:

"If I truly believed I was practicing medicine, . . . I could not do it."

"You were practicing nursing, in your mind," a lawyer said.

"Yes," Atcheson answered. "And in the mind of my professional body as well."

Although her work was reviewed in 1990 by the Alberta Association of Registered Nurses (AARN) and was found to be within the scope of nursing duties, the AARN was not much of a friend at the trial. They suggested that Atcheson acted "too independently."

The case was a landmark in the evolution of the nurse practitioner in Canada and it dominated the headlines just as the new profession appeared to be turning the corner, after its enthusiastic beginning was savaged by doctors and bureaucrats, and waned for 20 years. Her media support was an unprecedented testament to the sophisticated nurse practitioner role. An *Edmonton Journal* editorial proclaimed:

> Joyce Atcheson has a point. The Fort McMurray nurse was recently threatened with professional discipline because she was performing work reserved for physicians. It turns out that the real problem is not so much the work she did, as where she did it.....In isolated northern centres where doctors rarely visit, Atcheson and other nurses routinely handle some procedures normally reserved for physicians. But the same procedures conducted by the same person in Fort McMurray are declared off limits to nurses. Atcheson argues that either we have a double standard for health care in the North, or we have a double standard for nurses, and it is difficult to escape that logic.

What benefits?

There are over 100,000 nurse practitioners in the United States, a dramatic growth as a result of bottom-line performance criteria demanded by competitive forces, private sector accountability and driven largely by patient management practices of hospitals (private and public) and Health Maintenance Organizations (HMO). Rather than the tightly controlled information base in Canada, assembled by governments, hospital boards and professional organizations, there are thousands of public and private databases in the United States.

The enormity of the impact and effectiveness of nurse practitioners is measurable. Here are some benefits as cited by the American Academy of Nurse Practitioners:

- NPs cost 40 percent less than physicians and are particularly cost-effective in preventive care, counseling, patient/client education and case management.
- Patients under the care of NPs report reduced numbers of repeat episodes of illness.
- Research shows that nurse practitioners can manage 80-90 percent of what primary care physicians can do without the need for physician help.
- They write 42 percent fewer prescriptions than other providers.
- A study conducted in a large HMO setting in 1994 found that adding a nurse practitioner to the practice could virtually double the typical number of clients seen by a physician.
- Overall, when compared with the cost of MD-only teams, costs of using an MD/NP team in a long-term care facility were 42 percent lower for the intermediate and skilled care residents and 26 percent lower for those with long term stays. The study also showed significantly lower rates of emergency room transfers, hospital length of stays and specialty visits for patients covered by MD/NP teams.
- A year long study compared a family practice physicians managed practice and a NP managed practice within the same Managed Care Organization. The study found that the NP managed practice had 43 percent of the total emergency room visits, and 38 percent of the in-patient days, and the NPs total annualized per member monthly cost was approximately 50 percent less.

These claims should also be read with a degree of caution. This is what the American profession says about itself. But all Canadian experience confirms at least the general thrust of this data, if not the specific numbers. There is also a modern statistical nightmare afflicting health planning. Governments, medical plans, insurers, compensation boards and others play a shell game, listing and delisting covered services, and changing the rules with reckless abandon. The patients do not get better

— they just disappear from one insurer's list. These days, every time an employee changes jobs, pre-existing medical conditions usually get excluded from the new plan. Another negative number goes away. When any health management group boasts about its brilliance "curing" illness and restoring clients to productive lives based on statistics, a second look is well advised. Are these people genuinely better or were they simply pushed over the cliff? Who knows? Once disqualified from coverage, their condition is off the books, no longer able to inflate statistics.

Health budgets and the future

The greatest impediment to any change in health care is the word "budget." When an area of need is carefully defined, perhaps the plan for a multidisciplinary Community Health Clinic, with an integrated team of physicians, nurse practitioners and others, it is not difficult to get "approval in principle" for the business plan. In fact, most detached observers will be quick to show how serving the patient base would be much more cost effective than whatever currently exists, ultimately either saving significant sums, or substantially improving health services and outcomes. When these developments are funded entirely from new budgets (extra money from government), there is widespread support, as long as none of the existing fiefdoms have their income threatened. However, by the time a new idea gets pounded through the special interests of local doctors, hospitals, nurses, assorted health workers and unions, it is usually a pale imitation of whatever the original concept might have been. Tough health care managers close down costly, inefficient services and transfer the savings to more likely prospects. Unfortunately, such courage is extremely rare, because there is always a loftier personage who will cave under establishment pressure, if not a bureaucrat then most likely a politician. The hero gets stomped upon and embarrassed. Nothing substantive changes.

Roy Romanow's $15 million federal commission paid little more than lip service to the nurse practitioner role, acknowledging the advanced care nurse, while avoiding the minefield of role definition. This was the nervous — and therefore useless — posture his report took, too cowardly to address the obvious need for change in medicare's acceptance of non-MD health professionals. He acknowledged that the "comprehensiveness" commitment of the *Canada Health Act* needs review to more adequately recognize other health care providers. But we never learn who these "health care providers" might be. Romanow did observe:

Nurse practitioners . . . are trained to provide some health services that used to be the exclusive responsibility of physicians. Despite much rhetoric about interprofessional co-operation, in reality, the professions tend to protect their scopes of practice. Each profession appears willing to take on more responsibilities, but is unwilling to relinquish some duties to other professions.

Romanow did articulate a crisis in Canadian nursing, pointing out that the number of nurses has actually dropped during the past decade, in the face of unprecedented demand and growth in just about every area of health care. Enrollment at university schools of nursing has fallen by 50 percent. The Commission report stated:

For nurses, their pattern of practice has changed, but they have had little control over those changes. Fewer nursing administrators and less administrative support have resulted in an increased burden for nurses, leaving less time for direct care. Nurses have also been shifted in and out of their areas of expertise, from emergency rooms and intensive care to pediatrics and geriatrics, and from practice in teams in hospitals to individual practice in home care. . . . traditionally, decision makers have reorganized the pattern of practice of nurses pretty much at will, but attempts to change the pattern of practice of physicians are met with the stiff opposition of the medical profession who see this as a threat to their professional autonomy. . . .

For nurses especially, quality of work life is a serious concern. Morale has declined substantially and nursing organizations point to this as one of the reasons for a significant number of nurses choosing to leave their profession. They also suggest that the persistent low morale has an impact on the quality of patient care. Employers, unions and professional organizations are addressing these issues, but, in recent years, the relationships between these organizations have been less than positive and strikes have been regular occurrences in almost every part of the country. Physicians also have concerns about quality of work life, but they tend to have more direct control over their working conditions than do nurses.

The parallel study by the Senate of Canada's Standing Committee on Social Affairs, Science and Technology, chaired by Senator Michael Kirby was far better focused on both the problem and the solution. Where Romanow seemed not to be able to see that the nursing crisis had everything to do with lack of respect and MDs' turf protection, as well as grossly mismanaged health resources, Kirby's report quoted Dr. Duncan Sinclair, the Chair of the Ontario Health Service Restructuring Commission, in his testimony to the Committee:

> Having a doctor do work that a nurse practitioner or nurse could do is like calling an electrician to change a light bulb or a licensed mechanic out of the garage to fill your tank and check the oil and tire pressure — would they do a good job? They would do an excellent job! But would it be a good use of their time, training and expertise? It would not! It would constitute an expensive and inefficient use of scarce resources, both of money and the expertise of very talented people.

Kirby proposed an independent review of the scope of practice rules for the various health care professions, and cited nurse practitioners as a principal example. He said this needs to focus on "removing the barriers to fruitful collaboration" that now exist among health care professionals, preventing some from using the full set of skills for which they have been trained. "A federal/provincial/territorial initiative should develop national standards for terminology and scope of practice. It should include legislative requirements that support an expanded role for nurses and nurse practitioners," Kirby said.

The formal recommendation — applicable to a range of professions from nurse practitioners to optometrists, and from naturopaths to chiropractors — was as follows:

> An independent review of scope of practice rules and other regulations affecting what individual health professionals can and cannot do be undertaken for the purpose of developing proposals that would enable the skills and competencies of diverse health care professionals to be utilized to the fullest and enable health care services to be delivered by the most appropriately qualified professionals.

"Rising stars" — the new gatekeepers?

Another of the notable Canadian pioneers, Ottawa nurse practitioner Linda Jones was a guest speaker at the 1992 meeting of the Canadian University Nursing Students Association. Her speech was titled: *Nurse practitioners: Dinosaurs or rising stars?* Jones was frequently blunt. In the 1970s, she said, the thought seemed to be that they aspired to be "physician replacements," but the real role is simply an advanced practice nurse. "What's caused the great controversy is this medical function that we also serve ....But we call a spade a spade: we do make medical diagnoses. But more importantly, our roles are in health promotion and disease prevention," Jones said.

McGill University's Dr. Walter Spitzer in his 1984 article in the *New England Journal of Medicine*, warned:

> For the proponents of the nurse practitioner, the main obstacle to widespread acceptance of the idea is unlikely to be rejection by clients, but rather unawareness of the nurse practitioner's role on the part of the public. The lack of understanding and awareness is reinforced by shifting positions within mainstream nursing and among nurse practitioners themselves on the scope of practice, the demarcation of boundaries, the "cure vs. care" debate, and the controversies about minimal qualifications of practitioners. The disagreements seem to be divisive for nurses.

Does this explain how effortlessly medical doctor opposition was able to close down seven major university nurse practitioner programs? Has anyone ever sought public opinion on this? Surely the 100 percent success rate of nurse practitioners improving medical outcomes of clinics — most often in co-operation with medical doctors — and the consistent lowering of drug prescriptions, surgery and adverse events, is a topic the health system ought to be vigorously communicating to the public? Therefore, Dr. Spitzer's concern that public resistance may be a factor is only valid in the sense that the public is being given incomplete or dishonest information, entirely at the direction of the medical profession.

Yet it must be said emphatically, that nurses do not do a very good job selling the issues of vital importance to their own welfare. That they are admired is self-evident. They are usually number one in surveys of respect shown for different professions. But they fail to effectively leverage that popularity. Strong nurses' unions in some jurisdictions are tough in contract negotiations with government, but, generally speaking, with respect to medical doctors, the profession exudes a "battered wife syndrome," so desperate to be loved by medical doctors they will forgive any abuse that comes along.

This may still be the most significant challenge faced by the nursing profession, the nurse practitioner specialty and those within the health system who wish to advance the issue. Physicians must be convinced that they could multiply their effectiveness and satisfaction if each professional focused predominately on the area of their own expertise.

Most believe the role of the GP has eroded. It is...

- rarely of traditional "family" orientation any more because of public mobility and family breakup;
- pressured by rules requiring quantity of patients, not quality of service;
- confused in terms of local hospital planning, visiting privileges and regional dispersal of patients;
- increasingly geriatric, as a result of the only stable, local population being an aging one in most neighborhoods;
- more a brokerage for lab services, diagnostic centres and other medical specialists than a treatment centre;
- an order-taking operation for pharmaceuticals;
- losing the battle to impersonal walk-in clinics and hospital outpatient departments; and,
- of zero equity value for sale to another doctor.

The solution must be to entirely rethink the role. The centrepiece of a new tomorrow for health care could and should be the nurse practitioner, working in community clinics that have all of the necessary medical and health professional talent available at short notice. Preliminary assessment at the clinic, in a patient's home, at the workplace, upon advice from paramedics and other sources of intake, could be the nurse practitioner's forte, offering similar methodology as triage in emergency departments.

The new gatekeeper.

Minor surgery is that which is
performed on someone else.

9.
Closer to Home

*In Canada, there is a great deal of support to help people
die with dignity — living with dignity is the challenge.
This is where our system too often fails people.*

— WENDY ROGERS, an Ottawa physiotherapist

It is hard to imagine more ingenuous — if not clearly fraudulent —
rhetoric in the Canadian health system than the ocean-full of insin-
cere, empty words surrounding the issue of "closer to home". This means
moving patients away from acute care hospitals to less stressful, less dangerous, less costly and more convalescent-oriented environments, ideally
their own homes. Every health minister in modern memory has given
speeches on the topic. British Columbia even had a Royal Commission
that became so enthused it titled its report "CLOSER TO HOME."

Confronted with an accusation of inaction, every province and every
health minister could produce a fat brief showing all the things that have
been done for home and community care, as well as all the obstacles that
have prevented the evolution from optimizing its potential. Policies,
services and progress vary from province to province and even among
health regions within the provinces, but these small victories have not
come close to winning the war.

Bluntly put by professionals and caregivers on the front line, "getting
people to and from the bathroom," is all that is required to get large numbers of people back into their own homes. That one incapacity alone
keeps thousands of people in expensive hospital beds. With home counseling and tools available to therapists today, many of these patients
could be managed less expensively and in a healthier, more dignified
fashion.

Officials are extremely big with statistics, the scorecard by which
they and the politicians to whom they report measure their effectiveness.
We hear of millions of home visits, but what is the quality of each visit?

Five-minute social calls hardly replace 30-minute sessions with an accomplished professional. And that is what is happening in these cost-crunching days. The disparity between services provided those with extended health benefits and those without, is the difference between a four star hotel and a campground. Anyone who wishes to measure the imbecilic dishonesty of Canada's pretence to "equality" in medicare, ought to spend a day or two traveling with any home care professional.

Each province has aspired to evolve its own form of home care, usually working from the nucleus of a Community Health Centre (CHC). These take many forms and come up with a variety of acronyms. CHC is the conventional model. But Local Community Services Centres (CLSC) have a long history in Quebec. Health Co-operative Models (COOPs) make the patients and the communities "owners" of their collective service. Health Services Organizations (HSOs) are usually groups of physicians, without other professionals; Comprehensive Health Organizations (CHOs) add other professionals and Health Maintenance Organizations (HMOs) are most frequently American insurance models, but usually multidisciplinary according to choices of service made by managers. These are just a few of the acronyms one hears, as each jurisdiction and private groups attempt to address needs and provincial services.

Necessity sometimes evolves the best programs. In vast reaches of Canada, where physician services are rare, communities have had to work much harder to get more from community health centres. Similarly, in Saskatchewan, which was forced during the 1990s to close 150 hospitals, an advanced style of multidisciplinary community service ultimately emerged. What is strikingly similar from coast to coast is that the models which give patients, local residents, and "members" of the centre the most power over their own care, and the ones that operate in a multidisciplinary fashion — not entirely under the direction of medical doctors — are by far the best in every measurable statistic: cost, patient health, use of drugs and surgery and community satisfaction.

Ontario's home care network progressively evolved — in most areas more comprehensive than elsewhere in Canada — perhaps at its best in 1997, when 43 Community Care Access Centres (CCACs) were established across the province. The effort was to standardize services province-wide, a single point of access for people to link up with all the health and social support services they might need. The history in Ontario and elsewhere is that separate services often operated independently of one another: nursing, physio and occupational therapy, technical support (respirators), aids to the handicapped, and food and domestic services through social agencies. Sometimes charitable agencies and non-profit associations delivered care, sometimes professional. Some districts and professionals were unionized, some were not.

Ontario reorganization addressed all of that in 1997, but economic problems after 2000 forced the imposition of restructuring. The *Community Care Access Corporations Act* of 2001, introduced sweeping changes across the province. Central to the plan is the word "competition." In each of the Access Centres (now 42, two of which are hospital based), management boards are appointed and they are required to call tenders for the delivery of service. The system has gone through a period of uncertainty and it is hoped the end result will enhance both economy and quality, but it is too soon to tell. Some of the districts appear to be operating extremely well, but others are chaotic. The fear is that monitoring of quality such as access and levels of care, will be approached with far less enthusiasm than the efforts of bureaucrats to minimize costs, and the private sector firms to maximize profits. One worrisome byproduct so far is the unprecedented growth of independent fee-for-service professionals such as physio and occupational therapists, catering to patients (or their extended benefits plans) who now feel compelled to purchase what they used to receive at no cost. This is definitely a further escalation of two-level health care, one for VIPs and one for everybody else.

Community Care Access Centres are not to be confused with Community Health Centres. The CHCs co-ordinate programs and services with the home and long-term care providers, but they are far more health professional oriented, with doctors, nurse practitioners, dieticians, nutritionists and a long list of health specialists on call. Essentially, the CHCs are very large clinics, but far more multidisciplinary, and wellness oriented than hospitals. Ontario has some of the best in the world, but the distribution is hit and miss. In most instances, the evolution of CHCs in Ontario and elsewhere, had to overcome the opposition of the national and provincial medical associations. In most communities, fee-for-service doctors and the hospitals they dominate have been able to suppress CHC development.

Hospital without walls

Every few years, someone in Canada discovers a long-standing New Brunswick program and expresses surprise — more accurately characterized as "astonishment" — that other provinces have not copied the precedent. Senator Kirby's Committee was a recent discoverer. In 1993, reporter Ed Struzik wrote the following in the *Edmonton Journal*:

> HOSPITAL WITHOUT WALLS, A SMASHING SUCCESS! The New Brunswick Extra Mural Hospital is the archetypal hospital — it has no walls. Instead, it's an acute and long-term care centre of the future where people are admitted by their physicians to a bed in their own homes, complete with portable technology and personnel required for their condition.
>
> If it's a bold experiment in the eyes of some, it's one that's been running a long time. The hospital opened its doors, in a manner of speaking, back in October 1981. Faced with enormous demands on the health care system, the province of New Brunswick decided back then that it could no longer afford a virtually limitless program of expanding institutional services. So it looked to a community-based alternative which would see some people avoiding the hospital experience altogether while others return home after a shorter stay.
>
> "It's safe to say that there was a lot of controversy when we first opened for business," says Dr. Gordon Ferguson, the surgeon who's been the hospital's one-and-only chief executive officer. "We had to do a lot of missionary work, especially with the physicians." In the end, it was word-of-mouth from the patients that convinced New Brunswickers that this was a good thing. "The demand made it work," says Ferguson. "People who heard of a relative or neighbour next door being treated and recovering at home instead of a hospital wanted to have the same service."

Only one province has made dramatic strides in that direction and they did it in 1981. The New Brunswick Extra Mural Hospital philosophy (EMP) was ingenious in its theoretical simplicity, and clever in how it was made to fit into federal health financing policies. The home bed became a hospital bed, part of "doctor's rounds." The most extraordinary thing about the New Brunswick experience is that almost a quarter century of success later — while province after province has pedantically and repeatedly boasted they would achieve the equivalent — it remains unique. This is an indictment of health leadership coast to coast.

New Brunswick's numbers are impressive. During the fiscal year 2001/2002, 18,359 patients were treated in their homes and discharged. There were 453,813 home visits by health workers (respiratory, therapists etc.), including 321,905 of these by nurses. The New Brunswick statistics are hospital numbers, admitted within the definition of the *Canada Health Act* to a bed in their own home. These data must be separated from routine long-term care and social services statistics, which also help people in their homes. New Brunswick had a population of 730,000 at the time — the comparative Ontario numbers would be 306,000 hospital patients and 7.6 million home visits.

The Kirby/Senate of Canada report called attention to the New Brunswick program:

> It is often cited as a possible model for other jurisdictions. Designated as a Hospital Corporation under the New Brunswick Hospital Act, its services were eligible to be insured by the province. . . .Thirty service delivery sites provide for the delivery of EMP services to clients across the entire province. Staff includes clinical co-ordinators, liaison nurses, support staff, and field staff representing the disciplines of clinical nutrition, nursing, occupational therapy, physiotherapy, speech language pathology, social work, and respiratory therapy. All professional staff members are employees of the EMP who work in interdisciplinary teams. Support services such as homemaking and meals-on-wheels are contracted. Direct care staff provides the case-management function as well. Nursing services are available 24 hours a day, seven days a week, while all other disciplines deliver services Monday to Friday.

The New Brunswick Extra Mural mandate, when it was implemented in 1981, was the following:

- Provide an alternative to hospital admissions,
- Facilitate early discharge from hospitals,
- Provide an alternative to, or postponement of, admission to nursing homes,
- Provide long term care,
- Provide rehabilitation services,
- Provide palliative care, and
- Facilitate the co-ordination and provision of support services.

In a 2003 report, the program outlined its principal objectives as follows:

1. All New Brunswickers have access to home health care services, when required, in the home and community environment, in order to progress towards and maintain an optimal level of health.

2. Home health care is holistic in nature and is delivered through the provision of co-ordinated services. In order to meet the identified needs of the client, service providers recognize the contribution of other providers, establish effective communication and work together in partnership.

3. Home health care service must be delivered in an environment that is safe for the client and the EMP service provider.

4. The client's culture, experiences, knowledge and rights are central to, and carry authority within, the client/service provider relationship. Services provided are responsive to the needs of the client.

5. Home health care services are best provided through an interdisciplinary team with case co-ordination for each client and family.

6. A continuous quality improvement approach is essential in the provision of home health care services that are responsive to the changing needs of clients and the community.

7. Home health care services must support and incorporate the appropriate use of client self care and service providers, both formal and informal.

8. Relevant training and education of other health service providers, based on the needs of the client, are essential in the provision of quality home health care services.

9. Development and maintenance of an ongoing learning environment are essential to recruit and maintain competent, innovative, effective and efficient service providers.

The architect of the program in New Brunswick, Dr. Gordon Ferguson, had heard about innovative approaches in New Zealand. He and a colleague traveled there and returned home quite excited by the potential. A noted physician and surgeon, Ferguson's induction into the

Order of Canada was in recognition of his groundbreaking work in home-care. He headed the program he founded for more than 15 years and was a leader in the development and implementation of a team-based approach to patient services in his province. Ferguson died in 2004. The New Brunswick innovation, the first home care program accepted under the *Canada Health Act* of 1984, was reorganized in 1997 into a network of regional hospital corporations, and rehabilitation services were added.

Every province subsequently followed the New Brunswick lead and included a "home hospital" strategy, if not as a formal title, then certainly at the delivery of care level. But it is an extension of home care in these jurisdictions, and not as widely accepted by medical doctors. They have no choice in New Brunswick. Other provinces have been less willing to mandate standards of practice. New Brunswick, unfortunately, has not done as well as other jurisdictions in the evolution of the other dimensions of home and long-term care, including sophisticated CHCs, and the equal access for "non-hospital" patients to nurses, domestic help, therapists and other professionals.

Sublime to ridiculous

If New Brunswick offers the prototype of a better future, British Columbia should capture the gold medal for a blown opportunity. The late Richard Hatfield, former premier of New Brunswick (1970–1987), was once challenged in Vancouver about the benefits his province received as a so-called "have not" province. He responded: "British Columbia leaves more food on its plate than we ever get for dinner."

But the early 1980s were unkind to the west coast province. A savage recession descended, prompted by 20 percent interest rates and a collapsed real estate market. The calamity arrived in the early stages of planning for a 1986 World's Fair in Vancouver and many associated capital commitments. Premier Bill Bennett imposed brutal financial controls. Labor rebelled and a "general strike" was threatened.

In the health field, the pressure arrived on the desk of Stan Dubas, a new deputy minister. Dubas recalls that the first day on the job he was presented with an ultimatum from the finance minister — across the board cuts. "Cost containment was an unheard of phrase within Canadian health care at the time. Everybody was conditioned to inflationary increments and extra budgets for program expansion — it was automatic." The Bennett financial controls of the early 1980s were ruthless, and everyone in health care was in an uproar. But by mid-decade, not only was the World's Fair a triumph, British Columbia was again leading the Canadian economic parade, heralding in a series of balanced budgets and surpluses.

When health programs were able to expand once again, the legacy of the restraint era prompted many catch-up initiatives, along with new ventures. The inevitable consequence was inconsistency province-wide, and, in 1990, a Royal Commission on Health Care and Costs was appointed. The chair was Justice Peter D. Seaton of the British Columbia Court of Appeal. The commissioners heard more than 1,600 submissions, but the overwhelming theme by the time they came to write their report, was that avoiding acute care hospitals, wherever possible, or, once admitted, getting patients out faster, was the best single thing that could be done to improve health outcomes and cost savings. They urged a tiered system of progressively less intense environments: support for intermediate, long-term and palliative care facilities, community and home services. They titled their report *CLOSER TO HOME*.

The best evidence of the report's success was that every establishment group was horrified. "A lot of oxen get gored," said Robert Evans, PhD, of the University of British Columbia, a Commission member and, to this day, one of Canada's leading health economists.

The commission found that people who live in remote and rural areas had higher than average rates of infant deaths, accidental deaths, alcohol-related deaths, suicides, and homicides. They also had fewer health-care workers, fewer psychiatric beds and no alcohol or drug detox centres. In 1987–88 the medicare plan spent an average of little more than $200 per capita for people in remote areas compared with more than $300 for those in urban areas. Among the more contentious recommendations, the commission proposed:

- freezing all expansion of acute care hospitals, subject to review of the entire system;
- deliberately reducing the number of physicians and capping their income;
- encouraging the development of convalescent and long-term care facilities, but subjecting these institutions to the same scrutiny as what is required for major hospitals;
- expanding home care support;
- approving euthanasia under strict guidelines; and,
- replacing medicare premiums with an income tax surcharge.

Predictably, the acute hospital managers, health unions and the British Columbia Medical Association were quick to condemn the report. Said Dr. Gur Singh, a Kamloops neurosurgeon and president of the BCMA, "A more realistic title for the Royal Commission's report would be 'Throwing the Baby Out with the Bath Water'."

Journalist Carole Taylor, who subsequently became a Vancouver city councilor, chair of the Vancouver Port Corporation and chair of the Canadian Broadcasting Corporation, wrote in *The Vancouver Sun*:

> While hot topics like euthanasia, condoms in high schools, a mandatory lunch program for hungry kids, bike helmets for all and a revised one-drink limit for drivers have grabbed the headlines since the release of the Royal Commission's look at our health care system, the guts of this report lies deep in the back pages and between the lines of the full report. How are we going to revolutionize our health delivery system before it's too late?
>
> The principles enunciated by Justice Peter Seaton and other commission members are clear: Keep people out of hospital as much as possible. When admission is essential, let it be to a hospital close to home, except for tertiary care. (This term is generally used to describe the most complicated and serious cases such as heart transplants.) Open up the planning system to public scrutiny. Let communities have a real voice in how dollars are spent.

Reporter Barbara McClintock, in the Vancouver Province, added:

> The province should take a knife to health-care costs, and the place to start is with B.C. doctors, says the Royal Commission on Health Care and Costs. Victoria should cap the amount of money going to doctors, says the commission headed by Appeal Court Justice Peter Seaton. The increasing number of doctors in B.C. is one of the largest factors in growing costs, the commission notes, but there doesn't seem to be any legal way to limit the number of doctors.
>
> The only other approach to cost control, therefore, is to place an absolute cap on the total amount of money available for payment of physicians' services," writes the commission. The cap, the commission says, should be so strict as to ensure that more visits to doctors don't translate into more money for doctors.
>
> The commission says it knows doctors will be "distressed" by the recommendations, but warns that if the major cost item of doctors' fees

"continues to grow more rapidly than the economic base which supports it, we do not believe that the health-care system will survive in its present form."

Commissioner Evans suggested at the time that the release of the report, coinciding with a change of government, was fortuitous, an opportunity for a new administration to start with a clean slate. British Columbia was in excellent financial shape and many health reforms were starting to show dividends. The health budget was about $6 billion per year.

The New Democratic Party would remain in power for 10 years, wiped out in the 2001 election, losing all but two of its seats. During the interim, there was progress on few, if any, of the Seaton recommendations. The budget climbed to $8 billion, and almost all of the $2 billion growth was in the salaries of health employees and professionals. Elsewhere across Canada, the inflation-adjusted per capita costs for health had actually gone down from 1992–97. If anything, services in British Columbia had deteriorated, while costs soared. The biggest of the new capital projects, a giant acute care hospital in Vancouver stood vacant — a white elephant — a monument to incompetence. For 10 years, the motto of health management in British Columbia could be described as FURTHER FROM HOME.

The concept of increasing home care and building up the network of secondary hospitals and long-term care facilities, clearly collided with the interests of acute care hospital employees and their union locals. A landmark accord between the government and 55,000 employees, members of the Hospital Employees Union, the Health Sciences Association and the B.C. Nurses Union, guaranteed all existing employees their jobs. The government boasted that the unions, in exchange for the guarantee, pay increases and a reduction from 37.5- to 36-hour work weeks, agreed to permit the elimination of up to 4,800 positions.

Almost overnight, the deal added $500 million a year to the cost of health care — with zero benefit to patients; and, none of the staff cutbacks were realized. It may have been one of the most monumental managerial goofs and give-aways in the history of health care in Canada. But that was not the worst of it. The job guarantee to all 55,000 employees meant that they could bump down the system in order to retain employment. If community, home or long-term care beds enabled the reduction of needs in the acute hospitals, making employees redundant, these workers were guaranteed full pay for up two years and the first crack at any opening elsewhere in the system. Administrators of any facility that accepted government money or government subsidized patients, would have to employ the union members at full rates, bound by a contract of no relevance to them, which had been negotiated for the largest and most sophisticated acute care hospitals.

It devastated the whole point of simpler, less costly, more convales-cent oriented facilities, the kind that thrive on creativity and entrepre-neurialism. The best of these everywhere use volunteers, part-timers and assorted caregivers, in addition to the professional staff. Subjecting the administrators to acute care hospital salary structures, 36-hour weeks and a long list of union benefits, made them impossibly costly to operate. Private investment completely dried up. Government, desperate to main-tain the appearance of progress, faced the prospect of either financing unnecessary numbers of patients in acute care facilities, or finding tax-payer funds to construct all alternatives.

Medical doctors were equally uncooperative. Any time a proposal came forward to close down acute beds, there was a protest. MDs had grown comfortable with the placement of all of their patients in nearby hospitals, where they could see several at a time, during visits. Dispersing them through the community either meant uneconomic travel time or transferring the patient to other physicians. During the NDP's second term in British Columbia (1996–2001) they tried to get tough and faced a barrage of doctors advertising condemning them for putting patients at risk. Eventually, as always , the government caved in. The nightly sight of seriously ill patients on the television news, unwittingly negotiating on behalf of their doctors, wore the government down.

Perhaps the most significant failure in the years following the Seaton Commission was the lack of progress in home care. This was an area the NDP were enthusiastic about, but the fatter cats munching the budget pie left only pennies for this most cash-starved sector of the business. Without community infrastructure, home care goes nowhere. There needs to be an integrated program to make available as required, doctors, nurses, respiratory technicians, physiotherapists, occupational therapists, meals-on-wheels and even domestic care. There should be a "core" for regional services, optimally a Community Health Centre.

And there needs to be a healthy, co-operative attitude between pri-vate sector entrepreneurs, volunteers, charities, non-profit organizations and public employees. Some of the best home care services are provided by contractors, who agree to perform specific functions at a certain guar-anteed price, for a set number of patients. The employees of these firms usually have a personality and a lifestyle suited to flexible employment schedules, both in terms of their private lives and their work. They manage both odd hours of work and leisure time with ease. Managers of unionized operations are usually restricted by extreme costs for emergency call outs of staff who require full shifts of pay or double time for late night and irregular work. Private firms can be held to fixed prices. The public sector cannot so easily be held to account.

British Columbia unions opposed privatization in the home care field. But they were not happy with the NDP government either. They too, complained that the exploding costs surrounding the acute care hospitals, and all health workers elsewhere in the system, left nothing for them. In a thoughtful paper prepared during 2000 by several health unions and the Canadian Centre for Policy Alternatives - B.C. Office, this issue was addressed. Reminding readers of the 1991 Seaton Commission urging "the transfer of resources from hospitals to the community, to promote the benefits of early intervention, prevention and integrated, local care," the report protested that the Community and Continuing Care sector had been abandoned.

> Community and Continuing Care became a pivot of health care reforms across Canada. Legislators enacted regionalization strategies; researchers documented the health benefits of community-based programs; and Canadians themselves demanded holistic and preventive services that respected their needs as patients and families. Demographic and political conditions, such as the aging population and severe cuts to federal transfer payments, also focused attention on Community and Continuing Care.

Solid programs, the paper said, "relieve pressures on family physicians, emergency rooms, hospital beds and long term care facilities.. .and can resonate with the real-life needs and preferences of many Canadians . . . yet for all its fundamental importance, Community and Continuing Care is the most vulnerable and irrationally organized sector of our public health care system. It lacks both stability and status." It continued:

> The inspiration of 'closer to home' has been stifled by lack of infrastructure and dedicated funding for Community and Continuing Care. Today, British Columbians are reeling under the one-two punch of halfhearted reforms, in which many patients are quickly discharged from hospital only to be stranded without community services. As more

health services are delivered within homes and communities, more people will find themselves outside the shelter of Medicare: uncovered, uncared for and unable to buy private help. . . .rather than becoming more focused on prevention and early intervention, health care services in all sectors have become increasingly crisis-oriented.

Dubas, the deputy health minister in the years preceding the Seaton Commission, said that home care, without ensuring that infrastructure is first in place, can be a bottomless "big black hole" from a budget point of view. Family responsibility must be encouraged. Extra services to help bathe patients soon lead to a need to clean house and do dishes. And, if that is done, who is going to look after the front garden? If these services are provided — even occasionally — to one lonely patient, why should a taxpaying family across the street not also get financial assistance in the care for an ailing loved one at home? Each service generates a chain reaction of demand, requiring firm rules and rigid controls.

This is precisely what makes home care such an ideal area for harmonious public-private partnerships as in New Brunswick. In that province the 640 Extra Mural employees are public servants. But there is a network of private contractors working with them, providing both basic domestic and specialized services wherever it makes the best economic sense. What both sides of the equation know is that even extravagant costs in a well-managed community and home care model is much cheaper than the alternative. And, since the alternative is guaranteed by the *Canada Health Act*, the government would save money by changing the definitions of covered services.

As Dr. Evans said in a year 2000 speech in Alberta:

A national program of expanded home care is an option for taking further pressure off the institutional sectors, both in avoiding or further shortening acute care episodes, and in providing an alternative to long-term institutional care for the elderly. But tight management will be needed if expanded home care is to substitute for more expensive and less appropriate forms of institutional care, rather than being used as a way of adding on further services and costs — and incomes.

The failure to build the infrastructure first, and to establish clear, fair guidelines as to the services available and any "ability-to-pay" fees attached, is what most often dooms home care programs. During a 1997 health care forum, Dr. Judith Kazimirski, president of the Canadian

Medical Association, said: "I can't find beds for my patients when they urgently need hospitalization. . .I can't find home-care programs when patients are discharged quickly from hospital. I watch people waiting for hip-replacement operations. As far as people in my part of Canada (Halifax) are concerned, there is a crisis."

A Liberal government took office in British Columbia in 2001 and made major reforms to taxation and budget processes. Health care had risen from 33 percent of the provincial budget to 42 percent during the previous decade and the new administration was determined to hold the ratio at that level, or reduce it. Some of the most egregious pro-union rules governing long-term and intermediate care facilities have been removed. Tough deals have been signed with all unions except the doctors. In that area, the Liberals proved to be as spineless as their predecessors, arguing that a mediation report by the former Chief Justice of the Court of Appeal forced them to be generous. In 2002, in addition to various concessions on fees for procedures, and increments for special services, every doctor in the province received a cash bonus of up to $50,000. In an agreement reached in 2004, the doctors signed a two-year deal with no "general" fee increase, although a third year of the deal will go to arbitration if agreement can't be reached.

Major organizational changes have taken place in British Columbia, reducing the number of semi-autonomous health authorities from 52 — a well-meaning NDP effort to provide more local input to health management and planning, but which became an expensive bureaucratic monster — to five geographic zones and a separate authority for highly specialized province-wide services.

As for "closer to home," the political rhetoric is best described as "the usual." Firm statements have come from Premier Gordon Campbell and everyone in government to bolster home, community, long-term and intermediate care. Those within the system say that the vibes are good, but it is too soon to proclaim significant progress. However, a national authority on the topic, Nancy McKay of Bathurst, N.B., a past president of the Canadian Physiotherapy Association, describes B.C. as "one of the better examples" because home care is "organized; co-ordinated with the institutional side of the system; publicly administered; accessible to those who require palliative, early discharge post-hospitalization monitoring and care; interdisciplinary; and, it is not strictly physician run, with multiple points of entry."

As always, there is a power struggle for money that rarely involves patients, except to use sick people as props, during negotiations, to symbolize the "crisis" requiring attention. In 2000 as Dr. Evans said in his Alberta speech:

> A physician might respond to a patient's health crisis by taking a history, then developing a diagnosis, and finally recommending a therapy. Along the way, various observations and tests would be made to gather relevant data. Crises in the health care system, however, are typically approached in reverse order. First there is a recommended therapy, then a diagnosis may be inferred so as to justify that therapy, and the history and test results are often ignored, or simply fabricated.

The reasons for this perverse approach are, I think, to be found in the fact that health care 'crises' are commonly pressed into the service of a number of different agendas only tangentially, if at all, related to improving health care. In most cases the recommended therapy will involve spending more money, often quite a lot of it. But it is an accounting identity (not an economic theory!) that every dollar of expenditure represents, by definition, and without exception, a dollar of income for someone. Therefore all spending recommendations (up or down) are also recommendations with respect to someone or some group's income. 'More acute care beds' for example, means simply larger hospital budgets, since hospital capacity is now constrained more by money for staffing than by physical equipment.

Poignancy and tragedy

Nothing is sadder within the realm of putting people back into the community, than the track record of deinstitutionalization. Rarely a day goes by in any large Canadian city that a dead body is not found, hiding among dumpsters, inside culverts, under bridges or within public parks. In almost all of these cases, a trace of their personal history reveals that they have been in and out of institutions all of their lives. Most of them are mentally ill. Many forget to either obtain or take their anti-psychotic medication.

The movement began in Sweden during the mid-1960s and evolved into a global phenomenon. The most influential North American authority on the topic was a Syracuse University professor, Dr. Wolf Wolfensberger, who achieved international fame during the early 1970s as a visiting professor in Canada, at the National Institute on Mental Retardation (now Roeher Institute) on the campus of York University.

Wolfensberger and progressive sociologists, psychologists, psychiatrists and special needs educators worldwide, advocated "deinstitutionalization."

In the wake of the Academy Award winning movie *One Flew Over the Cuckoo's Nest*, and an endless series of horror stories emanating from institutions about general neglect, heavily sedated zombies, drug experimentation, lobotomies, sexual and physical abuse, and warehousing, rather than treatment, it was not a tough sell to the public. But the experts knew the problems. The advent of anti-psychotic drugs made it possible for schizophrenics and many others to maintain relatively normal lifestyles, but other institutionalized people were alcoholics; or challenged by varying degrees of mental retardation; or suffering from what is now commonly known as CMI (Chronic Mental Illness), conditions that defy easy definition or treatment. Many were prone to violence under certain circumstances and rarely predictable. There was a small group of severely mentally ill and the criminally insane who would never be considered for release.

The expert promoters of deinstitutionalization emphasized the need for community infrastructure. Some patients would need occasional institutional visits. Others would just need the benefit of group homes, stabilizing drugs and regular professional consultations. Most would need monitoring. Just about all of the institutional releases required educational catch-up, training and counseling, if not for work, then just in basic life skills. The experts argued that all of that should prove cheaper than the big draconian institutions that had earned derisive comments through history, the "nut house, loony bin, squirrel farm" and the plot lines for suspense and horror films.

Avant-garde post-1960s politicians latched onto "deinstitutionalization" like barnacles on the bottom of a boat, half of them aspiring to the glory of changing society, and others seeing only saved tax dollars. As usual, the floodgates were opened before the valley was prepared for the deluge.

The United States had 550,000 residents in mental hospitals in 1955. By 1985, that had dropped to 110,000 and just half of that a decade later. In Canada, there were 70,000 people in mental institutions in 1965 and just 20,000 by 1980. Comparative numbers are harder to assemble today because relatively few mental patients are permanently housed in institutions. Large numbers spend either a few days or most of their year in residence, but it is believed that the institutional population on any given day in this era is less than 5,000 in Canada.

One of the leading authorities on the topic is clinical psychiatrist, researcher and prolific author Fuller Torrey, MD, of Washington, DC, who wrote in a 1989 Harvard report:

> The homeless mentally ill are a product of the best of intentions followed by the worst of operations. They are the result of deinstitutionalization, the policy which evolved in the 1950s and '60s to shift care of the seriously mentally ill from state mental hospitals to community facilities. The policy is reasonable in theory, but in practice has proved to be a disgrace to the mental health professions and a national tragedy.

Dr. Torrey's famous 1988 book *Nowhere To Go: The Tragic Odyssey of the Homeless Mentally Ill* — still likely the most quoted and respected volume on the theme — was a blistering indictment of mental health managers. "The care of the seriously mentally ill in twentieth century America has been a public disgrace," he said, adding:

> Over fifty years of warehousing patients in inhumane state hospitals has been followed by almost forty years of dumping them into bleak boarding homes or onto the streets. It has been an era of remarkably poor planning and inept policy formulation. Professional self-interest has been confused with altruism, official inaction with benevolence, ideology with science, and ignorance with omniscience.

He quoted a *New York Times* article which said, deinstitutionalization had become "a cruel embarrassment, a reform gone terribly wrong," and a psychiatrist colleague who added: "the chronic mentally ill patient had his locus of living and care transferred from a single lousy institution to multiple wretched ones." Dr. Torrey listed these problems — all of them applicable to the Canadian history, and sadly, the situation today.

> .... the seriously mentally ill were dumped out of mental hospitals into communities with few facilities and little aftercare. And as soon as they were gone, the hospitals were closed down so that they could not return. Rather than deinstitutionalization, which implied that alternative community facilities would be provided, what took place was simply depopulation of the state hospitals. It was as if a policy of resettlement had been agreed upon but only eviction took place. How bad are the effects of the policy of deinstitutionalization— a policy that

affects an estimated two million seriously mentally ill people in the United States? Here are eight aspects of the problem:

1. There are at least twice as many seriously mentally ill individuals living on streets and in shelters as there are in public mental hospitals.
2. There are increasing numbers of seriously mentally ill individuals in the nation's jails and prisons.
3. Seriously mentally ill individuals are regularly released from hospitals with little or no provision for aftercare or follow-up treatment.
4. Violent acts perpetrated by untreated mentally ill individuals are increasing in number.
5. Housing and living conditions for mentally ill individuals in the community are grossly inadequate.
6. Community mental health centres, originally funded to provide community care for the mentally ill so these individuals would no longer have to go to state mental hospitals, are almost complete failures.
7. Laws designed to protect the rights of the seriously mentally ill primarily protect their right to remain mentally ill.
8. The majority of mentally ill individuals discharged from hospitals have been officially lost. Nobody knows where they are.

Dr. Torrey's bizarre postscript was to point out that the care for the serious mentally ill in 1963 cost $1 billion in the United States. By 1985, after disaster had occurred, institutions closed and the situation had become an unmanageable nightmare, the cost of mental health services in the same jurisdictions had ballooned to $17 billion, the preponderance of which paid to bureaucrats, managers and professionals, many of whom ought to have gone to jail for criminal negligence causing thousands of deaths.

In any North American city, perhaps worldwide, it is a regular sight to see indigent people wheeling shopping carts around loaded with their "treasures." Panhandlers abound. Most of these suffer mental illness. As unsightly as they may be, with extreme nuisance value, they are usually harmless. A few, particularly those who fail to take medication, can be violent, sometimes fatally so. Suicide rates are high. Church and other non-profit societies try vainly to feed and house them, and get them care when it is available, but these associations usually feel there is too little government support. Each person who dies becomes one less statistic for the authorities.

What is clear in just about every jurisdiction is that the richest, most powerful and largest bureaucracy — HEALTH — performed by far the worst of any in the deinstitutionalization issue. If a resident was lucky enough to fall under an education ministry, social services or even corrections (particularly juvenile), the chances of high quality re-entry to society mushroomed. These other departments either had a built-in infrastructure for handing-off clients to other processes, or — like social services — were quite accustomed to contracting with public and private agencies to look after institutional releases. Plans were evolved for each client and regular accountability and performance tracking were contract requirements.

But Ministries of Health knew only two gears: "Admit" or "Discharge." It is not hard to find outstanding examples of community management by health departments and individual mental health professionals, but successes were the anomalies. Usually, community programs could expect little more than lip service, the lowest rung on the ladder in terms of health priorities and funding goals. To this day, social services and corrections officials are bitter about the gross negligence of the health managers who continue to have the highest executive salaries — by far — and the richest budgets of all. It is thought that from 10–20 percent of all inmates in penal institutions should not be there. They are mentally ill. In the community, they fail to get the care they need and resort to crime. Business organizations trying to crack down on panhandlers and undesirables usually realize that there are precious few resources in the community, but fail to understand why alternatives cannot be provided. Police and jail are certainly not the answer. Police and corrections officers should not have to become surrogate mental health workers.

An American writer, responding to a public protest demanding more mental health facilities in the community, quoted Martin Luther King:

It is an historical fact that the privileged groups seldom give up their privileges voluntarily. Individuals may see the moral light and voluntarily give up their unjust posture, but, as we are reminded, groups tend to be more immoral than individuals. We know, through painful experience that freedom is never voluntarily given by the oppressor, it must be demanded by the oppressed.

Unfortunately, these poor folks are invariably leaderless, helpless, alone and impossible to organize into effective political action. So they die or disappear, in each instance helping the system manufacture the fraud of improved statistics.

Rx — the middle ground

British Columbia's former deputy health minister Stan Dubas, currently an executive in the field of long-term care, has a simple formula for the future:

- One Mayo Clinic quality diagnostic centre per jurisdiction, just a few of them coast-to-coast in Canada, based on either population concentration or regional service considerations. Each would have the best of ultramodern technical equipment, lab resources and health professionals.
- Far fewer and more narrowly defined acute care hospitals to deal with major surgery and the gravest of medical circumstances and particularly conditions where the course of treatment is uncertain.
- Continued development of a network of small surgi-centres, either private or public, should be encouraged. If private for-profit centres can provide procedures and follow-up care more effectively — cost and quality — the public system should not hesitate to contract them for the work. This should also apply to private diagnostic facilities.
- A much larger network of community based "convalescent" or intermediate-care hospitals across the country, where health and healing are the fundamental concern. The more detached these institutions are from the "illness" and "procedure" dominated acute care hospitals the better it will be for everyone.
- A rationalization of outpatient services, including both the elaborate emergency departments of today's major hospitals, as well as a preponderance of closer-to-home basic centres for emergency paramedical triage, routine accidents and community care. Dubas was among the first health managers in

Canada to finance and establish a regular physician clinic next door to a hospital outpatient department, to relieve emergency services from the pressure of walk-in patients with minor complaints. This should be standard practice.

Dubas realizes that the basic grid would be more complicated than that, because of the need for many specialized facilities including pediatrics, obstetrics, cancer centres, mental health, rehabilitation services and agencies such as the National Centre for Disease Control. However, the planning philosophy everywhere should also be to create physical separation between diagnostic, treatment, recovery and wellness modalities, facilities and personnel. Getting people out of acute hospitals should be the highest priority. "You never go to a hospital to get better," Dubas says. "The longer you stay in hospital the more likely it is that you are going to catch something."

It took a long time for the health system to recognize that the pressure to fully equip hospitals in all communities, with irrational duplication of assets and services, had nothing to do with patient care. It was for the convenience and financial benefit of the doctors and staff. They could cluster all of their patients under one roof and refer only the rarest of situations to other people and places. Far too many hospitals have CT Scanners (computed tomography) and other expensive equipment. MRI scanners (magnetic resonance imaging) are more rare, but they have become a booming business for private sector services. One of the reasons there are CT and MRI waiting lists in public hospitals is that health professionals like to work civilized hours, and less during the summer and major holidays. Many public hospitals make money by doing private scans during off hours. If each city, or each region, had fewer but more sophisticated diagnostic centres working 24 hours a day, public service would improve, privateering would diminish and everyone would be better off.

Those who continue to argue for large fully-equipped hospitals in every community suggest that both treatment and convalescence near home is desirable and that within the institution, the cultures can be separated. This is in fact an impossible myth. The culture of acute hospitals is dominated by the gravest circumstances within them, either the most perilous high-risk surgery, the mysterious infectious illness or the victims of major trauma in the emergency department. Everything in between is trivialized by and impacted by the higher priorities. Cure and treatment is the business. **Otherwise, keep out of the way**. And a growing body of evidence demonstrates that an alarming number of patients die or become ill unnecessarily because of this dangerous place of residence.

Therefore, the keys to "closer to home" are easily understood, but multiple services are required such as home care, Community Health Clinics, mental health services, a nearby convalescent/intermediate hospital with an outpatient department, and separate long-term care facilities. There must be access to the most advanced of diagnostic and treatment centres when necessary; but, where these are located is irrelevant to patients because transportation is far cheaper than acute care hospitalization.

"Bluntly put by professionals and care-givers on the front line, "getting people to and from the bathroom," is all that is required to get large numbers of people back into their own homes. That one incapacity alone keeps thousands of people in expensive hospital beds. With home counseling and tools available to therapists today, many of these patients could be managed less expensively and in a healthier, more dignified fashion."

"See .... it's all profit after the day's 40th patient .... even faster if you can sell an X-ray, lab tests, wart removal or whatever."

10.
MedLabs —
The Money Machine

We are now paying lab fees to medical doctors who not only never see the patient, they never see either the sample or the results. Most tests are computerized processes, flagging only the rare cases that need further expert analysis.

— An anonymous lab pathologist

A study conducted for the Government of British Columbia concluded in 2003 that taxpayers were paying $100–$150 million per year more than necessary for medical laboratory services. The consultant, Lillian Bayne and Associates of Toronto, was ever so gentle in report language, but the controversy it generated reverberated across Canada. British Columbians learned they were paying $116 per capita per year for lab tests, compared to the national average of $77.

The critics alleged that this situation — a combination of high fees negotiated with government by the British Columbia Medical Association and excessive utilization — represented a calculated, systemic, and long-term benefit to a relatively small number of corporations. The history of overly generous fees and over-utilization may stretch back decades and represent hundreds of millions of dollars extracted from the province's taxpayers. Before discussing the British Columbia anomaly in detail, it would be useful to put the modern medical lab business and science in perspective.

The scientists

Medical lobbyists and politicians bandy around the word "science" as if it is a brand their profession had purchased and nurtured as a sales tool. Most high quality medical practice is a combination of art, subjective judgment, intelligence, and technical skill. Science often provides the tools, but not the product. Radiology and advanced diagnostics are among the exceptions to all this, and pathology is another. These are the lab physicians and all of the biochemical scientists with whom they work.

The dominant television shows of this era focus on forensic investigations, crime scene analysis of blood, other body fluids, hair, skin, DNA and all related issues. There is less drama but equal science in the daily lab work at hospitals and medical laboratories. At the head of this parade of specialists are the pathologists: anatomical pathology (dissection and analysis of cadavers, organs and tissue); neuropathology (also, physical, involving the brain); general pathology (a catch-all for multiple general work and subspecialties such as forensic, endocrine, cardiovascular and just about every part of the body); hematological pathology (blood); medical biochemistry; and, medical microbiology.

National Centres for Disease Control and all of the lab links they employ have been high profile in recent history with concerns such as SARS, Asian Flu, Creutzfeldt-Jacob Disease (the human variant of mad cow disease, BSE — bovine spongiform encephalopathy), and swine flu. Local alert mechanisms watch for the most lethal forms of meningitis, necrotizing fasciitis (flesh-eating disease), infectious diseases, and other rarer threats. AIDS has become an industry in itself.

When critics question these days the staggering amounts of money being poured into laboratory medicine, none of them criticize either the science or the scientists. In fact, there is a shortage of them and based on pure market value, the most advanced of these professionals are underpaid by any comparison to the average earnings of medical specialists. In fact, the stars of this field of medicine, the best educated, most experienced, most competent with the most specialized area of knowledge and experience, are on salary, at hospitals, government laboratories, major corporations, research foundations and universities. The understanding of laboratory costs is something else entirely.

The money machine

It is often said that there is more wealth to be had from selling biscuits to the masses than caviar to the wealthy. Wal-Mart is more profitable than

Bloomingdale's. The wealth for private medical labs is in the routine tests ordered by every doctor every day. Just about everyone has trooped off to a collection centre at one time or another to provide blood, urine, and other specimens.

Depending upon what the referring doctor or hospital has requested, there may be 10 tests required from one blood sample alone. This is done by computer. No human hand gets involved in anything other than the drawing of blood or collection of the sample, the labeling, recording, transporting, and setting the analysis in motion. No doctor comes near it. In more than 90 percent of cases, no lab doctor will ever have anything to do with this sample. The computer delivers a reading. Most show no problem and a printout or computer file is referred back to the originating physician. The computer will flag areas of concern, but most of these are routine too. These also go back to the originating doctor.

The hospital or private lab these days must make considerable investments in technology and technicians, and service charges must bear this overhead in mind, but the lab physician, in these automated cases, does absolutely nothing. Why then are 10 fees collected on this one blood sample? Each of the 10 tests — one patient's blood — becomes a separate fee, including extraction, handling, testing, and doctor. The same process occurs with urine samples, from which multiple tests can be conducted. Why is any doctor fee appropriate if there is no doctor involved? What "value" does the lab doctor add? No one would question a fee if a flagged item requires professional attention and expert judgment.

The profitability of labs has everything to do with volume. That means convenient neighborhood locations, marketing to clinics and general practitioners, quality interpersonal contact with patients, concentrating the business on the most common tests and high technology to reduce the need of expensive professionals and technicians. It also means avoiding large geographic zones with sparse population (most of Canada). "Patient privacy" has also been an excellent business-development tool. If you can corner a geographic market and control patient records, not sharing with anyone else, you can lock in both the patient and their doctor. These are the items the for-profit labs exploit. In theory, the patient controls their personal records and gives permission to the originating physician, a lab or a hospital to use the data. But software and hardware is just now emerging which will enable the effective sharing of health records, avoiding duplication and increasing confidence levels in the accuracy of data.

The current lack of effective sharing creates a situation where government is required to develop its own premium lab services, not just for rare and sophisticated testing, but also routine services to hospitals and commercially non-viable areas (sparse or geographically dispersed client base) — no matter how pro-business the current political philosophy might be. Information sharing has been a cost nightmare. Patients arrive at hospital by ambulance and there is no information available. Sometimes the family doctor can be reached to share recent bloodwork and urine tests, but the hospital's risk management policy usually dictates complete new sets.

Ultimately, failure to deliver quality management and proper fees lies with government. It is not a public versus private sector issue. A sad consequence of this kind of story is that it feeds the arguments of those who oppose any privatization in health, a superb example that business cannot be trusted.

Just about everything government does in the laboratory field could likely be done more efficiently at less cost within a competitive private sector environment. It can and should be profitable for private firms. If a private company can deliver equal or better service at less cost than a public agency, government would be negligent not to pursue it. The problem is again that malignancy within Canadian health care: monopoly, protected fiefdoms and suffocating bureaucratic mediocrity.

Competitive bidding, as long as it is free of collusion among bidders, between private and public agencies ensures top quality, economy and efficiency. Government must set the standards and make the contractor meet or exceed the promises. The private sector operation of neighborhood collection centres, the management and delivery of samples, and even the high-tech analysis of results are easily definable services, both in qualitative and quantitative terms. But what fee is payable for professional input, if there has been no input in the first place — which there isn't in most cases? The items that make up lab fees are a concern including over-utilization and overpayment of fees.

The scale starts with "no input." Value — zero.

British Columbia — a world on its own

Government changed in B.C. in 2001 and a new health minister was soon apprised of the out-of-control costs of medical laboratory testing. Discussions were held with public sector pathologists and hospital administrators province-wide. Many were sharply critical of the system, and had been for years. Consultants were hired and they returned with alarming evidence. This led to the appointment of Lillian Bayne and Associates.

Citing 2001–2002 figures, Bayne reported that the national average per capita laboratory cost was $77 per patient, from a low of $73 in Saskatchewan to a high of $116 in B.C. The Ontario average was $90. She documented that "outpatient" costs in B.C. were rising at nine percent a year, while "in-patient" costs were growing at only two percent, consistent with the national average for lab services. Profits and dividends were soaring within the private lab sector, likely more from fees and the per-patient utilization than efficiencies.

Media and others who read her report concluded that there could be no other explanation than excessive charges. What was most puzzling and shocking was the vast span of history involved in this apparent systemic problem. Did public officials ignore the cost disparity between B.C. and other provinces? Were they so intimidated by the BCMA role in the issue they kept their blinders in place?

Lillian Bayne wrote:

All reviews have similar key findings, concluding that B.C.'s lab costs (estimated to be over $120 per capita in 2003/04)) are the highest in the country, and confirming B.C. has the highest lab services utilization rates of any province. One inter-provincial study found B.C.'s per capita expenditures were 50 per cent higher than the national average and increasing at a faster rate than anywhere else in Canada (34 per cent over the five years studied). All reviews also concluded B.C.'s laboratory sector suffers from a fragmentation of management, lacks system planning, has limited controls on expenditures, and is missing an adequate information infrastructure necessary for efficient management. . . . the reviews confirm there is clear justification and need for comprehensive reforms of this sector that represents more than four per cent of total provincial expenditures, approximately $473 million in 2002/03. If B.C.'s lab system was reformed to bring B.C.'s expenditures in line with other provinces and the Canadian average, government spending could be reduced by at least $100 million to potentially more than $150 million annually.

Following release of the report, an electrified buzz swept through the province's health industry. The private sector principals were known to be high quality firms and individuals, solid contributors to society, but

harsh words punctuated debates. The negligence of respective governments in permitting charges far above national standards is obvious. The
reader is left to judge how this came to pass.

- The provincial government, in negotiations with the BCMA sets
  the fees for lab rates in B.C., payable under the Medical
  Services Plan.
- Private labs handle $200 million of the estimated current $500
  million spent in B.C. for all lab services. The chair of the
  Finance Committee of the BCMA for 20 years or more has
  been and continues to be Dr. Donald Rix, the chair of MDS
  Metro Laboratories Inc. Rix and partners developed a large,
  independent lab business in B.C., eventually sold to the
  multinational MDS Inc., but he retained a significant personal
  shareholding in the B.C. operations.
- The second largest private concern, BC Biomedical
  Laboratories Ltd., was founded by Dr. Cam Coady in 1958 and
  is owned by 50 physicians. This company fundamentally serves
  the eastern side of Greater Vancouver and the Fraser Valley, but
  shares some geography with MDS. Some of the laboratory
  physicians (pathologists) on the public payroll who operate
  Fraser Valley hospital lab services are also partners and
  beneficiaries of the private sector competition. They receive a
  salary from the hospital authority, fees from the Medical
  Services Plan and shareholder dividends from BC Biomedical.
- There seems to be a geographic accommodation among them.
  BC Biomedical and Valley Medical Laboratories (a smaller
  physician-owned company in the Okanagan Valley) have joined
  a computerized patient information technology evolved by
  MDS Inc.
- There are other physician-owned labs in smaller B.C. centres.

As elsewhere in Canada, laboratory services divide between "in-
patient" and "outpatient." The "in-patient" work is within hospitals, and
government-operated laboratories, and the costs fall under ministry or
regional health authority budgets. Hospitals also provide "outpatient" lab
services, and for this their payment comes from the Medical Services
Plan. Private labs in British Columbia appear to "cherry pick" the opti-

mum locations and the most profitable services. They concentrate on urban areas and the most common tests. The Health Ministry and regional health authorities cover all of the most complex testing, the smaller population centres and the vast remote regions of the province. The approximate $500 million 2004 budget breaks down as follows:

- hospital "in-patient" — $200 million
- hospital "outpatient" — $100 million
- private "outpatient" — $200 million

The rates for specific tests and the fees paid to the pathologist or lab physician are negotiated by the BCMA. Hospitals have been major beneficiaries of the unreasonably high fees. Profits from their outpatient services have grown, but these funds have been pumped back into hospital operations and, indirectly, patient care. While the hospital-based lab pathologists — predominantly on salary — appreciated the windfall income available to enhance services, they nevertheless became the whistleblowers in this issue, motivating government to take a hard look at fees. The excessive profit in the private sector has gone into record increases in corporate share values, shareholder dividends, and physician-owners' bank accounts.

Following the Bayne report, the Government of British Columbia acted decisively. The highly respected Deputy Minister of Health, Penny Ballem, published an open letter in July 2003, in which she said, in part:

As many people have told us, B.C.'s current approach to lab services is fragmented, lacking any cohesion as a system. There are significant problems related to a lack of linked information and practitioner decision support systems. A common experience, for example, is the lack of access to the results of blood tests ordered by a family doctor in a community lab to a physician in a hospital emergency room. Such issues lead to unnecessary duplication and gaps in patient care. Providing an integrated approach will enhance physicians' abilities to provide prompt diagnoses and better patient care.

Currently in B.C., up to 27 different lab information systems are in operation and many are incompatible. In addition, our fragmented system is suffering from a current and worsening crisis in the supply of laboratory professionals, leading to gaps in expertise and difficulty, especially in rural areas, in covering population needs. As a result of

this and other issues, B.C. taxpayers pay more per capita for lab services than any other province, 50 per cent higher than the Canadian average. B.C. also has the highest use of lab service of any Canadian
province, with total lab expenditures now reaching nearly $500 million
a year and growing by 35 per cent over the past five years.

This situation is not sustainable.

Both the consultant Lillian Bayne and Deputy Minister Ballem carefully danced around the minefield of vested interests, meticulously cri-
tiquing "the system," but never any individuals. How could so few
people profit so handsomely, for so long, from this comparative higher
fee schedule? Why did they not question the role of the BCMA or the
inherent conflicts of interest within it? This could not have happened
without an extraordinary desire to accommodate the status quo. Since the
long-term higher fees reported represent many hundreds of millions of
dollars, surely an audit of some nature was warranted?

In any event, the B.C. government finally took decisive action. Using
regulatory powers under the *Hospitals Act*, the health ministry
announced an immediate cut of 8 percent in fees to lab physicians and a
further 12 percent for 2004. In addition, the government announced that
all lab services would be put out to tender. Let the free market determine
the proper price. Shockwaves rolled through the BCMA, MDS Metro,
BC Biomedical, Valley Medical Laboratories, and others who were profiting so handsomely on the status quo.

As usual, any time the cash flow of health businesses are threatened,
the public statements warned about the serious impact this would have
on patients:

MDS Metro said:

These plans jeopardize the community lab services 16,000 B.C.
patients depend on every day. . . . they could also compromise one of
the best lab service delivery systems there is — one that's been serving
patients in communities across the province for more than 45 years. . .
. but the government's other plans will also bring a period of complete
instability, turning today's system upside down. . . . If all this goes
ahead, the government's plan will result in six fragmented systems —
potentially providing six levels of service and access — and six new
bureaucracies to manage them. . . . Applying a competitive bidding
process to laboratory medicine comes at a very high risk — too high for

the number of patients and doctors who rely on this service. Price is always a major factor in any competitive bidding process. Lowest bids come with reduced access and service levels.

BC Biomedical said:

> We're not bidding on a commodity, we're bidding on how we look after patients.. . .while it's admirable that the B.C. Liberal government wants to save money, perhaps it better take a second look at the Olympics the province is hosting some 10 years hence rather than turning laboratory health testing into a medical green chain. . .a laboratory testing system based on the bottom line, which must necessarily be the case in a plan where competitors bid for lucrative contracts, would no doubt put immense pressure on lab technicians to work cheaper and faster. . . while on the face of it that might sound reasonable if the business concerned were assembling lawn chairs or radios, the decisions these lab techs make profoundly affect lives every day. . . if you or your loved one is undergoing a medical test, you want them to get it right the first time. Will stressed-out technicians be beneficial? Of course not.

The alleged concern for patients is standard in all health wage negotiations, including this one, but, if we are to understand the above correctly, it seems that the failure to have lab costs 50 percent more than the national average might endanger the 2010 Winter Olympics — although there is no statistically measurable health benefit to British Columbians resulting from the excessive and expensive testing compared to other Canadian provinces. Is BC Biomedical's warning about a "green chain" — a manual labor phrase from lumber mills —a characterization of the competitive market forces that achieve lower per patient costs everywhere else in Canada? Are patients there seriously at risk? The British Columbia Medical Association successfully challenged the arbitrary fee rollback as a violation of both health legislation and its contract with the government. In a direct letter to the health minister of B.C., the BCMA said:

> Your government's approach on the lab issue is the antithesis of meaningful engagement and discussion of policy and it does not stand the test of cooperation and consultation mandated by the Second Master Agreement. As you are aware, the Supreme Court of British Columbia found your action to be illegal. Your appeal of the Supreme Court's

decision on this matter further confirms your lack of willingness to work with doctors productively despite repeated efforts on our part to advance potential solutions that respond to your needs.

The government said that despite the court loss on the lab physician fee issue, it would press forward with competitive bidding. Out of the blue, the BCMA and the private labs responded by making a voluntary offer of a 20 percent rollback in lab testing rates. In theory, this should net a savings of $60 million on the $300 million "outpatient" lab services budget as billed by public hospitals, and $40 million from the private sector firms.

What stunned all observers was how quickly the government acquiesced. The directive came straight from the premier's office, bypassing the health minister and all of the public officials who had been involved in the negotiations. By conceding the "voluntary" rollback in order to preserve the monopoly, the private labs were confirming the allegations of their harshest critics. Instead of sending in the auditors to analyze this most suspicious of situations, government capitulated.

Among the mysteries here is why the BCMA fights this issue so desperately. There are fewer than 100 lab physician/pathologists whose income is based upon volume, fees for specific tests, out of a total BCMA membership of 8,000 doctors. Shareholding of the private firms is another group of doctors, but it still can only be a fraction of total BCMA responsibility. Yet, government officials say that the lab deal is a "huge" issue in all negotiations, but they fail to explain why to taxpayers.

In fact, as the BCMA and the government of B.C. finalized the 2004 contract for all fees and physician services, the memorandum of understanding had an attachment, a parallel document dealing with "related matters." The preface to this memo stated: "This Letter of Agreement is contingent upon the parties reaching agreement upon laboratory reform." Bluntly put, this implied that the annual physicians' contract was held hostage to the lab fee negotiations. The BCMA offered a 20 per cent fee reduction in order to prevent a public tender process for lab services.

This raises many questions. Over a long history, lab testing and other specialty referrals have occasionally raised concerns about cash kickbacks, bonuses, and gifts to referring doctors, but there has been no recent evidence of that in British Columbia. A former provincial deputy minister of health remembers a distant past when "open tabs" were created at prominent restaurants for select physicians to use at their pleasure. They never received a bill for food and beverages enjoyed at these premises. This was a thank you for referrals to a specific lab.

Among the most common ways to provide hidden benefits to physicians is the lure of cheap offices, upstairs from a drug store, lab collection depot or health products supplier, complete with financing on the friendliest of terms to equip the facilities. Major optical firms have been notorious for the benefits they have provided to ophthalmologists and other eye professionals.

The *Medical Laboratory Observer*, a Florida-based publication, recently detailed the history of lab kickbacks, including "cash, salary subsidies for lab employees, obscene sums of money for small or non-existent office space, medical supplies, and personal perks such as cars for physicians."

Today, physician "kickbacks" have been banned in eight Canadian provinces, and discouraged in the others. But the *Canadian Medical Association Journal* has published articles outlining the inconsistency of so-called "referral fees" from IHFs (Independent Health Facilities). These include non-medicare treatments such as some dermatology, surgery centres, diagnostic services and laboratories. Many such fees are paid and it remains a gray area.

The Montreal-based *National Review of Medicine* recently warned its health professional readers:

> AVOID THE SCAM — When all is said and done, provincial regulations, on the surface, appear to give the would-be kickbacker or kickbackee some wiggle room given where you practice. Rule of thumb: if it feels like a scam, it is a scam and you risk finding yourself in court even if it is only the court of good conscience.

While the recent B.C. medical laboratory controversy did not involve kickbacks, the 20 percent cut in fees is very real. Many of the province's hospital administrators and lab pathologists, who provided the evidence necessary to lower fees, are now also suffering the consequences of their own efforts. While they and the provincial laboratories had faithfully reported to government the true costs of tests — dramatically less than Medical Services Plan rates — these institutions nevertheless profited from the excess, which was the difference in what they reported and what government paid. The loss of this revenue has had a negative impact on public hospitals; it also meant the loss of funds available for allocation to patient care and services.

There are reports that the prospect of British Columbia business has attracted the attention of one of the largest biomedical testing firms in the world, Laboratory Corporation of America (LabCorp), and that this firm's representatives have made Freedom of Information requests under B.C. law to determine the inside story with respect to the local monopoly. LabCorp acquired Gamma-Dynacare during 2002, a prominent player in Ontario and Alberta and, recently, the successful bidder in Saskatchewan's two largest service areas. This story is not over.

Before moving from this B.C. situation to the national scene, it should be emphasized that from a service-delivery perspective and patient care point of view, both MDS Metro and BC Biomedical are outstanding operations with first class personnel. In fact, BC Biomedical has been cited in the *Globe and Mail's Report on Business* as the finest company to work for in Canada, heading the "Top 50" list for two years in a row, the first time any firm has achieved that.

Saskatchewan and the nation

At $73 per capita for lab services in the 2001–2002 comparison, Saskatchewan has the least cost in the country, and it may also be the most cost-effective service. Emanating from serious budget deficits over a decade ago, Saskatchewan combines all funding resources for lab work — in-patient and outpatient — in a common pool. The province assumes the responsibility for the actual scientific work, but contracts with the private sector for the service delivery system. Private firms do the blood drawing and acquisition of samples, the labeling, recording, and transporting.

Ontario's lab service structure most closely resembles that of British Columbia. Ontario has a mix of public and private services, organized into nine large health regions. There has been consolidation because of various government and hospital reorganizations and private sector mergers and acquisitions. A difference is that Ontario hospitals are not permitted to compete for the outpatient business. There are many small service providers and about 10 substantial concerns, including Gamma-Dynacare, now a subsidiary of the giant LabCorp in the U.S., and MDS Inc., also a subsidiary of an American firm. The private providers handle over 14 million patient interactions each year and provide a full range of laboratory services. The growth of costs in the Ontario private sector was so great during the 1990s that the government capped the budget, a short-term solution that has created long-term headaches. Private labs tend to dump the excess business on hospitals and public services, reducing levels of general service, and increasing budget pressures on the institutions.

The Atlantic Provinces and most of Quebec — aside from the larger urban markets — have primarily government- and university-based lab services. Both MDS and Gamma-Dynacare are prominent in Quebec. The Alberta system varies by region. Lethbridge, for example, is all public. Calgary has one large lab business, a public-private partnership with MDS holding 51 percent control. A strong government initiative in Manitoba created the province-wide Diagnostic Services of Manitoba to better integrate and standardize services to every region. Public labs dominate and compete with private firms in urban markets.

The principal issues

The nature of Canadian health management ensures that there will be different approaches in every jurisdiction, but the challenges are similar. The federal role has grown in recent years, often through the common sense agreement of all parties, simply because it is the best way to deal with the larger, international threats such as SARS and other infectious diseases. Several federal and provincial agencies do outstanding work in this field, but there was competition among the provinces to become the home of a world-leading National Centre for Disease Control, modeled upon the finest in the world, the Center for Disease Control and Prevention in Atlanta, Georgia. Winnipeg was selected to become the home of the Canadian agency, disappointing bidders from both Ontario and British Columbia.

Ambitions of the national program include:

- Far better co-ordination and information sharing among the provinces.
- Building systems that are far more patient based, than the usual practice today, controlled by physicians, hospitals, and service suppliers, entities that often operate independent of each other with respect to the same patient.
- Common information systems, not just within regions or provinces, but which can follow patients nationally as well. The issues here are legal, technical, and medical, involving patient privacy, but the fractured system today not only inflates costs, it can be fatal to patients.

- Each province is striving to ensure that testing is standardized. Distrust of different labs and results is causing needless duplication.

- Better harmonization of services between urban, rural and frontier areas.

- Over-utilization of testing is a major cost problem in major urban areas and centres where physicians are plentiful.

- Unavailability and under-utilization is an issue too, particularly in rural areas and urban ghettos. An effort must be made to ensure an evenness of service, from coast to coast.

- More of every professional and technical skill. There is an acute shortage of personnel. For the most advanced of credentials, the lag time between planning and results can be 15 years. The average age of lab physicians in Canada is far too old.

The value of a health-care card, programmed with each Canadian patient's medical history and current data, could be of inestimable value in quality service delivery. The privacy issue, from a legal and personal perspective, may prove to be an impossible hurdle, but would be a worthy goal. This standardization of the gathering of and access to information could, in itself, save the system small fortunes in the course of a year, and improve outcomes for patients.

"When critics question these days the staggering amounts of money being poured into laboratory medicine, none of them criticize either the science or the scientists. In fact, there is a shortage of them and based on pure market value, the most advanced of these professionals are underpaid by any comparison to the average earnings of medical specialists. In fact, the stars of this field of medicine, the best educated, most experienced, most competent with the most specialized area of knowledge and experience, are on salary, at hospitals, government laboratories, major corporations, research foundations and universities."

11.
Outcomes or
Incomes?

A new paradigm for medical practice is emerging. Evidence-based medicine de-emphasizes intuition, unsystematic clinical experience, and pathophysiologic rationale as sufficient grounds for clinical decision-making, and stresses the examination of evidence from clinical research.

— CENTRE FOR HEALTH EVIDENCE,
University of Alberta

Governments and insurers cut and change coverages, and then make statistical claims about reducing backlogs or cutting costs. Moving patients from one list to another, or erasing their specific concern from the radar screen, doesn't make them better. Any decision that does not have a positive result in patient care and health is a poor one. Our system is overwhelmingly concerned with administration and the pursuit of professional income, power, budgets and non-health goals — more so than the concerns of patients.

— DON NIXDORF, DC

Two decades ago, only the critics of health management ever used the word "outcomes" as a principal goal, or the phrase "evidence-based." They suggested that for every dollar spent, there should be a measurable patient benefit somewhere. They ridiculed a blank-cheque political culture which seemed to assume that ever-increasing amounts of money would improve the system. Since then, salaries of everyone in the public sector health system have soared to esoteric heights, drug companies post record profits, and the system consumes about 40 percent of provincial budgets, in addition to federal, corporate and personal expenditures.

What is the "evidence?" The health of Canadians is worse. Surveys indicate that an overwhelming majority believe the quality of services has deteriorated. Health treatment coverages are more restricted. Line-ups are longer. Embarrassing numbers of patients are jammed into hospital corridors and overflowing Emergency Departments are commonplace. Canada has dropped down on the quality list in every category of international health comparison, except one. We live longer, but the preponderance of Alzheimer's and other degenerative diseases, along with life-sustaining technology, create large asterisks worldwide as to the measurement of longevity. We are now 15th in infant mortality. What has been gained as a result of all the extra spending pumped into the people and corporations involved in health care?

Have you listened to the politicians lately? The terms "outcomes" and "evidence-based" are used with such abandon by politicians, bureaucrats and consultants — none of whom ever treat a patient — it is a veritable blizzard of rhetoric. The trendy phrase used to be "closer to home." After 30 years of dismal performance on that front, the conference and travel-obsessed marathoners, all on the public tab for top salaries, expenses and benefits, still seem convinced that they can talk disease into submission or, at least, that their fatuous efforts will keep the balloon afloat until they retire or move elsewhere. Even in the 2004 federal election, Prime Minister Paul Martin and virtually everybody else pumped the theme "more money" as if that automatically meant "better health care."

The analysis that matters must be the actual experience of each individual patient, and accurate statistics concerning groups and the general population. How do we ALWAYS ensure the most timely attention to needs, the most accurate diagnosis and the most effective treatment? Provincial health management does not come close to doing that. Our system gives physicians and hospitals a blank cheque to do whatever they please, irrespective of commercial motives, relative levels of competence, managerial efficiency or patient responsibility. We ensure that the principal financial beneficiaries of the system are given an absolute monopoly on both the money and the decisions. Governments attempt to control things from the sidelines with guidelines for hospital budgets, insurance coverages and payment infrastructure, but the doctor-patient and hospital-patient cost generators remain untouched, and shielded from competition and accountability (patient health results) within a monopolistic fortress.

The corporate world has its spectacular failures and we subsequently hear that whole businesses collapse or reconstruction succeeds. When health care produces its Corvairs, Pintos and K-Cars, do any heads roll that don't come from patients? Has anyone been fired as a result of the adverse events epidemic or chronic financial mismanagement? Is there even a system in place to investigate poor performance? How many thousands of families have been told that their loved one died because of "complications arising from the surgery," or "failing to respond to treatment," rather than the truth — possibly 50,000 deaths a year in Canada because of clear doctor and hospital mistakes. Will families ever see the official records that "adverse events" investigators studied in preparing their devastating report?

It is a macabre political game of brute power and self-interest. Politicians seeking votes. The federal government versus the provinces. The early history of medicare was that Ottawa pays and the provinces spend. The federal role legislates, regulates and directs what the money covers but it remains a jurisdictional tug-of-war. Medical doctors are likely the toughest union in Canada and they NEVER lose. Politicians always cave under the pressure. Other health unions, the most powerful of which are hospital-based, also drive hard bargains. All of them use "the patient" as the justification for their salary demands. In any jurisdiction, if you turn on the television news and you see stories about the "health crisis" with terrified, gravely ill-looking patients expressing fear that "the government" is not going to be able to treat them in a timely fashion, you can be certain that some union — usually the doctors — are negotiating something. The "health crisis" invariably disappears from the headlines as soon as the contract is signed.

We have a system which has little connection between expenditures and patient health. It operates on the daft premise that more doctor visits, more drugs, more surgery, more hospitals, more rehab centers and zillions of meetings, will somehow manage a positive net benefit. Doctors can crank up patient visits, tests and procedures according to their time availability and income needs. And the busier each side of this equation gets, the better it is for the people who work in hospitals, pharmacies, laboratories and all of the supplier industries.

If one were to attempt an assessment of the precise health of Canadians on any given day, the number and gravity of all injuries and diseases; work loss statistics; and, fitness and wellness concerns, we would have a foundation for accountability. Each policy and financial decision should then ask the question: will extra money for these professionals, for this service, for this federal-provincial agreement, for this facility, for this technology, for this research, for this university program, for this health delivery structure and a long list of other challenges, generate a positive patient statistic to ultimately justify the expense?

What do the politicians and bureaucrats mean when they use the phrase "evidence-based?" Here is some "evidence" that seems not to be worthy of government attention:

- Most modern-day studies into prescription drugs conclude that 50 percent are wrongly prescribed, either as a palliative to a persistent patient, a result of inaccurate patient reports, a duplication owing to poor information systems or, frequently, medical error or negligence. Thousands of needless fatalities occur in Canada each year as a result of this tragedy. Antibiotic use is at least double what experts believe to be appropriate. Prescription drug costs have grown in Canada from $10 billion to $22 billion in just over six years. Can system managers show any net benefit? This is a personal and economic tragedy so severe it ought to be a Royal Commission in itself. But the politicians are only discussing: who pays for more of the same!!!

- Nurse practitioners and clinics operating under the medical management of salaried doctors, prescribe about one third fewer drugs, and generate far much less in laboratory costs, hospitalization and surgery. Their health-outcome results are better than the average attained by more traditional fee-for-service approaches. Surely this meets the criteria of "evidence based?" Since this has been a documented fact for 35 years, why have governments succumbed to medical associations and discouraged expansion?

- British Columbia enjoys the lowest dental hygiene costs in

Canada simply because it was the first province to permit dental hygienists to be independent. Most dental hygienists continue to work within dental practices, but a few set up their own businesses. The fact that people didn't have to go to a dentist for hygiene lowered the cost for everybody. Simple competition. Why should expensive dentists have a monopoly on teeth cleaning?

■ Internal medicine specialists among MDs, public health doctors, dieticians, nutritionists, chiropractors, naturopaths, other alternative therapists and some who bill themselves as orthomolecular doctors, have been advocating healthy lifestyles for 40 years, invariably against the bitter opposition of the health establishment. Vitamin proponents — many of whom are now legendary heroes of health history — were ostracized like criminals. Yet we see alarming headlines today about obesity, diabetes, heart disease and many other related health issues. We continue to pump the preponderance of our money into cures. The "evidence" — but not the intent — is that we set out to generate illness so that the monopolies, entirely obsessed with drugs, diagnostics and surgery, can remain overworked, overstressed and overpaid.

■ If optometrists are just as skilled in routine eye examinations and sophisticated diagnostics as ophthalmologists, less expensive and more accessible to the public, why do we not legislatively insist that the optometrist is the principal gatekeeper for eye care? In fact, medicare and private insurance coverage of optometry has been steadily eroded, but the ophthalmologist is "free." However, the latter may require a visit to a family doctor for a referral and a six-month wait for an appointment. The "evidence" is that government protects the most expensive and often the least appropriate caregivers, multiplying costs and eroding public service.

■ Evidence indicates serious problems within the medical laboratory field. In some regions of the country, the owners of private labs (often doctors or multinational corporations) are making fortunes. There have been allegations of kickbacks, obvious conflict of interest and share bonuses to individual doctors, and handsome profits to medical associations that negotiate lab rates as part of the medical plans. A serious problem has been lack of information co-ordination to avoid duplication of tests (hospitals often order complete sets of tests, since physician information is either unavailable or not trusted). Outstanding work is now being done by both public and private laboratories in new information-sharing technologies, standardization of testing to eliminate duplication, and ever more sophisticated science and technology. As well, it is an area where too much competition can be chaotic and counterproductive. But, just like pharmaceuticals, it is also a field laced with suspicious profits and secret insider deals.

■ Although obstetricians cite the "too posh to push" movement among busy mothers as the reason Caesarean section rates are averaging 20 percent of births in Canada and as high as 30 percent in major urban areas, most health critics say it is predominately to do with MD convenience and scheduling. Yet the CMA has done everything in its power to curtail the growth of midwifery and nurse practitioner services in the country. The head of obstetrics at a major Vancouver hospital expressed public shock in September, 2004, when he returned from an absence to discover that 42 percent of births at the hospital in August had been by Caesarean.

■ If two-thirds of all patients in an acute care hospital are there for diagnostic purposes, observation or in recovery mode, why keep them in such expensive beds and expose them to iatrogenic illness? The "evidence" is that they should either be home or in a convalescent and/or diagnostic facility, saving money and improving health. The concentration of patients in large central institutions serves only the convenience, income and power base of bureaucrats, large unions and doctors.

■ Studies in Canada and the United States have demonstrated that the number one killer in society — as great as any disease, and far worse than crime or traffic statistics — is iatrogenic illness. These are misadventures caused by the health care system, in hospitals, clinics and doctors' offices. If this is the case, why is there not an obligatory re-examination of physicians' competence, as there is for most professions in Canada where errors can be life-threatening to the public? Why are Canadian governments paying most — if not all — of the malpractice premiums for medical doctors? Surely this blank cheque in the face of thousands of annual deaths-by-mistake must border on acute governmental irresponsibility, if not insanity?

■ Finally, and likely the most easily proven example of waste, is the fact that over 30 percent of all visits to general practitioners are for back and spine related problems. The spine structure and central nervous system covers 60 percent of the human body. Historically, medical doctors have had little or no training in this area, other than basic anatomy and organic disease (not neuro-musculoskeletal concerns, which represent 95 percent of patient issues) The one-third of "visits" does not imply one-third of budget. Far from it. Major diseases and serious accidents cost so much per patient that statistics get skewed. However, the 30 percent figure is vital in health planning. It means that 30 percent of all patients are knocking on a door that virtually guarantees high public cost and the least patient benefit, with increased likelihood of iatrogenic incidents. Back, neck, spine and related central nervous system issues are what chiropractic doctors spend at least four years learning. Family physicians and the chain reaction of service referrals (physiotherapists, orthopedic surgeons, labs, the drug industry, radiologists, hospitals) view with alarm the potential loss of this patient intake.

Evidence-based? Very trendy of you, Mr. Politician. Any idea what you are talking about?

If "evidence" meant anything to the health ministers, the drug industry horror show featuring drug recalls, runaway costs, and serious patient health issues would be the subject of a national emergency investigation. Evidence would guarantee an expansion of coverage for optometry, nurse practitioners, community health clinics and chiropractic under medicare. What is actually happening is the reverse. The only critical evidence is that politicians are terrified of medical associations and all of the drug and institutional money that surrounds MD control of the health industry.

Injury and accident insurers

There have been many professional studies into the caseloads of insurance companies and workers compensation boards and the most effective treatment of victims with spine and related problems: whiplash, back injuries and pain. The evidence of studies is overwhelmingly in favor of chiropractic care.

In fact, any compensation board at any time could review past records and trace average recovery times for patients of a similar complaint category, who were treated by medical doctors, physiotherapists and orthopedic specialists, with those who saw a chiropractor. If WCB managers ever do that, the results are never made public. And the procedure for adjudicating complaints and assigning treatment, never changes. This is yet another medical monopoly. Chiropractic services are covered by most compensation programs, but only if the patient, their union or company safety office demands it. And, since many of the claims result in disputes, the only hope a patient has of a satisfactory outcome is to humor the MDs who run the system. Compensation boards jealously guard all records — even those sanitized to remove patient names and identifying data — on the grounds of "patient privacy"; but, critics believe the secrecy has everything to do with maintaining the medical doctors' domination of decision-making. Whenever these records are made available for third party review, they consistently demonstrate better outcomes with chiropractic and with the patients more quickly able to return to productive lives.

Most private auto insurance companies in the United States and some in Canada, are no better when it comes to evidence-based decision making. Industry ideology emphasizes that actuarial science insists upon the most appropriate and most economical form of resolving issues. If this were true, auto insurers would make greater use of chiropractic doctors; but, the insurance industry and particularly the government-owned Canadian auto insurers, put too much decision-making into the hands of medical doctors. They are a substantial source of income. When any matter becomes the subject of a claims dispute, the insurers usually find medical doctors to support whatever argument they wish to make. Insurance companies have many profitable and mutually-dependent linkages to the medical profession in life insurance, malpractice issues, capital facilities and evidentiary courtroom work.

The Insurance Bureau of Canada reports that "soft-tissue" injuries — the more accepted colloquial term is "whiplash" — costs insurers and policyholders $4 billion per year in Canada, including legal fees, claims paid to victims and $1 billion paid to health professionals and rehabilitation services. The Bureau has publicly stated that this latter sum "is not very well spent."

The phrase "soft-tissue" is an insurance industry invention, with no practical basis in health science. Soft tissue could describe every cell of the body. Somewhere in the not too distant past an insurance "spin merchant" came up with a devious way of implying that if an X-ray doesn't show a broken bone, there is no evidence of torn or ruptured muscles, or an artery is not spurting blood, the victim is a fraud and a malingerer. It could be said that cancer is a "soft tissue injury" or a "lifestyle-generated" condition. Tens of millions of people who have suffered debilitating pain and — frequently — total incapacitation, know the dishonesty of these insurance industry attempts to evade responsibility.

However, there is another side to the story. A Toronto psychiatrist and author, Dr. Andrew Malleson, whose book *Whiplash and Other Useful Illnesses* documents a long history of professionals, medical and otherwise, who have turned the indefinable into profitable career paths. Following is an excerpt from a Malleson paper entitled: *Health Care Entrepreneurs in Search of Work*:

> Cars and human bodies do not mix well. People in fast-moving hunks of metal involved in collisions easily get hurt. In the United States, about 50,000 occupants of vehicles are killed each year, and for each person killed, many more are injured with varying degrees of severity. Neck injuries are the most common form of motor vehicle injury. Indeed, it is claimed that 85 percent of all neck injuries result from vehicle collisions, and, of these neck injuries, 85 percent result from rear-end collisions.
>
> The true incidence of whiplash injury is unknown. At the low end the estimate is one million new cases annually, generated by about 12 million motor vehicle accidents. The high-end estimate is that as many as five million Americans sustain a whiplash injury each year, from which three million do not fully recover. In 1994, 2.6 million American citizens were reported to have chronic pain as a result of whiplash injury, and in 650,000 cases this pain was reported to be severe and ongoing. The massive American insurance company State Farm estimates that the annual cost of whiplash in the United States is somewhere between $US 13 billion and $US 18 billion.
>
> The term "whiplash" was first used to denote the motion of the head and neck induced by forces of acceleration or deceleration, though the term has since come to signify the injuries induced by this motion. The head is said to be jerked violently backwards or forwards, by forces sufficiently powerful to cause serious neck and brain injury even in the absence of any direct blow to the head or body. Delicate nerve cells in the brain and spinal cord, once destroyed, never recover, so

their loss can have disastrous consequences. Many authors report that whiplash causes deterioration of cognition, memory, and behavior.

The literature describes a range of serious whiplash neck injuries: fracture of vertebrae, rupture of intervertebral discs, painful separation of the intervertebral disc from the vertebral end plate, damage to the vertebral arteries (two of the four arteries that supply blood to the brain), acute bilateral internal carotid arterial dissection, and rupture of the esophagus to name just a few.

In the huge majority of whiplash cases, however, no such injury can be demonstrated, and the symptoms are then attributed to "a musculoligamental sprain or strain of the neck." The condition is called "common whiplash," a condition in which demonstrably serious injuries such as neck fractures and dislocations are, by definition, absent.

Dr. Malleson is no kinder to chiropractors than he is to colleagues in the medical profession, for what he views to be, in an alarming number of cases, exploiting a phantom injury for personal profit. Less than reputable lawyers, insurance fraud artists, assorted malingers and health professionals have done well in the whiplash field. It has been good for Malleson too, not merely in book sales, but also as a guest speaker at insurance conventions and as an expert witness in court. One presumes that these have been profitable ventures.

In view of the millions of legitimate victims who have suffered acute pain and either temporary or permanent disabilities, the insurers and their boosters should step carefully. It would be far more useful to study the evidence of how honest people are most effectively treated, rather than how the dishonest rip off the system. Whiplash is not a fantasy created by avaricious lawyers, health professionals, crooks, and whiners. It's real. And in most areas where Malleson's identifiable "acceptable" injury prevails — fracture of vertebrae, rupture of intervertebral discs, painful separation of the intervertebral disc from the vertebral end plate, damage to the vertebral arteries (two of the four arteries that supply blood to the brain), acute bilateral internal carotid arterial dissection, and rupture of the esophagus, etc. — medical consultation and case management would be preferred. But with respect to the more enigmatic "soft-tissue" problem, the chiropractic profession would welcome any comparative study into the effectiveness of treatment modalities. Medical managers of insurance company claims departments usually ensure that this never happens in any systematic way.

Hard evidence

It is difficult to constrain the excitement now that Canadian politicians have discovered the phrase "evidence-based" related to health decisions, but it still seems almost always the case that the best research takes place in the United States. We reported in a previous chapter about a Florida study of 20,000 compensation board records in 1960. It concluded that the average patient under chiropractic care returned to work in three days, while the patients under medical care took nine days. The compensation costs were 311 percent higher per average case in the physician-care group.

A 2003 study, conducted by researchers from American Specialty Health and Health Benchmarks, Inc. compared the experiences of 1.7 million patients in a California managed-care plan: one million members without chiropractic coverage and 700,000 with chiropractic coverage. Patients were divided into six groups, based on whether they had chiropractic coverage and whether they received chiropractic or medical care for their neuro-musculoskeletal conditions.

The researchers discovered that chiropractic care in the managed-care setting was more cost-effective on a number of levels:

- **Total health-care costs.** Patients with chiropractic coverage experienced 12 percent lower costs than care provided to patients without chiropractic coverage. Much of this reduction was attributable to favorable patient selection.
- **Low-back pain treatment episodes.** Patients with chiropractic coverage experienced 28-percent-lower costs than patients without chiropractic coverage.
- **Fewer in-patient stays.** Patients with chiropractic coverage experienced 9.3 stays per 1,000 patients, versus 15.6 stays per 1,000 patients for those without chiropractic coverage.
- **Fewer MRIs.** Patients with chiropractic coverage experienced 43.2 MRIs per 1,000 patients, versus 68.9 MRIs per 1,000 patients for those without chiropractic coverage.
- **Fewer low-back surgeries**. Patients with chiropractic coverage experienced 3.3 low-back surgeries per 1,000 patients, versus 4.3 surgeries per 1,000 patients for those without chiropractic coverage.
- **Fewer radiographs.** Patients with chiropractic coverage experienced 17.5 radiographs per 1,000 patients, versus 22.7 radiographs per 1,000 patients for those without chiropractic coverage.

The study was headed by Doug Metz, DC, chief health services officer of American Specialty Health and Health Benchmarks, Inc., and
Craig Nelson, DC, MS, senior health services research scientist. Several
distinguished medical doctors were part of the review process, and the
results were published in the October, 2004, edition of the American
Medical Association's prestigious *Archives of Internal Medicine* magazine. According to Dr. Nelson, these findings could translate into a
$US 47.5 million savings over four years for the 1.7 million member
managed-care plan, if all 1.7 million members were provided with chiropractic coverage.

There were other interesting findings:

- The inclusion of a chiropractic benefit attracts slightly younger
  and slightly healthier subscribers.
- Most of the chiropractic care provided is a direct substitution
  for medical care.
- The cost per episode of chiropractic care for back pain and neck
  pain is much lower than for medical care.

Overall, the inclusion of chiropractic benefits results in a much more
conservative management profile of back pain (less surgery, in-patient
care and advanced imaging). The AMA's *Archives of Internal Medicine*
article reported:

> Access to managed chiropractic care may reduce overall health care
> expenditures through several effects, including (1) positive risk selec-
> tion; (2) substitution of chiropractic for traditional medical care, par-
> ticularly for spine conditions; (3) more conservative, less invasive
> treatment profiles; and (4) lower health service costs associated with
> managed chiropractic care. Systematic access to managed chiropractic
> care not only may prove to be clinically beneficial but also may reduce
> overall health care costs.

The authors said that a comprehensive study of scientific literature
demonstrates that chiropractic spinal manipulations have superior results
than "conventional treatment" and that not one study suggests results
"substantially worse." Irrespective of insurance coverage variances for

chiropractic care and sometimes greater costs to patients, "there is significantly higher patient satisfaction compared with patients who receive conventional treatment."

Also in relatively recent history, prominent American sociologist and statistician, Dr. Donald N. Muse of Washington, DC, produced a landmark work which concluded that the average medical cost for American families can be cut in half if a chiropractor complements the care of a family physician. Dr. Muse, who has worked for the U.S. government, Congress and Health Maintenance Organizations, said the study analyzed six million Medicare claimants, isolating from that a group of 1.5 million who had chiropractic care during the year. The group with chiropractic as part of their health treatments represented 26.8 percent of the total sample but cost the system only 16.7 percent of the total. The average per capita for medicare health costs for families who never see a chiropractor was $8,100 per year, but just $4,400 if a chiropractor was part of the care program.

But Dr. Muse said it is a hard sell to convince major employers to bypass the gatekeeping — and monopolistic — role of conventional medicine to include chiropractic in the coverage. He said it took the insistence of the U.S. Congress, before the Department of Defense would cover chiropractic care for the substantial number of military people with back and musculoskeletal problems. "They did a demonstration and on every single measure — satisfaction, outcomes, cost and everything else — chiropractors won, so (in 2001) the Department of Defense, reluctantly, and I emphasize the word 'reluctantly' — because Congress sort of shoved it down their throat — said 'OK, we'll do chiropractic in the military.'"

These American studies confirm the world's leading research in this field, conducted in Canada by Dr. Pran Manga of the University of Ottawa, the work that is reported at length elsewhere in this book (see chapter 15). Manga emphasized that medical doctors receive little or no education at all about the human back. Mistreatment results in needless and damaging use of both surgery and pharmaceuticals. He added: "The management of our health care system is so inefficient that we not only fail to put patients in the hands of those professionals most qualified to give the best treatment, we actually insure that the most expensive and least qualified person provides the care."

Manga, Muse and most visionaries attempting to create a model for optimum future health care, advocate multidisciplinary approaches, extracting the best from each contributor, and focusing wherever possible on the highest value area of their individual expertise. Another of these is Chicago-based health management consultant, university teacher and public lecturer Linda Eldridge. A leading American innovator in the development of multidisciplinary health care models, she has produced important papers for a long list of clients, including the American Medical Association. The authoritative and outspoken advocate of alternative approaches to health care advises HMOs, workers' compensation organizations and major employers.

In one highly publicized project, Eldridge achieved dramatic results within a 600,000-member Health Maintenance Organization, reducing hospital admissions by 56.8 percent, hospital days per thousand by 73 percent and outpatient cases by 67.8 percent. The focus of this program was the integration of Complimentary Alternative Medicine with the best of conventional medicine. The planners said, "let's promote quality physicians who use non-pharmaceutical and non-surgical treatments as their primary modality. Let's not reach for drugs first. Let's not reach for the knife first because they have serious repercussions and consequences. They can do great good but they also can do great harm."

What emerged was an integrated model including conventional medicine, chiropractic care, massage therapy, acupuncture, stress management, nutrition, herbal medicine, homeopathy, cranial sacral therapy, ayurvedic medicine and traditional Chinese medicine. She said they would have included naturopaths, but Illinois doesn't license this profession. The model "combines the best of both worlds and scientifically documents the clinical outcomes and cost savings." The HMO was able to measure the results in the dramatic lowering of costs for its insured population.

Eldridge said chiropractors are vital as a primary portal for patient entry into this program, since a third or more of all health professional visits relate to spine or musculoskeletal problems and since chiropractors "share a scientific base of knowledge with their MD counterparts, they focus on prevention and optimal health training and they are non-pharmaceutical and non-surgical in their approach." The results of these multidisciplinary approaches were stunning, a model that has since been copied by many American HMOs. Unlike Canada's national health insurance that is cutting back on all the alternative forms of care, American HMOs are increasingly financing less expensive and more effective therapies.

"When we take a look at our success, it's because we've been able to integrate it. .... you don't limit access, and you don't prohibit utilization.

And you take a look at the diagnoses, you set high standards, you focus on primary care, you integrate the data and then you document the savings," Linda Eldridge said.

Cancer — the "Everest" of health care

The attack and management of some issues become an industry so awesome in scale, the economy — in whole or in part — would collapse if a solution were ever found. An example of this would be the so-called "War on Drugs." It is said — and not facetiously — that the economy of Florida would be in ruins if all the rich crooks, police officers from dozens of agencies, lawyers, court workers, prison guards, social workers, rehab workers, realtors, car dealers, yacht brokerages, money launderers, bankers and hundreds of other spin-off beneficiaries, suddenly lost their raison d'être. If the drug cash flow stopped, many legitimate businesses would be ruined and tens of thousands of criminals and people within the justice system would be out of work. The business press in British Columbia now estimates that the cash flow from marijuana grow-ops likely rivals forestry and tourism as the province's principal industries.

The medical equivalent to this must be cancer. Could we ever afford the cure? How many institutions and laboratories would be redundant? How extreme would be the unemployment and surplus of highly qualified specialists, scientists, technicians, nurses, care givers and suppliers? What would all the research foundations worldwide do? What other focal point would so dynamically charge the emotion and commitment of donors: governments, universities, corporations and individuals? One estimate cites that $US 1.2 trillion was paid to health professionals, HMOs, and hospitals in North America for cancer treatment between 1971 and 1998. During recent history, cancer has cost between 13 and 14 percent of the total health budget per year in Canada and the United States.

In a 1971 State of the Union Address, President Richard M. Nixon, made a proclamation which he believed to be as visionary and do-able as John F. Kennedy's pledge, a decade earlier, to put a man on the moon. Nixon said: "The time has come in America when the same kind of concentrated effort that split the atom and took man to the moon should be turned toward conquering this dread disease. Let us make a total national commitment to achieve this goal." The floodgates of federal U.S. spending opened and governments and institutions around the world scrambled to keep up.

No one has any idea how much has been spent globally on cancer research since it really went big league during the 1950s. It may also surpass a trillion — one million million dollars. No enterprise, with the possible exception of major world wars, has consumed as much investment as cancer.

Scripps Research Foundation reported in 2002:

> Much has been discovered and reported on cancer in the last 30-odd years about its causes, prevention, detection, and treatment — but the battle lines are still drawn. And in the last three decades we have learned above all that cancer, like war, is hell.
>
> Cancer is still one of the leading causes of death in the United States. It is the second leading cause of adult mortality and the leading cause of child mortality for children under the age of 15. According to statistics compiled by the National Institutes of Health, the overall cost of cancer was over $US 180 billion in the year 2000 alone, a figure that is dwarfed perhaps only by the human toll. One new cancer is diagnosed every 30 seconds in the United States, and every 90 seconds another American dies of cancer.
>
> Many of our greatest successes in the struggle against cancer have come from basic research aimed at understanding the fundamental molecular and cell biology that produces the condition.
>
> We have learned that cancer is not a single type, but rather over a hundred different errors in cells of various tissues caused by various sorts of mutations. Some mutations turn on or increase the activity of certain key genes, increasing the expression of metalloproteinases for instance; others downregulate them, shutting off production of receptor proteins. Common to tumor cells is their resistance to normal programmed cell death. Thus they continue to live and proliferate. After certain mutations occur, a cancer cell grows out of control, dividing over and over and forming a solid tumor — or, with leukemias, an every increasing number of circulating tumor cells in the blood and throughout the body. Tumors often damage the tissues where they are located and most metastasize and migrate locally and through the bloodstream — and these are the tumors that claim so many lives every year.

Substantial progress has been made in diagnostics and treatment modalities, and the management of many cancers, most notably breast, prostate, most forms of leukemia and many other less common varieties. In jurisdictions where testing is consistent, systematic and habitual among patients, cervical cancer has been virtually wiped out. Early detection and public education has greatly increased the chances of success with most forms of the disease. And the massive investment in research labs, scientists, universities, biochemistry and diagnostic technology has had countless positive spin-offs for other health issues. But, as the population ages, greater numbers of people are living long enough to develop cancer. Progress has been frustratingly elusive with some of major cancer killers such as lung, liver, pancreatic, colorectal or melanoma.

So the challenge is relentless. Major cancer investment decisions are made in every affluent country of the world. How much is enough? How much is the basic fair share our country — no matter how small — should accept? It is sometimes said that Canada is too often content to be a parasite, paying lip service to research commitment, but happy to glean the results of successes elsewhere, a comment emphatically rebutted by Dr. Manga. "About 50 percent of university-based or related research in Canada is biomedical. Just as our provincial budgets spend a disproportionate amount on health, averaging 42 percent of annual budgets, research appropriations are distorted for questionable reasons. Virtually none of this research is spent on alternative therapies or areas that might promote healthier lifestyles," he said.

In the context of this chapter, however, what kind of cost-benefit analysis exists anywhere with respect to cancer spending? We know that insurers (government and private), corporations and families are frequently stunned by the cost of drugs and treatment cocktails, some of which are purely experimental. Most of us want every possible effort made to assist any afflicted family member, and, sometimes, in the final stages, it can be a gloomy, expensive business. It is estimated that the average cost of treating one lung cancer patient in the U.S. is $US 175,000 per year. Oncologists often comment that in most cases, it is not the cancer that finally kills, but rather the overwhelming toxicity of the drugs, and a weakened body and immune system that can no longer fight off even the least offensive virus. Tough decisions are made by doctors and medical managers every day. But no one doubts or questions that hundreds of millions of dollars worth of excessive and pointless treatment takes place. This is highly profitable for doctors, hospitals, drug companies, the manufacturers and operators of technology and related businesses.

Animal welfare crusaders have commented that nothing raises money like a picture of an imperiled and bloodied baby harp seal, a fluffy ball, a death too horrible to contemplate. Raising money for big, fat, ugly sea lions is tough sledding. In the medical and charitable foundation field, cancer is the General Motors, with more different foundations, agencies and fundraising machines than most diseases have dollars. A photo of a cancer-afflicted child charges the tear ducts of humanity and money rolls in, because each and every one of us identify with this terrible disease. The odyssey of the great young Canadian, Terry Fox, has achieved a legacy that does the entire country proud, for Terry inspired the emotions of the world.

Unfortunately, there are scores of diseases that tear families apart, but which do not have much volunteer help to provide support, or affluent charitable foundations to seek solutions. It is not possible to imagine how far medical science might have advanced if even some of the cancer billions were invested elsewhere. Only cancer and heart disease have become formidable industries. Lung and related respiratory problems, diabetes and a few others are on the radar, but they are faint blips by comparison.

There are several distortions that go into the appropriation of research funds. Pharmaceutical companies and other private firms are interested only in end products that would justify the investment, and progress reports to help make company shares attractive. Charitable foundations also seek profile, and achieve it by embracing popular causes. Scientists and researchers are forced to follow the money. Granting agencies establish tough criteria to ensure cost-benefit accountability of any funding, to the point where the bureaucratic process of seeking budget can consume as much time and energy as the research itself. But at least there is definition to specific projects. There is an odd kind of market-driven force at work. Show biz and emotion bring in the money and capture vote-seeking political attention and public budgets. Universities and other research agencies hoping to swim in the mainstream, structure themselves to be part of the larger enterprise. For-profit private health companies invest in these resources to gain additional help in achieving patentable products.

Therefore, it becomes the sole responsibility of government referees to ensure even-handed attention to all health challenges and responsibilities. Maybe a few million — pin money — transferred from cancer research to something else might have much higher prospects for genuine achievement? Similarly, in the management of health care dollars, more attention might be paid to the prospect of beneficial outcomes. Too often, it seems, blank cheque spending surrounds hopeless cases, benefiting no one but the doctor, drug companies and other suppliers.

Health Care or Wealth Care?

A Vancouver conference during 2002 inspired this book. It was titled "Health Care or Wealth Care" and the subtitle essentially asked the most pregnant question: "Is it all about money?" Speakers included British Columbia's health minister, a national bank economist, prominent American and Canadian economists, and the president of the British Columbia Federation of Labour. Delegates consisted of a wide range of health professionals, labor leaders, bankers, health insurers, Members of Parliament and public officials. The priorities of health decision makers were questioned, the principal accusation being that the shopping list of vested interests is always paramount. Is the priority ever "the patient?"

The overwhelming conclusion was that we should fight to preserve Canada's universal health care, but that it is more imperiled by monopolies, bureaucracy and waste, than any threat from treatment costs. Priorities are entirely out of whack. It starts with political motives at the top and works its way down through layers of turf wars and self-interest, each community within fighting to preserve its niche, increase income and gain power.

Any system that started with "the patient" would soon start looking from the ground up. There are communities and communities within communities. Every major company and its union is a health centre that could radiate good health management throughout many families. Each school, university or public institution has an opportunity to become a quality health focal point, and, if well supported by nurses and first aid assistance, both an educational and early warning resource for issues. Our health system faces extraordinary pressures as a result of preventable venereal disease, malnutrition, cigarette smoking, alarmingly high rates of abortion and a whole series of issues that should be tackled through sensitive, intelligent and well-financed school health education. But petty and bigoted adult sensitivities almost always trash any attempt to do useful health and lifestyle education in the schools.

In terms of "outcomes" and value for money, and in view of the limitless billions of dollars that seem to be available for prominent western diseases, a global view is appropriate. Based on 50 years of history, and even the current statistics, a small investment in a sewer line in India, or a water reservoir in Ethiopia, would create more additional person-days of positive health longevity than 10 times or more that amount spent on popular pursuits in the industrialized world. Foreign aid as a percentage of GDP has gone backwards in both Canada and the United States. The U.S. spends one tenth of one percent of GDP on foreign aid. Canada gives just three-tenths of one percent of GDP.

In fact, closer to home, if that modest appropriation were to be invested into school meals, nutrition and a health education program in a ghetto school district, the statistical results for society would be greater in every respect: healthier, longer and more productive lives for many, rather than descending into subsistence lifestyles, or crime. Efforts to stamp out tobacco usage have been constrained by the explosion of young women smoking, and failure to make bold strides against atmospheric toxins. Failure to invest heavily in health education among children, with both money and political courage, is doubtless a major contributor to the growth of AIDS and other sexually transmitted diseases, unwanted pregnancies, malnutrition, and knowledge about all health services available in society, not just those promoted most heavily in public advertising.

Focus on outcomes, not incomes, and evidence-based appropriations of funds. Nothing rivals the public support behind cancer initiatives, both in terms of public policy and with hard cash. Research funding, public education and aggressive treatment belong at or near the top of the priority list for investment. The concern here is balance. Make sure that expenditures are subject to proper scrutiny, both in terms of project or treatment value, and relative to all of the other health issues desperate for funding.

"Have you listened to the politicians lately? The terms 'outcomes' and 'evidence-based' are used with such abandon by politicians, bureaucrats and consultants — none of whom ever treat a patient — it is a veritable blizzard of rhetoric. The trendy phrase used to be 'closer to home.' After 30 years of dismal performance on that front, the conference and travel-obsessed marathoners, all on the public tab for top salaries, expenses and benefits, still seem convinced that they can talk disease into submission or, at least, that their fatuous efforts will keep the balloon afloat until they retire or move elsewhere. Even in the 2004 federal election, Prime Minister Paul Martin and virtually everybody else pumped the theme 'more money' as if that automatically meant better health care."

NEWS ITEM:
Doctors advise avoidance of megavitamin theories.

Doctor Linus Pauling, 1975   2005

12.
Antitrust Victory

On August 27, 1987, Judge Susan Getzendanner, United States District Judge for the Northern District of Illinois, Eastern Division, found the American Medical Association, The American College of Surgeons, and The American College of Radiology, guilty of having conspired to destroy the profession of chiropractic in the United States. In a 101-page opinion, Judge Getzendanner ruled that the American Medical Association and its co-conspirators had violated the Sherman Antitrust Laws of the United States. Judge Getzendanner ruled that they had done this by organizing a national boycott of doctors of chiropractic by medical physicians and hospitals using an ethics ban on inter-professional cooperation.

— Official summary of federal court ruling

I n 1865, Sir James Paget wrote the following warning in the *British Medical Journal*: "Few of you are likely to practice without a bone-setter for a rival; and if he can cure a case which you have failed to cure, his fortune may be made and yours marred. Learn then to imitate what is good and avoid what is bad in the practice of bonesetters." Spinal and bone adjustments were not known as either chiropractic or osteopathy in those years, but the competitive threat to medicine was there from the beginning. The relief patients received from these alternative healers had a direct impact on business.

The stunning growth of chiropractic in North America following World War II was greeted with alarm by the American Medical Association. This powerful lobby set out to secure its dominance, if not its exclusivity. A charmingly titled Committee on Quackery was created in 1963 and its prime aim was ruled by Judge Getzendanner in 1987 to be an illegal boycott and conspiracy. She added, "The committee worked aggressively — both overtly and covertly — to contain and eliminate chiropractic as a profession." During this period, a number of illegal measures were embraced by the AMA as official policy. These were intended to:

- prevent medical doctors from referring patients to chiropractic doctors;
- prevent acceptance of referrals of patients from chiropractors;
- prevent chiropractors from obtaining access to hospital diagnostic services, including X-rays, therefore forcing chiropractors to buy their own equipment;
- prevent chiropractic doctors from membership on hospital medical staffs;
- prevent medical doctors from teaching at chiropractic colleges;
- prevent collaboration between the two professions on medical/chiropractic research;
- prevent any co-operation between the two groups in the delivery of health care services; and,
- discourage, if not prevent, any relationship between established universities and chiropractic education.

This strategy would ultimately lead the AMA to one of the most costly and devastating defeats in the history of United States health care. (The Committee on Quackery was disbanded in 1974, after a disastrous series of legal and public relations embarrassments. But the AMA announced that it had been successful because it had slowed down the growth of chiropractic.) Trial evidence showed that the defendants took active steps, often covert, to undermine chiropractic educational institutions, conceal evidence of the usefulness of chiropractic care, undercut insurance programs for patients of chiropractors, subvert government inquiries into the efficacy of chiropractic, engage in a massive misinformation campaign to discredit and destabilize the chiropractic profession, and they engage in numerous other activities to maintain a medical physician monopoly over health care in the United States. AMA activities were declared unlawful in the 1987 federal court decision, but the AMA did not know when to cease and desist. They persevered with an ill-fated appeal until, in 1991, the United States Supreme Court flatly refused to even listen to their arguments.

An ugly monopoly

Before relating the history of the chiropractic antitrust action, it should be noted that the AMA and its supporters did not discriminate. They resented and opposed all other health professions equally, particularly those that demonstrated value to patients. Medical associations in Canada — less overt but using the same material in a covert fashion — have done precisely the same things but, unlike the U.S., monopolies tend to be tolerated if not encouraged. Aided by wealthy benefactors from the drug and equipment supply industries, along with the hospital, university, research and government sectors, medical doctors consistently and successfully strive to make it impossible for anyone to compete with them.

Optometrists were the first to score victories against the AMA.

A 1955 resolution adopted by the AMA House of Delegates read as follows: "RESOLVED, that it is unethical for any doctor of medicine to teach in any school or college of optometry, or to lecture in any optometric organization, or to contribute scientific material to the optometric literature, or in any way to impart technical medical knowledge to non-medical practitioners."

In 1964, Dr. Cyrus Bass of Chicago, an optometrist, launched a $US 90 million lawsuit under the *Sherman Antitrust Act*, but before filing the lawsuit, Dr. Bass asked two patients to cooperate in an experiment. He wanted to see how deeply rooted was the discrimination against optometry. He mounted a test of ophthalmologists, certain that they would behave unethically if they thought optometrists were involved. His experiment called for the patients to go to an ophthalmologist, get their eyes examined, and obtain the prescribed glasses. Then they would go with these new glasses to a second ophthalmologist, have their eyes examined again, and obtain the glasses he prescribed. Of course, the patient would tell each ophthalmologist that his glasses had just recently been prescribed by an "optometrist." The first patient visited six ophthalmologists and obtained five prescribed glasses. The second patient, a diabetic, visited six ophthalmologists and also received five pairs of glasses. The diabetic patient told these ophthalmologists that he was suffering dizzy spells, but only one of them indicated it might be caused by the diabetic condition and recommended he see his physician. In addition to the new glasses, five ophthalmologists offered unsolicited derogatory remarks about optometry in general. Two of the ophthalmologists were visited by both patients, thus bringing to eight the number of ophthalmologists prescribing glasses. Eight ophthalmologists were either unable to agree on the diagnosis of a simple eye refraction, or were practicing fraud.

The devastating test was made public, embarrassing not only the ophthalmologists involved, but it also exposed the AMA policy. This was to become evidence in the antitrust suit, but an agreement was reached out of court and the AMA policies with respect to optometry were changed.

The Chicago Five

Chicago is the de facto headquarters of the United States health industry. Despite big lobbying offices in Washington, D.C., the AMA, the leading health publications, many of the largest Health Maintenance Organizations, related associations and health-based industries, have their head offices in the Illinois city. Medicine and health have a high profile in business, media and community culture.

Not only did the optometrists' antitrust challenge originate in Chicago, it was there where chiropractic began to fight back. Dr. Chester A. Wilk, a chiropractor who had authored and self-published a 1973 book entitled *Chiropractic Speaks Out*, an unemotional history of his profession, with positive messaging about how the therapies work for patients. Wilk became incensed by the AMA discrimination and equally angry at his own profession for failing to fight back in an aggressive fashion.

The legal fight had its roots in the early 1960s when Wilk encountered routine discrimination as he attempted to care for his patients. He found himself asked to contradict outrageously inaccurate criticisms of his profession. He did not know at the time, but he was encountering a massive, dishonest propaganda campaign launched countrywide by the AMA's Committee on Quackery. Wilk noted a similarity of reports all over the United States, regurgitating the same precise language and incorrect data. It could not be a coincidence, he accurately forecast. Trial evidence would confirm that this was all part of a deliberate, nationwide distribution of false and inaccurate statements, encouraging local professionals and organizations to fan the fires of anti-chiropractic debate. In a 1996 book titled *Medicine, Monopolies, and Malice*, he categorized these findings under seven headings:

1. **Innuendoes** — statements implying or suggesting a wrongdoing by a chiropractor that, if challenged, could not be supported by fact.

2. **Material taken out of context** to create an image worse than, or different from reality by removing key facts surrounding an issue.

3. **Half-truths / portions of truth** manipulated so as to create false impressions or conclusions, never telling the whole story.

4. **Obsolete material** that represented outdated statements of earlier chiropractors as to the thinking of modern chiropractic.

5. **Obscure sources** that were cited as authoritative — such as random, bizarre comments made by some unknown or obscure chiropractor — were used to hold all within the profession up to ridicule and embarrassment.

6. **Incidental exceptions** to the rule presented as commonplace occurrences.

7. **Outright lies** — Wilk characterized the disinformation as "the same tactic Nazi propagandists had used" more than twenty years earlier on the principle that the more outrageous the falsehood, the more believable it becomes.

Wilk's research uncovered a 1964 AMA lobbying campaign that convinced the National Education Association, under the guise of "consumer education," to place material in schools all over the country. Buried within this literature was a sharp attack on chiropractic.

When he challenged legal and public relations strategies of the American Chiropractic Association which, in his view, expressed insufficient outrage and inadequately promoted the benefits of chiropractic, he was urged to soft-peddle, rather than risk an establishment backlash. His proposal to take legal action had more critics than allies within the chiropractic profession.

The chiropractors who initiated the suit (known as the "Chicago Five") were Wilk and Drs. Patricia Arthur, James Bryden, Steven Lumsden and Michael Pedigo. (Dr. Lumsden suffered ill-health early in the legal marathon and reluctantly withdrew. He remained a supporter throughout.) Dr. Pedigo, among the profession's most respected leaders, later became president of the International Chiropractors Association. The case is widely referred to as "the Wilk case." Engaged as legal counsel for the plaintiff chiropractors was lawyer George McAndrews, son of a chiropractor and brother of Jerome F. McAndrews, DC, then an officer of the ICA and subsequently president of renowned Palmer College of Chiropractic in Davenport, Iowa. Strong support later came from the ICA and through the fundraising activities of the National Chiropractic Antitrust Committee. The American Chiropractic Association opposed the action for years, arguing that more could be attained through lobbying, but finally joined the cause in the later stages.

Tenacious McAndrews piloted this case through 14 years of trials, appeals, stops and starts. Although they lost the first round in Chicago, there were dividends for chiropractors and their patients right away. Media reports drew parallels to fights by optometry and others against the predatory monopolistic activities of the AMA. Policies of the AMA began to change:

- **1978** – a medical practitioner could without fear of discipline or sanction refer a patient to a duly licensed chiropractic doctor.
- **1980** – a medical doctor could also choose to accept or to decline patients sent to him by a duly licensed chiropractor.
- **1986** – a medical practitioner could teach at a chiropractic college or seminar.
- **1987**– it became ethical for a medical doctor to professionally associate with a chiropractic doctor. This has not previously been communicated by the AMA.

The case eventually arrived at the loftier perches of United States jurisprudence, the federal District Court of Judge Susan Getzendanner, concluding with her landmark ruling. Following the 1991 refusal of the United States Supreme Court to consider an appeal of Judge Getzendanner's decision, Dr. Pedigo said: "The all-out assault on chiropractic waged by the AMA and its co-conspirators was actually an undeclared war on the sick people who dared to challenge the arrogance and ignorance of the medical community by seeking help from doctors of chiropractic. The AMA's actions have tarnished the image of medical physicians everywhere. As we have in the past," he added, "we renew our request that medical physicians and chiropractic physicians join their respective areas of expertise for the good of their primary constituency: the people of the United States who experience poor health, those who find themselves confined to hospitals, or those who generally wish to maintain themselves in an optimum state of health."

Dr. Wilk was more concerned after the victory by AMA attempts to put a positive spin on a crushing defeat. "They don't have to love us," Wilk said in an interview with *The Chiropractic Journal*, "but they'll have to respect us and respect the law....you can't just take the spots off the leopard and expect it to be tame. They'll still be dangerous, but at least they're not going to be so open because their lawyers are going to tell them 'shut up or you'll go to jail'." Wilk emphasized in this interview that the fight is not with average MDs, but rather with the "reactionary" AMA leadership.

It must be emphasized that the medical associations in Canada have been equally venomous toward chiropractic as are their AMA colleagues, but far more subtle, covert and pervasive. Medical doctors have been encouraged to avoid chiropractic referrals. MDs prefer to send patients to physiotherapists, who provide muscular relief without solving the root problem; but, most important, always send the patient back to the MD, the principal source of physiotherapy referrals. When patients go to chiropractors, they rarely ever return to the MD for back or spine-related problems, thus threatening income from one third of all medical visits. The medical associations have done everything in their power to oppose any affiliation between a Canadian university and a college of chiropractic. When medical lobbies attempt to diminish chiropractors on grounds that their professional education lacks the benefits of major universities, science labs and other appropriate educational opportunities, the accusers never explain how actively they work to prevent this access.

"Unscientific" and "dangerous"

When layers of rhetoric are scraped away from the arguments by medical organizations against chiropractic, and even the core thought processes of individual physicians in both Canada and the United States, two words ultimately appear: "unscientific" and "dangerous." When official organizations and supposedly well-researched papers use these words with respect to chiropractic, it can only be described as untruthful and fraudulent. With respect to individual physicians, it is a matter of deeply ingrained bias. There is resentment that millions of patients openly demonstrate dissatisfaction with what MDs offer, by preferring to pay a chiropractor than get "free" treatment from a medical physician. An associated ethical issue is that when patients report to their family physician that they have benefited from chiropractic care, this information rarely becomes part of the permanent medical records. This omission could have detrimental ramifications upon future care, as subsequent health professionals review the patient's history.

The question of "danger" — cited by medical doctors — is both insulting and ridiculous. It either demonstrates a professional myopia bordering on psychiatric disorder, or a vacuum of intellect. No health treatment, including chiropractic, is free of risk. Mistakes are made. Chiropractic regulatory and licensing bodies deal efficiently with complaints and appropriately discipline offenders, as required by law governing the profession in various jurisdictions. There are patients who claim and can demonstrate that they had been ill-treated and even claim the occasional tragedy. But — compared to what? Medical doctors? This is like comparing a school yard wrestling match to a world war.

The only evidence necessary to prove this point is actuarial science, the precise calculation by insurers of where dangers lie in our society. Malpractice insurance premiums cost chiropractors mere pennies compared to the insurance cost for each medical doctor. There are hundreds of medical malpractice cases for every action against chiropractic. Yet the medical lobby is so influential with media that any negative chiropractic story — no matter how rare or isolated the case may be — makes the headlines, while routine death and disabilities caused by medical misadventure in hospitals, clinics and MD offices, seem to be ignored. Perhaps the mistakes of medicine, principally involving drugs, anesthesiology and surgery, are simply so commonplace that they are no longer news.

The more pervasive, subjective and insidious criticisms of chiropractic concern the obsessive use of the word "unscientific." The pretentiousness, and dishonesty, of the critics is underscored by the assumption that "medicine" and "science" are synonymous. This is categorically untrue. Definitive studies have calculated that more than 80 percent of conventional medical practice is guesswork, albeit educated guesswork. There is science in technology, chemistry and a battery of other research and diagnostic tools available to all health professionals, but there is no science in the subjective judgment of physicians. We seek professional help because of the practitioner's knowledge and experience, not some formula best left to computers. Whether a certain drug or treatment is appropriate to a given situation is a matter of judgment by the professional; but, once applied, no one ever knows for sure if or how it will work with each individual patient. Everybody's system, genetic composition, lifestyle, nutrition and physiology is different and will react uniquely to treatment.

Chiropractic never has any difficulty delivering truckloads of scientific confirmation to any hearing or venue, the testimony of independent experts with degrees from prestigious institutions, doctorates in medicine, sociology, science, history and related disciplines. Each time, once fairly adjudicated, the profession earns yet another endorsement. Just as in medicine, most of the theories, practices and treatments are based on judgment and experience, not precise science. Chiropractors spend four years intensely studying the neuro-musculoskeletal system of the human body, more commonly described as the spine and the central nervous system. Aside from basic skeletal anatomy, medical education virtually ignores this. Advised that Dr. Pran Manga, a noted health authority and professor at the University of Ottawa, said that typical medical education reduces the back to mere hours of attention, a prominent Canadian physician and member of the Order of Canada, replied: "if that, and I missed that lecture."

Dr. Wayne Jonas, MD, Director (1995–98) of the United States Office of Alternative Medicine, National Institutes of Health, was once asked if there was science behind chiropractic? He replied: "The answer is yes for some treatments and no for others, but the amount of science is increasing. . . . controlled trials and guidelines based on quality clinical research. .. . provides a sophisticated summary of the evidence for chiropractic and medical management of back pain. Would that we had such evaluations for all conditions treated in mainstream medicine." Dr. Jonas added: "In their major area of practice, the evaluation and treatment of musculoskeletal problems, chiropractors have better training and experience than conventional physicians do."

If the medical profession could be as "officially" analytical and critical of itself as it is of chiropractic, public health would substantially benefit. In a 1996 book *What Doctors Don't Tell You*, Lynne McTaggart reported startling facts concerning back surgery. She said that Professor Gordon Waddell, orthopedic surgeon at Glasgow's Western Infirmary in Scotland, "scathingly" summed up an appalling track record: "...dramatic surgical successes, unfortunately, apply to only some 1 percent of patients with low back disorders. Our failure is in the remaining 99 percent of patients with simple backache, for whom, despite new investigations and all our treatments, the problem has become progressively worse."

McTaggart wrote:

For back patients who undergo surgery, 15 to 20 percent will fall into the category of 'the failed back' — the official name given to people with chronic, considerable back pain that doctors can't fix. Some 200,000 to 400,000 patients go under the knife in the United States every year. That translates into 30,000 to 80,000 Americans every year who will emerge from back surgery in considerably more pain than before they went to their doctor.

The most overwhelming endorsement of chiropractic is related to outcomes. Some of the important evidence follows.

- One of the earliest outcomes-based studies related to chiropractic was conducted in 1960 by the First Research Corporation, a nationally recognized independent research firm. Entitled, *A Survey and Analysis of the Treatment of the Sprain and Strain Injuries of the Back and Neck in Industrial Cases*, this consisted of almost 20,000 Florida workers compensation records. The average patient under chiropractic care returned to work in three days, while the patients under medical care took nine days with compensation costs that were 311 percent higher.

- A particularly significant study of chiropractic was conducted between 1978–1980 by the New Zealand Commission of Inquiry. In its 377-page report to the House of Representatives, the Commission called its study "probably the most comprehensive and detailed independent examination of chiropractic ever undertaken in any country." The commission reported itself "irresistibly and with complete unanimity drawn to the conclusion that modern chiropractic is a soundly-based and valuable branch of health care in a specialized area." It confirmed that spinal manual therapy in the hands of a registered doctor of chiropractic is safe and effective in relieving musculoskeletal symptoms such as back pain, and other symptoms known to respond to such therapy, such as migraine. The commission found that chiropractors are the only health practitioners who are necessarily equipped by their education and training to carry out spinal manual therapy and that it is in the public interest and in the interests of patients that there must be no impediment to full professional co-operation between chiropractors and medical practitioners.

- Comparative Studies. Key testimony in the Wilk case came from by Per Freitag, M.D., PhD, professor of orthopedics, who outlined a study monitoring the length of average orthopedic in-patient stays at John F. Kennedy Hospital in Chicago, incorporating chiropractors into their patient care program, and Lutheran General Hospital, which does not utilize chiropractic. According to the research study, the average length of hospitalization for patients at JFK Hospital was five to seven days compared to 14 days at Lutheran General. Dr. Freitag testified that the only difference in care was the inclusion of chiropractic. Also offered into testimony during the case was evidence that the maternity ward of JFK Hospital was demonstrating significant success with the use of chiropractic care in place of intradermal steroids. According to the study, the use of epidural steroids to relieve pain was markedly reduced where the expectant mother received chiropractic care in the prenatal period and in the labor and delivery rooms.

- Chiropractic training. In addressing the question of the relative merit of chiropractic training as opposed to medical training, Freitag told the judge that, in his opinion, the anatomy and dissection labs at National College of Chiropractic were superior to those at the University of Illinois Medical School, and that chiropractors have a better understanding of musculoskeletal ailments than do medical doctors.

- Another Wilk trial expert was Dr. John McMillan Mennell, orthopedic surgeon, professor at eight medical schools and noted author, who testified that major chiropractic colleges were equal in academic excellence to the best medical schools in the nation he had examined. He also noted that a new medical resident in a hospital normally spends no more that four hours training on the musculoskeletal system and may actually have no training at all in some cases.

- A University of Saskatchewan study of spinal manipulation was conducted by a noted orthopedic surgeon Dr. W. Kirkaldy-Willis and chiropractor Dr. J. David Cassidy in 1985. This involved 283 patients at a specialized university back pain clinic who had not responded to previous conservative or operative treatment. Daily spinal manipulations were administered and the effects of this treatment were assessed at one month and at three months. Results revealed that 81 percent of the patients became symptom-free or achieved a state of mild intermittent pain with no work restrictions. Kirkaldy-Willis and Cassidy, along with Haymo Thiel, D.C , M.S., also conducted a 1993 trial at the Royal University Hospital in Saskatchewan and concluded that "the treatment of lumbar intervertebral disk herniation by side posture manipulation is both safe and effective."

■ A 1990 report published in the *British Medical Journal* outlined a study conducted by T.W. Meade, a medical doctor, which concluded, after two years of patient monitoring, "for patients with low-back pain in whom manipulation is not contraindicated, chiropractic almost certainly confers worthwhile, long-term benefit in comparison with hospital outpatient management."

■ A Utah workers' compensation study conducted by Kelly B. Jarvis, D.C., Reed B. Phillips, D.C., PhD, and Elliot K. Morris, JD, MBA, compared the cost of chiropractic care to the costs of medical care for conditions with identical diagnostic codes. Results were reported in the August 1991 *Journal of Occupational Medicine*. The study indicated that costs were significantly higher for medical claims than for chiropractic claims; in addition, the number of work days lost was nearly ten times higher for those who received medical care instead of chiropractic care.

Dr. John McMillan Mennell's testimony at the antitrust trial delivered a remarkable contrast between the education of doctors, chiropractic versus medical. An orthopedic surgeon, professor and textbook author, he was asked by the AMA lawyer whether he had said that medical doctor education consisted only of "four or five hours" of manipulative therapy with respect to the back.

Mennell: "I think I said zero hours, didn't I, for the most part?"

When asked how much of the of the body consisted of the musculoskeletal system, the professor replied 60 percent. Exasperated, the AMA lawyer then asked: "Is it your testimony that it is your understanding that the entire medical school curriculum is devoted to 40 percent of the body?"

Dr. Mennell was blunt: "Yes, sir."

Three Distinguished Canadians

There is an Oswald Hall Award at the University of Toronto, an honor so respected that the most cursory of Internet searches will encounter numerous academic Curricula Vitae in which past winners proudly

record the fact. Dr. Oswald Hall and two other noted professors and sociologists, Dr. Merrijoy Kelner and Dr. Ian Coulter, then both within the
Faculty of Medicine at the University of Toronto, collectively analyzed
chiropractic in 1980. Dr. Kelner, who has earned countless honors in a
distinguished career, and who has served on several national commissions and initiatives related to health, is, today, Professor Emeritus at U
of T. Dr. Coulter, who figures prominently elsewhere in this book, is
presently a researcher for the Rand Corporation in Los Angeles, and a
professor at two California institutions.

They reported their findings in the book *Chiropractors, Do They
Help?* Hall, Kelner and Coulter praised the quality and thoroughness of
chiropractic education and soundly criticized the medical and health
establishment for campaigning to keep chiropractic away from major
universities. Then they hypocritically argued that chiropractic education
is weak in biological sciences, chemistry, and laboratory infrastructure
available only at publicly-funded universities and research facilities.

The authors expressed admiration that despite this opposition, "during their years at chiropractic college, students are repeatedly encouraged
to think of themselves as potential members of the health care team.
They are told they should "work together with physicians, nurses, dentists and others to promote the health of their patients."

These distinguished social scientists discovered the paradox of chiropractic:

> Among all the healing occupations chiropractic occupies an intriguing
> and unique place. For most of its history it has been the target of bitter
> attacks by the established healing occupations. It has been denounced
> as a hoax, and its members have been described as quacks and charla-
> tans. The officials of the state have frequently refused it recognition,
> and chiropractors have, at various times and in various places, been
> jailed and fined for following their occupation. In those few instances
> where chiropractic has been studied it has usually been viewed as a cult
> or sect, something wholly outside the edifice of accepted healing occu-
> pations.
>
> How is it then, in the face of this hostile reception, that the number
> of chiropractors has grown and their clientele has increased?
> …Chiropractic survives on its own resources while the larger and more
> powerful health occupations increasingly need financial help from the
> state in order to carry on.

"What are you going to do Mr. Premier?"

"Simple. Find out how much the doctors want this time."

"I don't understand."

"Well, once the contracts are signed . . . . no more health crisis."

13.
Extorting Universities

*When doctors enter the arena of politics or finance or the
law, they may have no more expertise than other citizens,
yet they often adopt the guise of scientific authority. This
phenomenon has been described by Dr. H. E. Emson in his
textbook on doctors and the law: "The assumption of
unwarranted expertise is often an extension of one of the
facets of the total doctor-patient relationship — the desire
of the patient for a parent-figure, and the willingness of the
physician to assume this role. . . . the doctor is conditioned
from the first days of training to assume this position of
omnipotence and omniscience, and it is remarkable how
many intelligent and independent people, finding
themselves in the position of a patient, will rapidly revert to
a state of dependency." He warned doctors: "Do not
pretend to be an expert when you are not."*

— GEOFFREY YORK

The *Globe & Mail*'s Geoffrey York, among Canada's leading journalists for a generation, now based in Beijing, authored a blistering
condemnation of medical politics in a 1987 book, *The High Price of
Health*. Among the points he hammered home was the undeserved and
unearned respect demanded by the Canadian Medical Association, its
provincial derivatives and other physicians' groups. The extract above
should be engraved on a sign on every health minister's desk. More
pathetic than the MDs' delusionary posture on public policy, is the attention politicians pay to their invariably myopic, mercenary and ill-
informed opinions. York adds:

A paternalistic attitude might have therapeutic value, but doctors extend
the same attitude to the arena of politics and public policy. They assume

that the taxpayer and the voter can be guided as easily as the patient. Organized medicine has taken a paternalistic attitude towards Canadian public policy for more than 50 years. In 1934, for example, the Canadian Medical Association argued that it was natural for doctors to control health policy. "This is not a selfish motive because what is best for the medical profession must be best for the public," the CMA said.

York reminds readers that in the United Kingdom, the tradition was that medical doctors were referred to as "Mister" (and presumably these days also "Ms." and "Ma'am"), a legacy from major universities where they were the victims of discrimination. It was believed that medical doctors were not particularly learned nor well schooled in anything important. Rather, they were skilled tradesmen and should be treated accordingly. One of the reasons that medical schools have a heritage of autonomy is that the real scholars believed that they — unlike pure scientists — did not belong on the campus in the first place.

Organizations representing physicians oppose anything that threatens the power base and income of the current monopoly. Through various generations, the Canadian Medical Association has, at one time or another, opposed:

- Women (as doctors)
- Jews (restricted numbers of doctors)
- Medicare (a Bolshevik plot in the Tommy Douglas era)
- Vitamins
- Immigrant doctors, by creating impossible hoops and hurdles to qualify, unless needs are so great in some areas government overrides restrictions.
- Osteopaths (unless conscripted into the medical profession)
- Chiropractors
- Optometrists
- Midwives
- Physiotherapists (unless MD fee comes first)
- Massage therapists
- Naturopaths
- Orthomolecular medicine
- Dieticians (unless MD fee comes first)

- Nurse practitioners (unless MD fee comes first)
- Salaried doctors in public clinics or group practices
- Podiatrists
- Acupuncturists
- Meddling by pharmacists in patient health issues

This is just a partial list. The forward to York's book was written by a distinguished physician, Dr. Philip Berger, who wrote about the anguish suffered by the pioneers in Canada who dared to suggest a better way of practice than fee-for-service. Berger, instrumental in Toronto's now world-acclaimed South Riverdale Community Health Centre, wrote about discrimination against Jews in his native Manitoba, although he said it preceded his career. But he added:

> Though blatant discrimination ultimately failed in Manitoba, the Canadian medical profession has maintained firm hold of its territory. . . .midwives, chiropractors, nurse practitioners and others have fallen victim to the dominance of physicians. Immigrant doctors have been severely restricted from entering the Canadian profession by governments with the support and approval of medical associations. Even salaried physicians at community clinics have come under attack from the medical establishment. The clinic movement in Ontario ground to a halt as a result of the intervention of organized medicine in the mid-1970s.

In a chapter titled, "The Campaign Against Salaried Doctors," York cited the example of several Community Health Centres in Canada that dared to defy the manner in which the medical associations dictated how practices ought to be conducted. A celebrated case — to this day — is the Sault Ste. Marie Group Health Centre, which was founded in 1963 by United Steelworkers of America union members who worked at Algoma Steel. Because of this large group practice, they felt they could hire all of the doctors and specialists they needed to provide a uniform level of care, in which health and healing were the highest priorities, not just cut and drug. The belief was that dedicated salaried doctors would spend more time with patients, and would make decisions without any personal income motive.

The campaign against them was brutal. The Ontario and the Canadian Medical Associations bought full-page ads in newspapers.

Doctors all over the Sault area warned patients they would be at their peril. Unconscionable pressure was placed upon any doctor the new clinic tried to hire. For years, the clinic was blocked from acquiring an anesthetist, since none could risk being ostracized by doctor-controlled hospitals. That meant that surgery couldn't be performed on the premises. To the eternal credit of the Steelworkers Union, the Sault Ste. Marie Group Health Centre persevered and prevailed. Other pioneering clinics were not so successful. Most were drummed into submission by the medical associations' scare tactics with patients, and through the bullying of doctors, hospitals and bureaucrats.

Today, the Sault Ste. Marie Group Health Centre (*www.ghc.on.ca*) has 60 doctors and associates. It is not surprising when one traces the roots of this patient-directed enterprise, to find a doctor whose passion was "public health" not "fee-for-service." The founding medical director Dr. Thompson A. Ferrier, was a Pennsylvania native who added a Masters Degree in Public Health to his medical credentials, while working for the United Mine Workers Welfare and Retirement Fund. Before his death in 1993, he was the recipient of honorary degrees from prestigious universities in Canada and the United States. A leader and visionary in the field of community health care, several scholarships and awards carry his name.

Modern medicine is often a paradox. There is now a vast list of drugs and treatment practices, once enthusiastically embraced by physicians, that are now defunct. Conversely, the profession has always vigorously opposed alternative therapies, including many now universally accepted as effective. An example is the multi-billion dollar international business of vitamins and nutritional supplements.

Dr. James Lunney, a chiropractor and Member of Parliament, recalls a discussion he had many years ago with noted Toronto orthopedic surgeon, Dr. Robert Salter, a member of the Canadian Medical Hall of Fame. Salter was a pioneer in the area of Continuous Passive Motion, modern ways of treating fractures, avoiding the dangers inherent in completely immobilizing limbs. Joint and bone mobility assists circulation and cell repair, however passive that motion may be. Dr. Lunney said that during the course this discussion of his groundbreaking work, Dr. Salter made the following observation: "there are three phases you go through when you introduce a form of treatment that does not fit the current medical model. The first is universal rejection — who do you think you are; it's always been that way! The second is equivocation — well, maybe! And the third is universal acceptance — well, of course, it's obvious!'"

The unhealthy monopoly

The most authoritative history chronicling the evolution of physician power is Dr. Ronald Hamowy's book *Canadian Medicine: A Study in Restricted Entry*, published by the Fraser Institute in Vancouver. While the CMA and its sycophants at Canadian universities were quite accustomed to dismissing journalistic critics — even those as accomplished as Geoffrey York — Hamowy was quite another story. After studies at Cornell and the City College of New York, Hamowy obtained his doctorate at the University of Chicago under an economic legend, Friedrich A. Hayek, and then studied law at the University of Paris and Oxford. At Oxford, he was a student of Sir Isaiah Berlin, one of the 20th century's most noted philosophers and advocates of individual human rights.

Professor Hamowy was at the University of Alberta (he's a Professor Emeritus at U of A today, in addition to being a distinguished scholar at New York's Cato Institute) when he took on the medical profession's persistent mantra, that their central control of health issues was in the public interest, with the purely humanitarian goal of protecting patients from the scourge of pretenders offering false remedies. He described his results as follows:

> Its conclusions dispute the widely held belief that the various statutes and regulations raising the requirements for medical licensure were, in the first instance, enacted to protect the public from so-called incompetents. The historical data provides substantial evidence that the profession's motives in raising the standards of entry into medical practice and in instituting policies that prohibited advertising or any sort of price competition were almost purely ones of economic self-interest.

Economist Dr. Walter Block, at the Fraser Institute when Hamowy's book was published, wrote a précis of the findings for both the foreword of the book, and also an article in *The Financial Post*. Dr. Block wrote: "[Hamowy] contends that the function of medical licensing in this country is not so much to ensure physician quality as to limit entry into the field, so as to increase the income, power, and prestige of those doctors already in practice. According to the evidence amassed in this book, the Canadian medical establishment at one point or another in its history has:

- banned price and other advertising for licensed doctors;
- set minimum price schedules;

- acted to prevent "overcrowding" or an oversupply of physicians by setting up a whole host of irrelevant criteria for licensing — examples include a knowledge of grammar, mathematics, Latin, history, philosophy and other academic studies, language requirements, citizenship, etc.;

- outlawed the uncontrolled study of medicine, even for those who do not intend to practice;

- placed roadblocks against foreign doctors practicing in Canada where they would compete with domestic physicians;

- been content with imposing entry examinations only. If the certification of quality were the true goal of these exams, they would more likely be required of practicing physicians at least every decade or so. For, says Hamowy, there is little guarantee — certainly not on the basis of testing — that a 70-year-old doctor is still qualified, merely for having successfully passed an examination 40 years earlier;

- fought against prepayment contract practice, opposed doctors testifying for plaintiffs in malpractice suits, and discouraged charity work as undermining minimum fee schedules and professional prestige;

- raised medical student fees in order to increase the costs of entry into the profession;

- succeeded, from time to time, in raising physicians' income levels beyond that of other, equally skilled, professions in Canada.

Hamowy's concern about MDs' continuing education has been raised by other critics. Chiropractors, nurse practitioners, optometrists and a long list of other health specialties require regular educational upgrading and examination, but the self-appointed "protectors of the public" will not accept mandatory scrutiny. Where medical specialty associations some-times advocate periodic review of qualifications, testing is voluntary because membership is not required. What makes it so preposterous is that in every round of fee negotiations with government, doctors manage to extract extra funds and bonuses for Continuing Medical Education. Physicians on the staff of hospitals and government agencies often get travel expenses related to this, in addition to the generous gifts the phar-maceutical industry and equipment suppliers have offered over the years. But there is no follow up. There is no audit to ensure that these funds and bonuses are spent for the purpose intended. One 1980s Ontario study concluded that the competence of 49 percent of doctors over the age of 70 was in doubt, but no effort was made to either upgrade them, ensure that they only practiced within the range of their competence, or, in some instances, compelled them to retire.

Two of the University of British Columbia's renowned economists Dr. Robert Evans (health) and Dr. William Stanbury (competition, monopolies) observed in one report: "It is taken for granted that airline pilots, for example, are subject to periodic examination of both physical and occupational capabilities.....Anyone suggesting lifetime licensure for airline pilots would be greeted with derision. Yet for surgeons, demonstration of competence at the beginning of the career is considered adequate."

The historic discrimination against immigrant doctors, even those with outstanding credentials, is defended with the understandable bias in favor of our own native-born graduates. But even when the medical schools cannot meet the demand, and in the face of remote communities desperately pleading for doctors, the medical associations are intransigent. Hamowy demonstrated that it was all about supply and demand, just like agricultural marketing boards plowing under excess crops to preserve high prices.

Today's four-year medical school will cost the average student $50,000 in tuition alone, but the country invests at least $500,000 in the development of each new doctor, not including the multi-hundreds of millions spent on capital costs. University medical schools and hospital training facilities are huge government investments. And, when doctors go to work, the public provides the vast majority of the tools and facilities they use to earn their income. With that in mind, immigrant doctors may well be the best bargain around. When it suits their purpose in fee negotiations, medical associations warn that if we don't give them what they want, we will risk the "brain drain" to the U.S. and elsewhere (it's always phony posturing and never statistically relevant), yet when it is suggested that immigration will balance the loss, they oppose that too. Apparently, the "brain-drain" only flows in one direction. When we gain a physician from elsewhere, the CMA view is that Canadians are being benevolent, doing someone a favor.

A serious flaw in the Canadian health care system is that doctors drive the demand. Through their management of patients, and not-so-subtle suggestions of diagnostic procedures, drugs and surgery, they are able to keep themselves and their associates busy, whether the services are needed or not. There are dreadful statistics throughout the North American health market. Gall bladder surgery, shown by studies to be unnecessary 80 percent of the time, causes more fatalities than any other surgical procedure. Most patients are advised only that it is minor surgery. Caesarean sections are once again approaching 30 percent of all births in major urban centers in Canada. It was five percent in 1967. A "Too Posh to Push" movement puts the blame on mothers, but the C-section is far more convenient and profitable for daily medical schedules than the uncertainty of natural childbirth.

Evidence is overwhelming that increased numbers of doctors in a community has little relationship to the quality of life or the health statistics, but if the increase is in the fee-for-service category of physician, costs, drug utilization, surgery and the pressures for capital construction of facilities will all soar to new heights. But, on average, the community will be no better off. Comparative studies of patients under group health care practices with an identical community of patients under fee-for-service physicians, always concludes — without exception — that there is dramatically less surgery and less drug consumption when MD's income is not a factor.

This has led many United States Health Maintenance Organizations to insist upon a second opinion from a doctor with no financial interest in the outcome, before approving any elective surgery. Geoffrey York quoted Joseph Califano, the former U.S. secretary of health, education and welfare:

> In many communities the standard is: when unsure about treatment, put the patient in the hospital and when you can, cut. When there is doubt about diagnosis or a more complex ailment is found, the uncertainty increases, and so does the incentive to do more tests, prescribe more pills, perform more surgery. However well motivated the physician's urge to do something to help the patient, it costs billions of dollars in unnecessary procedures.

And, may we add, more than minor cost and inconvenience for the "statistic" — patients and their families.

The arch-enemy

According to Geoffrey York's 1987 book:

> . . . of all the health professions in Canada, one occupational group has always suffered the harshest attacks from physicians. These are the chiropractors. "Organized medicine has been more hostile towards the practice of chiropractic than towards the practice of any other major healing group," the Ontario Committee on the Healing Arts reported in 1970 after its four-year inquiry. "Innumerable spokesmen for organized medicine have contended that the practice of chiropractic should be sharply limited or abolished." Two sociologists from the University of Toronto have described how the chiropractic profession has been forced to endure "the most strenuous efforts of the medical profession to destroy it."

Major inquiries and Royal Commissions in Canada (Hall, 1964; Lacroix, 1965; Hall, 1981; Ontario Committee on the Healing Arts, 1970), New Zealand in 1979 and in just about every country in the free world, have confirmed the validity of chiropractic and most have sharply criticized the inaccurate, dishonest and monopolistic posture of the medical establishment. Among these was the conviction of the American Medical Association in 1991 under the *Sherman Antitrust Act* for conducting a predatory monopoly in the United States. Every provincial government in Canada has passed legislation establishing the chiropractic profession. If there was even a hint of accuracy in the frantic screams of the medical associations, these laws would not exist.

The best illustration of shameless and deliberate medical hypocrisy is the subject of "university" education:

- It is standard rhetoric of medical associations, in attempts to discredit chiropractic, to point out that no chiropractic college is affiliated with any major North American university, the implication being that the profession is therefore inferior and perhaps even questionable.
- The medical profession passionately fights to sabotage any proposal by any university to include chiropractic as a faculty.

This dishonesty was among the keys to the U.S. antitrust conviction, and the Royal Commission findings in Canada, but the AMA and the

CMA brush off these defeats as if they were merely irritating insects and no one in Canadian government seems to have the courage and determination to put a stop to it.

There are 24 chiropractic colleges worldwide accredited by the Council on Chiropractic Education (CCE), all but eight located in the United States. There are two in Canada, two in Australia, one in France, one in Denmark and two in the United Kingdom. But there is chiropractic education in Japan, Brazil, South Africa and many other countries, each working their way toward the prized CCE accreditation. The only two in North America that are not fully independent are the Colleges of Chiropractic within the small University of Bridgeport, Connecticut, and the 11,000-student Trois Rivières campus of the University of Quebec.

Unbiased scientists have frequently given testimony before formal government commissions about how impressive and thorough are the facilities and the scientific curricula of the independent chiropractic colleges. Some of them are world famous, such as the Palmer College of Chiropractic in Davenport, Iowa; the National University of Health Sciences in Lombard, Illinois; and, the Canadian Memorial Chiropractic College in Toronto. As noted in the previous chapter, a respected professor of orthopedics, Per Freitag, MD, PhD, said the (then named) National College of Chiropractic had anatomy and dissection labs that were superior to those at the University of Illinois Medical School.

That being said, chiropractic colleges have an average student count of about 800 per campus, and, unlike public universities, they are fully autonomous. Rarely does public money ever come to their assistance. Students pay about $20,000 a year in this country and $US 15,000 tuition in the United States. Standards are high and many programs require an undergraduate degree to get in. Living entirely on their own resources, it is not possible to evolve the major scientific laboratories and related professional services that are taken for granted at mainstream universities. The education is fundamentally clinical and there are few resources for research. As a result, leaders within the chiropractic profession have long desired affiliation with large universities.

The model may well be Australia's 57,000-student Royal Melbourne Institute of Technology, established in 1887. RMIT has a complete range of facilities and labs for the study of biology, chemistry, and health sciences from nursing and midwifery to radiology. The emphasis is on non-medical health professions. Chiropractic students benefit from the surrounding infrastructure, the research capability and interacting with other health specialties. Its College of Chiropractic offers the following:

- Undergraduate teaching in the Chiropractic Stream of the Bachelor of Applied Science (Complementary Medicine);
- Postgraduate course work teaching in the Masters of Applied Science programs in Animal Chiropractic, Chiropractic Pediatrics, Musculoskeletal Management and Sports Chiropractic;
- Chiropractic teaching clinic; and,
- Research and research supervision in Masters and PhD programs. Major areas of research interest include clinical neuroscience; clinical trials of effectiveness, outcome measures and safety; competency-based professional standards and assessment, and chiropractic education; nutritional aspect of health care; and, psychosocial aspects of clinical practice.

In the wake of Canada's disappointment in the 2004 Olympics, many looked to Australia in some wonderment. How can this country, with half the population, an economy half the size, located far from the nucleus of world economic power, rank with the global giants in sports success? How, in fact, can minuscule budget Australian movies win so many Academy Awards and evolve so many international stars, while most CBC and Canadian productions have been an embarrassment beyond our borders? Could it be that the Australian market is more open and adventurous, less suffocated by establishment mediocrity, paranoia and protectiveness?

Proposals to evolve chiropractic schools within established North American universities have mostly come from the business development departments of these institutions. Chiropractic has been invited. These are usually campuses that do not have a School of Medicine, but which would like to emulate what has been done in Melbourne, with an exhaustive array of nonmedical health specialties, including all of the technologies, naturopathy and the exploding "wellness" business. Cash-strapped universities look with envy at the financial success and autonomy of the small chiropractic colleges, and the growth of the profession both in the number of doctors and the patients they treat. It is truly a boom area of health sciences.

So these universities issue the invitation, and the fun begins. It takes little time before the province/state and national medical associations hit the warpath. They call in all of the chips, including Big Pharma and doctor-run foundations that finance a high percentage of university research

activity. They threaten governments and university administrators, haul-
ing out decades worth of totally fraudulent and discredited papers from
past campaigns, the same material that offended the United States
Supreme Court, the New Zealand Royal Commission and Mr. Justice
Emmett Hall in previous generations. The same tiresome anti-chiropractic critics who show up for every battle arrive on the local scene.

These are paint-by-number campaigns, a traveling battle wagon.
They reach within the targeted university for distinguished friends that
share their bias, or those totally dependent upon drug financing or medical establishment largesse. They use the issue as a negative in all negotiations with the responsible government, with respect to fees and public
health services. They invest extravagantly through their media relations
infrastructure to obtain anti-chiropractic stories in local press, not at all
shy about reminding publishers and broadcasters how much money the
drug industry and medical establishment invests in their publications and
programs. By comparison, the drug-free chiropractic profession has few
economic resources and thus little clout.

Finally, within each campus, the medical establishment can find,
intellectually speaking, a nut who is obsessed with this topic. There is
always a history, sociology or psychology professor who has attained
legendary local status by questioning anything even slightly out of the
ordinary. These are the same people who in other generations supported
the flat earth until they fell off the edge, debunked doctors who washed
their hands, ridiculed Harvey's theories of blood circulation, laughed at
the idea that small doses of a disease would kill off life-threatening
encounters and who wrote copious tomes about the fantasies of spiritu-
alists, psychics, faith healers and more conventional scientists who proclaimed that the human body was surrounded by a visible energy field.
Debunking this was fair game until the Russians spoiled it all with
Kirlian photography (clear photographs of human aura). Today's magnetic imaging resonance and positive electron tomography render to the
garbage heaps countless numbers of past doctoral theses by these university defenders of orthodoxy, who seem not to understand that the
essence of science is to explore the unknown, not merely defend what we
already understand. In any event, they still have chiropractic and naturopathy to assault as "quacks" and "cults," and the medical profession can
be a good source of funds wherever the battle is engaged.

The Canadian Memorial Chiropractic College has long desired to
become part of a mainstream university. At least informal conversations
— and, in a few instances, serious campaigns — took place concerning

affiliation with the universities of Guelph, Waterloo, Waterloo Lutheran, Queens, Ryerson Polytechnical, Toronto, McMaster, Trent, Brock, Ottawa, Western Ontario, Victoria and York. Only the most serious of these conversations became the subject of anti-chiropractic campaigns by the medical establishment. Some of the proposals didn't fit either the business plan or the available financial resources of the institution, or, from a provincial perspective, the overall post-secondary education plan. In the meantime, chiropractic has thrived, despite far less coverage under medicare and extended health plans and the belligerent opposition of the medical establishment. Cutbacks in coverages — private and public — have escalated in recent Canadian history. There were 2,200 chiropractors in Canada when Geoffrey York's book was published in 1987. He emphasized that this was double the 1,100 who were in practice in 1971. There are over 6,600 chiropractors today. And that is what the CMA concern is all about. Over five million Canadian patients go to chiropractors by choice and most often pay for the treatments willingly, either directly or through insurance plans.

What seems lost in all this — as always — is paramount concern for patients. Canada's chiropractic education and research would be immeasurably enriched by a university association. Presumably the quality of care would also improve, a benefit to individuals, their employers, their families, and society. The self-sufficiency of chiropractic would enrich universities, easily amortizing any public investment through both direct revenues and spin off economic impact. Today, half of all Canadians who enter the profession, graduated from American institutions. Not only would Canada be able to serve its own chiropractic educational needs, we would be able to profit from educating chiropractors for the rest of the world. Nonmedical universities, through chiropractic, could enhance their resources and capabilities on all health and bio-scientific fronts.

Canadian Memorial Chiropractic College (CMCC)

Now world renowned in the field of chiropractic education, the Toronto college was established in 1945 to set standards for the profession in this country. The goal has been to become a scholarly institution, conducting both education and research. Most chiropractors in Canada — without any direct benefit to themselves — have generously contributed funds, through their provincial associations, for the development and advancement of this college.

Entrance to the CMCC is extremely competitive, and requires at least three years of undergraduate university education in qualifying sciences. The chiropractic program is four years of full-time education. Therefore, chiropractors require a minimum of seven years post-secondary education. Each year about 450 candidates apply for just 160 first year positions. It is Canada's only English-language program, but admittance to the University of Quebec in Trois Rivières is an even greater challenge with, typically, 900 applicants competing for 45 positions. This all generates another sorry statistic: more than 800 Canadian students a year are forced to leave the country to attend chiropractic college in the United States. Calculating the cost of Canadian families supporting them abroad this may represent a negative economic impact of $50 million a year or more, the equivalent of an 800-student chiropractic campus in this country. The other loss is the ability to educate our young people under Canadian standards and inculcate them with this country's professional health culture, rather than merely giving them an examination upon re-entry.

Successful students at the Canadian CCE accredited chiropractic schools will eventually complete no less than 4,400 hours of instruction and clinical experience. Chiropractors receive training in the sciences necessary to understand, diagnose, and treat conditions of the neuro-musculoskeletal system. CMCC education follows three learning stages.

- **In the first year**, chiropractic students are trained in the health sciences, including: anatomy — the structure of the body; physiology — the functions and activities of living matter, such as organs, tissue, and cells; histology — the microscopic study of tissues and cells; biochemistry — the chemical processes in the body; and, pathology — the study of diseases.
- **In the second year**, the study of health sciences is complemented with course work involving adjustive techniques of the spine and pelvis.
- **For the third and fourth years**, chiropractic students conduct an investigative research project, continue studying the sciences, and receive extensive clinical training.
- **Postgraduate chiropractic specialties** exist in clinical sciences, radiology, rehabilitation, and sports chiropractic.

The faculty at the CMCC is interdisciplinary, and many faculty members are cross-appointed with medical schools.

Ian Coulter and the University of Victoria

In any list of Canadian casualties as a result of the "brain drain," the name Ian Coulter, PhD, should be on it. A senior medical sociologist whose research had entailed nursing, dentistry and alternate therapies, he is a former Assistant Vice-Provost of Health Sciences at the University of Toronto. He co-authored in 1980, along with two other University of Toronto professors, a book entitled *Chiropractors: Do They Help?* Later he would become president of CMCC. Today, Dr. Coulter is a senior researcher with the RAND Corporation, based in Los Angeles, a professor in the School of Dentistry at the University of California in Los Angeles (UCLA), and a research professor at Southern California University Hospital School.

He became executive vice-president of the Canadian chiropractic college, and subsequently president, because he had a vision of what interdisciplinary approaches to health care might evolve. He wrote papers in late 1988, hopefully heralding an age where health and wellness took priority over constantly reacting to and treating symptoms. Coulter envisaged a partnership between a great university and the Canadian Memorial Chiropractic College, evolving a research and graduate educational program that could offer the first PhDs in the world in specialized neuro-musculoskeletal research.

This vision was coincidental to that of Howard Petch, PhD, then the president of British Columbia's growing University of Victoria. Petch envisaged "Complimentary Health Professions," to augment the existing School of Nursing and health-related sciences, dealing with everything not looked after by the University of British Columbia Medical School in Vancouver. Proposals were encouraged from optometrists, who wished to establish a Western Canada School of Optometry, and CMCC.

At first, the British Columbia government, the official opposition, and the decision-makers at the university were enthusiastic. Dr. Coulter prepared lengthy dissertations about his vision for future integrated health services and what an extraordinary step it would be for this Toronto institution, developed with funding from chiropractors coast to coast, but predominately Ontario, to sponsor such an important move to the west coast. Independent British Columbia economists calculated that the economic impact to Victoria would be $38 million (1990) dollars, as a result of minimal capital investment, easily amortized by the self-sufficient college. That would be about $60 million in 2004 dollars. Everybody cheered the opportunity, a coup for British Columbia.

Dr. Coulter delivered a learned presentation, ostensibly to define the philosophy of CMCC and chiropractic, but which really was a forward-thinking view of how everyone ought to perform within the healing arts.

> Much has been said about the philosophy of chiropractic, most of it, incorrectly. . . . There is no single philosophy of chiropractic and our profession is as split philosophically as any other. At best, there are some broadly shared "philosophical" principles.

- The first has historically been termed vitalistic philosophy. Simply put, this philosophy accepts that health is a natural state and departure from this state is viewed as the failure of the individual to adapt to one's internal and external environment without adverse biological consequences. This position embraces the notion that the body has an innate tendency to restore and maintain health by homeostatic mechanisms, reparative processes, and adaptive responses, subject to both genetic and acquired limitations. Vitalistic philosophy underlies numerous health paradigms and much of the contemporary work on the immune system. It has its clinical counterpart in the belief that the role of the practitioner is that of a facilitator and captured in the aphorism "I treated the patient, God cured him". Andrew Still, the founder of osteopathy expressed it best in his statement "health comes from within or not at all."

- A second, and related philosophy, has been termed holistic health care. This premise accepts that the health of the individual cannot be reduced to biological structures, nor treated by simply focusing on symptoms. Conversely, it accepts that health is the biological and mental expression of a complex interaction of biological, physiological, social, and spiritual factors. The clinical importance of this perspective is the whole individual in the focus of the health practitioner not simply the disease process (dis-ease as opposed to disease).

- A third philosophical premise is as old as Hippocrates and captured in his remark "physician do no harm". It can best be described as therapeutic conservatism and accepts that the best care is the least care. Given that iatrogenic illness now comprises over 30 percent of all illnesses in North American society, it is a principle worth restating.

- A fourth philosophical predilection is for natural remedies. Traditionally, chiropractors have legislatively been described as drugless practitioners and as functioning without the use of surgery and/or drugs. In chiropractic, this proposition is also highly related to the concept of therapeutic conservatism and both are logically related to the notion that the body does have natural defensive mechanisms, and although not always operative or successful, they should at least be given the opportunity to function prior to radical interventions.

■ Last but not least, the College embraces the philosophy of critical rationalism. This is the philosophy that underlies science itself and is the belief that through reason, and its application in the world of our five senses, we can come to understand and act upon, nature. However, it is much broader than simply the contemporary notion of scientific research. It covers all those contemplative, reflective, experimental processes which, through systematized reasoning, attempt to create a body of knowledge and a discipline.

Emphasizing the opportunity that would be possible in partnership with the University of Victoria, Dr. Coulter lamented the "investigative silence" surrounding the area of the muscular-skeletal system. He said:

> For example, if we compare the research on the respiratory system, cardiovascular system, circulatory system, and the immune system (to take but a few examples) to research on the muscular-skeletal, the contrast is overwhelming. The spine and its related structures has not been of particular interest to biomedical researchers. This is an incredible situation if one considers the volume of the body taken up by the spine (60 percent), and ponders even for a minute on the nature of the spine as the weight bearing mechanism of the body, and its housing of crucial neurological elements (eg. the spinal cord), and its associated musculature. Further, 80 percent of the population will suffer a back problem at some time in their life. As a cause of lost time from work, it is second only to the common cold and economically probably surpasses the cold in lost productivity. Yet no centre currently exits anywhere in Canada for the study of muscular-skeletal disorders. If CMCC and UVic were to create such a research centre it would be leading the world by this very act alone.

Years would pass. Dr. Coulter departed CMCC in 1990. There would be a British Columbia election. The British Columbia College of

Physicians and Surgeons and whatever allies it could influence within the university, government and media, did not exactly kill the venture. Each chapter of the story became cause for further research, discussion, and delay. Government support remained officially in place — the new Premier elected in 1991 was committed in writing — but it was half-hearted, reluctant to interfere with a university process. Finally, in 1992, the University of Victoria advised CMCC that it had chosen not to affiliate. The proposal from optometrists fared no better.

The visionary president Howard Petch's vision of an advanced, multidisciplinary health sciences program at UVic is no further ahead today than it was in 1990. In fact, the university has gone backwards in stature, even deeper into the shadows of the University of British Columbia and Simon Fraser University on the mainland.

Suckers for punishment?

CMCC closed the British Columbia file in 1992 and, along with their supporters on the west coast, returned to their primary mission. It took a while for bruises to heal and for business development resources to return to a healthy state. But the university quest was not over — and may never be over until the dream is fulfilled.

York University: In 1994, initial talks took place in Toronto concerning the prospect of affiliating with CMCC. Several scientific professors in the Toronto academic community had worked or still worked at the University of Toronto, York and CMCC, and a few of them taught at more than one institution at any given time. The schools were well known to each other. The UVic files were still fresh and every conceivable issue available for inspection. In 1995, a letter of intent was signed between York and CMCC. For the next six years, first under the auspices of York's Faculty of Pure and Applied Science and subsequently at the Atkinson Faculty of Liberal and Professional Studies, the affiliation supporters pressed their case. The same exhausting, expensive attrition that killed the UVic proposal set in. Each new round of questions or criticism created yet another committee, another study and more delay. York finally rejected the proposal in 2001.

British Columbia Institute of Technology (BCIT): The 50,000-student degree-granting polytechnical institution began discussions in 1996 with the British Columbia Chiropractic Association with a view toward developing a complete new school of chiropractic medicine to serve western Canada. The Dean of Health Sciences at BCIT, Dr. George

Eisler, became an enthusiastic supporter. BCIT had established itself as a vital link in health education, training most of the technical expertise needed in the province, including nursing and a long list of advanced nursing specialties. A chiropractic doctorate would not only elevate BCIT's health sciences, it would add to the growing list of degree programs enhancing the "university" stature the institution was acquiring. This proposal began and concluded in a positive frame of mind, with little of the anguish surrounding previous university efforts, although the medical peanut gallery did their best to sabotage the proposal. Eisler and BCIT had hoped to add chiropractic, naturopathy, and Traditional Chinese Medicine, but the plan was abandoned because of budget concerns amid a difficult provincial economy. Informal conversations continued during the next two years with nearby Simon Fraser University (SFU), and particularly its respected School of Kinesiology within the Faculty of Applied Science, and these proved to be hopeful but not fruitful. Many SFU kinesiology graduates have gone on to become chiropractors, most obtaining their doctorates in the United States.

In both the University of Victoria and York University proposals, the decision against chiropractic affiliation was by an extremely narrow vote, but the multi-year campaigns were debilitating in other ways. The postscript to this is that Canadian Memorial Chiropractic College escaped the frustration of university alliances, at least temporarily, and launched a redevelopment plan of its own in 2001. A new $30 million Toronto facility opened in 2004, with more space and resources for every program consideration. As always, chiropractic paid its own way, unlike the almost 100 percent taxpayer-financed realm within which MDs earn their living.

The current chair of CMCC's Board of Governors is Dr. David Olson of North Vancouver, the fourth British Columbian to hold the position in the college's 60-year history. "This is one 'national' Canadian organization that has always made a sincere effort to serve the entire country. The attempt to affiliate with the University of Victoria 15-years-ago was a testament to that philosophy. I am very proud to be part of it and most of us in the profession have personally contributed to its development."

Florida State University (FSU)

After years of preliminary study, the State of Florida approved a $US 9 million start-up budget in 2004 for a College of Chiropractic at Florida State University, the 38,000-student campus located in the state capital,

Tallahassee. It promised to be a development for the profession to rival the significance of the program at the Royal Melbourne Institute of Technology in Australia. FSU is a complete university, in every sense, including a College of Medicine, established in 2000.

But it was a curious development. Critics claimed that it came about entirely as a result of one powerful politician, State Senate Majority Leader, Dr. Dennis Jones, a chiropractor. FSU never asked for the program and there seemed not to be a great deal of enthusiasm emanating from the university. In fact, concern was expressed by some that the affiliation would impair the credibility of its young medical school. Following is an excerpt from a 2003 FSU student newspaper article:

> "No chiropractic school in the country is affiliated with a medical school," Provost and Executive Vice President of the College of Medicine Dr. Lawrence Abele said. "It's much closer to a nutrition and movement science than to medicine. The curricula is different enough that it's just not a close fit."
>
> Although chiropractic is a relatively new profession (beginning just over 100 years ago), it is now a recognized profession that is licensed in all 50 states. Millions of people utilize chiropractic services. According to www.aecc.ac.uk, chiropractic is now the third largest primary health care profession in the world.
>
> Due to the questions surrounding the legitimacy of the profession, starting a chiropractic school at FSU could potentially affect the University and its academic reputation. However, it has been made clear that Florida State's chiropractic school would be top-notch.
>
> We told the Florida Legislature that if we are going to do this, we are only going to do it as a first-class, quality program that will have a science and evidence-based curricula," Abele said. "It won't be cheap, but we won't do it any other way; that wouldn't be fair."

An article in the *Tallahassee Democrat* suggested that the new FSU chiropractic college could become the best in the world and even act as catalyst to inspire co-operative relations between doctors of chiropractic and doctors of medicine. Several medical physicians and distinguished biomedical scientists, who are also chiropractors, have endorsed more amicable relations among all of the "life sciences," and research projects that could investigate issues. Here is an excerpt from that article:

> "Chiropractic (medicine) was seen by many people for some time as

quackery at worst and something that might help, but not kill them at best," said (Dr. Partap) Khalsa, who has a chiropractic degree along with a doctorate in biomedical sciences.

"But the chiropractic profession has transformed into a more accepted health-care option in the past few decades," Khalsa said. "Many doctors regularly refer their patients to the chiropractor down the street — especially those with lower back pain. The federal government now has millions to spend on research into chiropractic care."

FSU's school plans to be on the cutting edge of producing new scientific evidence, which will in turn change how and what chiropractic colleges teach. And that possibility thrills Khalsa, a trained scientist and graduate program director for the biomedical engineering department at Stony Brook State University of New York.

Despite official approvals, Legislature votes and the forceful public support of Governor Jeb Bush, the chiropractic college at FSU was killed at the end of January, 2005. The university's Board of Governors voted 10-3 against it, after one of the most bitter campaigns on record. Opponents rallied 500 professors to sign a petition. One of them created a fictitious campus map, locating the chiropractic college next to schools devoted to "Bigfoot," faith healing, UFO studies, crop circles and other objects of cult interest or superstition.

The uphill climb
A sample of anti-chiropractic media may add a taste for what has been involved in the campaigns to evolve university affiliation.

Since York University does not have a Faculty of Medicine or even a large-scale health program, we sought information about chiropractic from external experts. Most were associated with the National Council Against Health Fraud (NCAHF) which is headquartered in California. The reference material they provided at once dispelled the most common misperceptions of chiropractic. The average person — even an educated health-care worker — is not aware how prevalent anti- and pseudoscientific attitudes are within contemporary chiropractic. Support for the status quo is normally rationalized in the following way: since our government licenses and partially subsidizes chiropractic, how can it not be okay? In the first place, licensing is not intended to confer scientific legitimacy, but rather to protect the public from incompetent practitioners. In the second, some governments eagerly subsidize therapies such as therapeutic touch which are demonstrably pseudoscientific.

Within a couple of weeks, we had become sufficiently well informed to apprehend that an affiliation with the CMCC would have deleterious consequences for Science at York. A letter was written to the administration by three professors expressing our grave concerns about the affiliation proposal. The administration ignored our letter, but in mid-February we managed to convince the FPAS through a democratic process to strike a committee to study the "academic implications" such an affiliation would have upon our Faculty.

— A York astronomy professor in 1998

It should be noted that the National Council Against Health Fraud is more smoke than fire, a noisy self-justifying lobby operating from an office that is not much more than a glorified mail-drop in a Peabody, Massachusetts, industrial park. The organization disputes claims that its roots were with American Medical Association's Committee on Quackery, established in 1963, and that it gets funds from Big Pharma. Despite the notable lack of distinction of this organization's most loquacious and ubiquitous speakers, chiropractic critics invariably quote it as an authority.

What is consistently amazing is how supposedly reputable university professors and physicians, desperate to demean the chiropractic profession, latch onto totally discredited allies. The 25-year antics of Montreal physician Dr. Murray Katz, demolished by a New Zealand Royal Commission and other venues, were described in an earlier chapter. But two of the most prolific voices within the so-called National Council Against Health Fraud have also been routinely exposed. The "coalition" was defeated in an attempt to bring an action in Los Angeles against a health food manufacturer; but, in the process it attempted to get Dr. Stephen Barrett and Dr. Wallace Sampson considered as "experts" in the case.

At the end of 2001, a the California Supreme Court had this to say about Barrett:

> . . . As for his credentials as an expert on FDA regulation of homeopathic drugs, the Court finds that Dr. Barrett lacks sufficient qualifications in this area. Expertise in FDA regulation suggests a knowledge of how the agency enforces federal statutes and the agency's own regula-

tions. Dr. Barrett's purported legal and regulatory knowledge is not apparent. He is not a lawyer, although he claims he attended several semesters of correspondence law school. While Dr. Barrett appears to have had several past conversations with FDA representatives, these appear to have been sporadic, mainly at his own instigation, and principally for the purpose of gathering information for his various articles and Internet web-sites. He has never testified before any governmental panel or agency on issues relating to FDA regulation of drugs. Presumably his professional continuing education experiences are outdated given that he has not had a current medical license in over seven years. For these reasons, there is no sound basis on which to consider Dr. Barrett qualified as an expert on the issues he was offered to address. Moreover, there was no real focus to his testimony with respect to any of the issues in this case associated with Defendants' products.

And this about Sampson:

While he stated that he teaches a university course on "alternative medicine," Dr. Sampson admitted that the course does not instruct on how such methods may be practiced, but rather is a course designed to highlight the criticisms of such alternative practices. Therefore, the Court finds that Dr. Sampson has relatively thin credentials to opine on the general questions of the proper standards for clinical or scientific research or other methods of obtaining valid evidence about the efficacy of drugs. The Court further finds that Dr. Sampson lacks experience in the field of homeopathic drugs, which renders his testimony of little or no weight in this case.

Back to British Columbia, there was the following excerpt from the *Canadian Medical Association Journal* in 1999, quoting a B.C. general practitioner:

. . . the BCIT proposal was particularly alarming because of the institution's role as a training facility for most of the province's X-ray technicians, physiotherapists and other health professionals would be reduced. But for a highly reputable institution like BCIT to grant degrees in unscientific therapies would have been a much more dangerous development. . . because it would have cast doubt on the academic reputation of BCIT's entire health sciences program. . . . the move would have jeopardized the close working relationship between doctors and BCIT-trained technical staff. He is relieved that, for whatever reason, BCIT has abandoned the plan. There has been a bandwagon of enthusiasm for alternative therapies. . Now there is some rethinking of it all. It is a very welcome sign.

Note the threatening tone in the above with respect to other health care students at BCIT. The message is clear: "If BCIT approves chiropractic education, medical doctors and hospitals will not hire you." What possible relevance might it have to the competence of a laboratory technician or CT scanner specialist, the fact that chiropractors were educated on the same campus? Obviously, none at all, but this blackmailing posture is central to all provincial medical association campaigns. Aside from everything else, their tactics are crude. The public and politicians are quite familiar with threats to withdraw services, and insensitivity toward patient suffering. Behind the scenes, the coercion is a vicious, relentless process wherever they have influence.

And, this 2003 Florida letter to the editor:

Ever since Daniel David Palmer, a self-styled "magnetic healer" gave birth to chiropractic in 1895 by applying force to a protrusion on a janitor's back (which he claimed cured the man's hearing loss), spinal manipulation has been the chiropractor's standard treatment. (Florida law allows the use of manipulation to treat all but a handful of diseases.) Manipulation has its devotees among the public and many will swear that it "works". This is known in scientific research as "anecdotal" evidence, but for a medical treatment to be scientifically valid it must stand up under far more exacting examination. While chiropractic employs the language of medicine — physician, diagnosis, subluxation, board certification, for example — at present the hard science behind chiropractic practice is between slim and nonexistent. This is partly because, as a consultant's report commissioned by FSU itself points out, chiropractors have never rigorously researched their methods.

One of the most humorous of all broadsides came during the early stages of the University of Victoria discussions. A sports columnist in the local newspaper quoted a university coach, who lamented that it had been a bad week. Two of the university sports teams had suffered embarrassing losses and the College Senate had approved moving forward on chiropractic education. It wasn't clear which of these events was seen by the coach to be the gravest calamity. This coach, in addition to being unable to win on the playing field, failed to understand that professional and Olympic-class athletes are among the most enthusiastic consumers of chiropractic treatments. There are few teams without at least one regular chiropractic doctor. Here is the excerpt:

> According to (the coach) chiropractic does not belong in a "university setting:" especially at UVic. If an application from the Canadian Memorial Chiropractic College to move its Toronto-based school to UVic is accepted it could "put the university's reputation at stake," he said. No other university in North America has a school of chiropractic and (the coach) doesn't think UVic should become the first. After all, he reasoned, medicine does not recognize the practice of chiropractic.
>
> Actually there are medical doctors who do acknowledge chiropractors and are even willing to work alongside them. The villain is not the doctors themselves but the provincial medical association trying to look after its own selfish interests instead of the health of the public. Many people have benefited from regular visits to chiropractors. In fact, some of the more high profile of. . . the school's athletes, who have done more for UVic's reputation than any academic, owe a portion of their success to chiropractic care.
>
> Fortunately for UVic, its president is more sympathetic to the chiropractic proposal. Howard Petch even says the chiropractic college meets university standards and that he would rather have UVic promoting preventive health professions such as chiropractic than opening up a medical school.

First, Do No Harm!

The full-time medical politicians and financial extortionists recklessly toss around the word "science" with callous disregard for facts or even common sense. "Chiropractic is unscientific," they chant. Many of the tools and treatments used by medicine do represent pure science, and there are many physicians whose work is entirely scientific (pathology, imaging, genetics, research) but the vast majority of medical doctors — absolutely and completely — do not. Their professional judgment is what makes them valuable to society and patients, the experience to diagnose what ails a patient and then to choose a proper course of action. It is educated guesswork, the product of education, training, and experience.

Cutting out a tumor in the hope of curtailing the spread of cancer, or amputating a leg to halt the progress of infection, are gambles in each case. Because the biology and genetic composition of each patient is different, no matter how much science created a drug, it will not behave the same in any two bodies. When drugs are mixed, either deliberately in so-called treatment "cocktails" or inadvertently by patients, all of the science goes out the window. As statistics demonstrate, there is far more danger in all of that, than anything ever proposed by chiropractic.

A 1997 television movie starring Meryl Streep should be required viewing for all health professionals. Written by Ann Beckett and directed by Jim Abrahams, *First Do No Harm* traces the experience of a mother and a young son with epilepsy. Local doctors try an endless series of drug remedies and the boy gets progressively worse. The treatments escalate to experimental cocktails and the boy nearly dies. The mother becomes frustrated and desperate, and starts her own research into the existing literature on treatments. She learns about the Ketogenic Diet developed at Baltimore's acclaimed Johns Hopkins Hospital, a nutritional remedy used successfully by many patients over several decades. But her local doctor calls the Ketogenic Diet "unscientific" and says she would endanger the boy's life by transporting him to Baltimore.

More drugs are pumped into him and Mom becomes more frantic. When she tries to snatch him from the hospital she is apprehended by security. The local doctor then threatens to apply to court for legal guardianship, a court order asserting that the mother is endangering her son's life. The hospital plans exploratory neurosurgery, a look into the brain to see if anything can be spotted that doesn't show up in the X-rays.

Finally, a family friend, Jim Petersen, — a professional pilot but formerly a doctor and still licensed to practice — confronts Dr. Melanie Abbasac, the villainous local doctor. Dr. Abbasac says she couldn't understand the "foolishness" of subjecting the boy to an unproven therapy, the dialogue was as follows:

> DR. PETERSEN: Of course you don't, since so many in our profession choose not to look beyond the limits of drugs and surgery . . . that's what made me change careers but I kept my medical license current.

> DR. ABBASAC: I assume you know that all of the evidence in favor of the Ketogenic diet is anecdotal; there is absolutely no scientific evidence that this diet works?

Dr. Petersen: When you say "scientific evidence" you mean double blind studies. Then I have to ask you, where are the double blind studies on the effects of the interactions between all of the drugs you have had Robbie on — where are the studies on the surgery you propose as a result of the electrocorticogram . . . . Doctor, to arbitrarily pretend that your treatments for epilepsy are science and then argue against the Ketogenic diet seems to be the cruelest of double standards. When you and I became doctors we swore an oath that said 'first do no harm'.. these folks want to try to control their son's seizures by changing what he eats instead of drugs and surgery, and I think they deserve that chance.

In what was said to be "based on a true story" with proceeds going to epilepsy charities, the pilot flew the boy, the mother and a nurse to Baltimore. Doctors there first detoxified the patient and then began the Ketogenic Diet. The lad never had another seizure, and resumed a normal, happy, and active life.

The Ketogenic Diet has been widely used elsewhere as well, successful in approximately 50 percent of cases, including the Mayo Clinic since 1921, primarily in childhood epilepsy. Mayo reports, "The mechanism by which the Ketogenic Diet works is unknown. The high-fat, low-protein, no-carbohydrate diet mimics some effects of starvation that seem to inhibit seizures. The diet is very rigid and carefully controlled, and must be supervised by a physician — sometimes in a hospital setting."

"Mr. Premier. Would this be a good time to discuss your decision to cut chiropractic from medicare?"

14.
The Doctor of Chiropractic

A body that is free of nerve interference has more power to heal, think and metabolize. Ninety percent of the stimulation and nutrition to the brain is generated by movement of the spine.

— ROGER W. SPERRY, PhD
1981 Nobel Laureate for Medicine

What is this enigma that seems to be able to grow its base of professionals and satisfied patients more rapidly than any other sector of health care, despite every impediment imaginable in terms of official obstruction and efforts to minimize insurance coverage? Why are there 10 students waiting for every opening in a Canadian chiropractic college, and a successful professional practice in just about every neighborhood? How is it that chiropractic care — including its sophisticated educational resources — can be entirely self-sufficient, while medicine seems unable to generate a professional heartbeat without government or charity money? What is it about the word "chiropractic" that reduces the American Medical Association and Canadian Medical Association to a state of apoplexy, including a conviction of the AMA for antitrust behavior in the United States?

There is no enigma. For a vast range of disorders, chiropractic works and medicine often does not. Ignorance is a difficult cross to bear and, bluntly put, potentially expensive in lost business.

Back and spine-related issues represent almost one-third of all visits to health professionals. Virtually all of the five million patients of Canada's 6,600 chiropractic doctors are refugees from medical doctors, who failed to provide any help despite multiple visits and procedures, invariably involving drugs, and far too often resulting in needless, dangerous surgery. Patient health is less important to medical associations than the "ownership" of the care to be provided.

The knowledge and skills of modern medicine and all of its associated technologies cannot possibly be understated. It is so frequently brilliant and awe-inspiring that society fails to see a reactionary subculture that opposes anything it does not understand and dominate. If medical schools don't teach it and if it is not a customary treatment, it must be wrong by definition. What is most often missing in western medicine is the comprehension of the central nervous system. The health establishment attempts to denigrate, for example, 5,000 years of Chinese experience with acupuncture and other remedies, all aimed at helping the body heal itself. Traditional healers believe that natural processes must be given an opportunity to work before invasive techniques, such as drugs and surgery, are even considered.

The chiropractic profession passionately embraces this theme. The basic concepts can be described as follows:

- The body has a powerful self-healing ability.
- The structure (primarily that of the spine) and its function are closely related, and this relationship affects health.
- Chiropractic care is given with the goals of normalizing this relationship between structure and function and assisting the body as it heals.

The most frequent care provided by chiropractic doctors is for back pain, suffered by all but a few people at some point in their lives, and on a recurring basis by a significant population. Years of science, hundreds of thousands of case studies (including peer-reviewed evidence-based scientific examinations), and formal government inquiries worldwide have repeatedly endorsed the efficacy and value of chiropractic spinal adjustments. Spine-related injuries occur from many circumstances including:

- Whiplash associated disorders from a car accident
- Work place injury
- Sports injury
- A slip or fall
- Poor posture

- Physical weakness
- Tension, anxiety, nervousness
- Back pain from pregnancy
- Children's activities

The word "neuro-musculoskeletal" is a fancy way of describing the spine and the central nervous system. More than a century of experience has demonstrated that the treatment of obvious spine issues by a Doctor of Chiropractic, can often bring relief from other common symptoms, such as:

- Back pain
- Headaches (migraines)
- Neck pain
- Disk problem
- Sciatica and leg pain
- Numbness and/or tingling upon waking up
- Shoulder, arm and hand pain
- TMJ (jaw joint) pain
- Carpal tunnel syndrome
- Dizziness
- Fatigue
- Knee pain

History — a Canadian footnote

The word chiropractic comes from a combination of the Greek words "chiro" and "praktikis", meaning "done by hand." From the time of Hippocrates, who is regarded as the founder of medical inquiry, "treatment by hand" was an accepted form of therapy. The first recorded references to spinal manipulation occurred in ancient Greece. But it was a Canadian grocer and self-described "magnetic healer" from Port Perry, in Durham County just to the northeast of Toronto, who would found what would become a durable mainstream health profession.

Daniel David Palmer, born in 1845, had moved with his family to the small town of Davenport, Iowa. By the late 1880s he had established a practice as a "magnetic healer," but his curiosity knew no bounds. Palmer encountered two patients who displayed symptoms apparently linked to spinal problems. One had suffered deafness associated with a

spinal dislocation. On September 18, 1895, Palmer corrected the dislocation and his patient recovered his hearing. A second patient suffering from
heart disease improved after adjustment of a spinal dislocation which
Palmer believed exerted pressure on the nerves leading to the heart.

Palmer generalized from these experiences and founded chiropractic.
His theory was that decreased nerve flow may be the cause of disease,
and that misplaced spinal vertebrae may cause pressure on the nerves. He
started educating others, founding the Palmer School and Cure in 1897
and, by 1902, the school had graduated 15 chiropractors. D. D. Palmer
defined chiropractic as "the science of healing without drugs." One of his
early students was his son, Bartlett Joshua Palmer, who joined his father
in conducting classes. Upon completing the course of study, B. J. (as he
came to be known throughout the world) developed what is now the
internationally renowned Palmer College of Chiropractic, with several
campuses. D. D. Palmer died in 1913 and B. J. remained prominent until
his death in 1961. In 1995, Canada Post honored the 100th anniversary
of chiropractic with a postage stamp commemorating the work of Daniel
David Palmer.

Both Palmers were eccentric intellectual adventurers, far more fascinated by the inexplicable "cures" generated by the body's nerve system
than by the predictable and satisfying healing of spine problems through
manipulation. Chiropractic was controversial from the beginning and
many chiropractors, including Palmer, were prosecuted for practicing
medicine without a license, although eventually it was recognized that
chiropractors were not practicing medicine but chiropractic. Their passion and this pursuit haunts chiropractic to this day, both a curse and a
blessing. Every chiropractor regularly encounters positive situations that
defy scientific explanation. They become the subject of theory and belief,
but should not be advertised as scientific certainty.

Both medicine and chiropractic are relatively young professions,
with far more yet to be learned than whatever has been discovered.
Chiropractic, as did the British osteopathy, evolved from the "bonesetters" who go back in history as far as ancient Greece. The Palmer
advance was the focus on the nervous system and ancillary healing.
Medical historians usually begin the "modern" chapter with William
Harvey's discovery of blood circulation in 1628, but they tend to forget
how primitive the trade remained right into the twentieth century.
Despite Lord Lister's determined efforts, few surgeons bothered to even
wash their hands between procedures, until the final years of the nineteenth century.

Health professions, most notably those established by legislation, have all evolved in relatively recent history, most of it within the last century. In North America, the delivery of health care and the education, licensing, and regulation of practitioners is exclusively a provincial or state responsibility. Various agreements exist between governments and professional associations to honor each other's credentials. Federal law in both Canada and the United States is primarily associated with the transfer of money and functions — agreed by states and provinces — that can be better handled collectively (epidemiology, food production standards, pharmaceutical approvals, most research and so on). Provincial legislation creates the legal mechanism by which educational requirements are determined, schools accredited, and programs established. Following from that are the qualifications for registration. This process is similar in democratic countries worldwide.

The definition and application for each profession emerged historically from distinct services or treatments for identifiable body systems or structures. Each profession has obvious limitations of education, scope of practice and experience. Medical doctors are concerned fundamentally with diseases, injuries and organic issues. Most would like to be more involved in overall patient health, but the reality is that society uses and rewards private practice and clinical doctors only for treatments, procedures, and related services. Therefore, their education concentrates almost exclusively upon diagnosis, injuries, surgery, and drugs. There is little about vitamins in medical education, and similarly little about neuro-musculoskeletal system.

As medical science becomes ever more specialized, the problem gets worse. Study after study has demonstrated that professionals will find a disproportionate and unreasonable volume of problems within their narrow area of expertise, since they lack the training and experience necessary to take an overview. Work at Harvard, Oxford and elsewhere dating back over a century, demonstrates that when autopsies are done, the error-rate of original diagnosis is as high as 80 percent. The general practitioner error is a problem of volume.

If the overwhelming number of patients have the same few problems, or the dominant external stimuli is about a narrow range of popular drugs, diagnostic bias moves in those directions. With specialists, a focus on symptoms frequently misses the root cause. The presumption of the health specialist is that the referring physician has the holistic view and correctly defined the needed treatment, but this is decreasingly true as family practice fades, and impersonal medical care grows.

The function of the spine and related nerve system is primarily the expertise of the chiropractic profession, as defined by government studies and Commissions around the world. Alberta legislation — *The Chiropractic Act* of 1923 — was the first in Canada and among the first in North America to formally recognize and regulate the profession.

Science and health professionals

Despite all of the high-level discussions concerning medicare, hospitals, technology, and science, health care remains predominantly a practitioner-patient paradigm. While individuals are encouraged to enhance their own wellness through lifestyle, healthy eating and exercise, we turn to health professionals in all disciplines when there is a need for information, counseling or care. Whatever the motivator be it disease, illness, accident, or discomfort of any kind, action ultimately requires the services of a health provider. Most commonly, this is the family physician or outpatient department of a hospital; but, in millions of cases each year in Canada, it is also a chiropractor, an industrial nurse, a paramedic, a dentist, a physiotherapist, a pharmacist, or others who may be the first contact. Other necessary help swings into gear once a problem is correctly defined: in rapid fashion, care becomes not a patient and "the system," it is a matter of an individual and a health provider, in an important, private interpersonal relationship. Primary contact with a chiropractor is usually through a referral from a family member, friend, or co-worker who has been satisfied with the health care they had received.

Critics of chiropractic regularly question the scientific foundation of the profession, oblivious, it seems, to the realization that very little of any health professional's practice is based upon science. Richard Smith, the editor of the *British Medical Journal*, wrote in 1998 that only 15 percent of all medical interventions were based upon science and that only between one and five percent of all treatments "reach scientific soundness and clinical relevance." Smith further debunked articles in medical journals, stating that only five percent of these achieved minimal scientific criteria, and fewer than one percent of alleged medical scientific reports in 20,000 other journals investigated worldwide. Yet medical doctors and their supporters regurgitate quotations from these questionable authorities to demonstrate that their daily work is based upon science.

A scientist beyond dispute (PhD in neurophysiology), a medical doctor and specialist (neurology) and Doctor of Chiropractic, is Scott Haldeman of Santa Ana, California. His grandfather, father, and brother-in-law were all chiropractors. Born in South Africa and raised in Canada, Haldeman acquired his medical degree at the University of British Columbia, and, in addition to the private practice of neurology, he is a professor at both the University of California, Irvine, and the University of California, Los Angeles (UCLA). He has authored one of the most important textbooks in the history of chiropractic.

In a 2000 speech, he addressed the topic of science and chiropractic. Dr. Haldeman said that relatively recent history has seen chiropractors widely accepted with high quality scientific meetings that are often co-sponsored by medical institutions. He cited the fact that meetings of the World Federation of Chiropractic are co-sponsored by the World Health Organization (WHO), and the creation of a WHO Collaborating Centre Task Force on the Cervical Spine and Related Disorders. "Chiropractic has moved rapidly from the outskirts into the mainstream of health care," he added. "The independent reviews of research and clinical practice by such agencies and commissions as the AHCPR (Agency for Health Care Policy and Research), the New Zealand commission, the Australian, Danish and British government guidelines for treating people with back pain or spinal problems have included input by chiropractic authorities and many of the procedures practiced by chiropractors have received favourable recommendation."

But, Dr. Haldeman also reminded the profession of how far it had come:

> Chiropractic, in its early stages, had some very colorful and interesting theoretical perceptions. The most widely quoted theory was that one could seek chiropractic care for anything that was wrong and that chiropractic would make it better. It was also widely believed that everybody should be seeing a chiropractor on a regular basis even if they were healthy. This concept led to the situation where chiropractors became outcasts to the medical system. These claims were often repeated in flamboyant advertising in newspapers and resulted in complete separation of chiropractic from the rest of the world of health care that was unable to accept this point of view without some research support.

And he issued this challenge:

> Today we are starting to enter the era where science is driving theory. Scientists and clinicians are developing new theory out of the scientific knowledge that is evolving. This new theory is based on the results of

prior scientific investigation. At the same time, clinical research is beginning to drive practice. What we are allowed to do in practice and what we will be permitted to do in practice in the future will be dependent upon what we can prove to be effective. Those methods of practice that are shown to be valid and effective will be permitted whereas those practices that are not shown to be valid will be discarded, not paid for, or discredited. This process of investigation should result in the development of new techniques as well as new methods of treatment. This is already happening in the practice of medicine and it's about to happen in chiropractic-science. This is going to start driving the direction of clinical practice as well as theory. If chiropractors do not accept this change many will find themselves in a kind of culture shock as the demands to follow this pattern pick up momentum. It must be realized that scientific research is forming the basis of the theories that direct further research and which therefore direct clinical practice. It should allow for an evolution of the thought process on how patients should be managed to the benefit of both patients and chiropractors.

Right now chiropractors can go before any audience and say that there is sufficient science to discuss the neurological and clinical effects of the adjustment. It is no longer credible for anyone to state that 'there is no scientific basis for spinal manipulation or the chiropractic adjustment'.

You and your spine

Common vernacular about the human back is almost entirely wrong. Since there are no laymen's terms to adequately explain back problems, we hear phrases such as "my back went out," or "I slipped a disk" or "I pulled a muscle." These phrases are entirely meaningless to a professional.

Critics focus on the word "subluxation" as used by chiropractors, an abbreviation of the term Vertebral Subluxation Complex (VSC). Subluxation is essentially a mechanical event or behavior of the joint components that has both local and remote influence on health and symptoms. This can be caused by unusual events or strain, such as car accidents, improper lifting, and work injuries. But common things such as emotional stress, nutritional deficiencies, poor posture, or sitting in front of a computer for a long time can bring on an occurrence. Patients' back problems occur from circumstances as routine as sleeping on a sofa or towel-drying one's hair. The action in these events includes an unusual motion or position of the spine or a portion of it. The effects become felt upon the associated tissues. Since the bone or vertebra do not have a clear pain sensation, the complaint is not that "my four and five lumbar are hurt" but rather that "my muscles" or "my leg" is sore. Many health problems, including subluxations, are subtle in the early stages of development. It's the same way that a cavity or heart problem can be overlooked before causing pain or other warning signs, a spinal problem may develop and exist for years before causing difficulties.

Neither the Oxford nor Webster's dictionaries attempt to define "subluxation," not unusual for medical and scientific terms. But a standard medical definition might be "partial dislocation without loss of contact between joint surfaces." But the chiropractic definition goes further: "a complex of functional and/or pathological articular changes that compromise neural integrity and may influence organ system function and general health." And thus the controversy.

The foundation of chiropractic is based upon the scientific understanding that human body functions are governed by the central nervous system, a conduit that mediates activities of body structures and other organs through the influence of its voluntary and involuntary subsystems. It is through such mediation that the central nervous system, namely, the brain and the spinal cord, detect abnormalities in the body, through manifestations such as the experience of pain. Chiropractic treatment, therefore, is directed at different body malfunctions through specialized positioning and adjustment procedures involving the spinal column and the associated nervous system.

Understanding the spine and nerve system is relatively simple in concept, but physically more difficult to envisage. It is not generally seen, felt, or touched. People don't complain about "lumbar" aches. Instead we hear about muscle pain, lumbago, disks, sciatica, strain, sprain, and a long list of other complaints, real or imagined, and related loss of activity or functions. The chiropractic view of the back begins with the 24 vertebrae between the head and pelvis. The spinal nerve roots, blood vessels, and other tissues including muscle, ligament, and disk are interrelated leading to many possible health outcomes. Cranial nerves for example, associated with the brain and skull, descend to the neck to join with nerves that leave the cervical spine. This anatomical knowledge is crucial if one wishes to understand chiropractic care. Numbness or tingling in the arm are clues to other concerns. While the source of difficulty may be an area of two or three vertebrae, too often health professionals treat the symptoms and not the cause.

Most people are aware of the importance and general role of the nerves of our body. The common understanding of spine problems involves the lower back (around our belt line). Over 100 years of clinical/patient experience provides clear knowledge of symptoms: loss of movement, muscle pain or spasm. Advance stages of the same problem, disk and nerve involvement, frequently cause numbness or tingling pain in the right or left leg. Despite the intransigence of the medical establishment, which continues to deny reality and fail patients, there is now no doubt at all anywhere about the most effective way to treat these conditions.

Among the most outstanding studies was the 1993 Manga Report (formally titled, *The Effectiveness and Cost-effectiveness of Chiropractic Management of Low-back Pain*), funded by the Ministry of Health of Ontario. The bibliography to this report had 400 references to reports and studies providing a comprehensive understanding of the condition, treatment, and outcomes. The study and outcomes associated with the diagnosis of the lower lumbar spine (subluxation) and the primary treatment (spinal adjustment) clearly demonstrate the best recovery for these conditions. There is less comprehension that the techniques so universally effective in treating the lower vertebrae, are of equal value for all 24 vertebrae of the spine, and a vast array of related neuro-musculoskeletal conditions.

The prime responsibility of any health professional is accurate diagnosis. It is more important, in fact, for any doctor, including chiropractors, to discover and understand what "not to treat" than it is to merely proceed with routine procedures. While many patients will make a primary visit to a medical doctor or a clinic for a "check-up," most first time visitors to a chiropractor arrive with a specific complaint. The chiropractor will attempt to obtain as detailed a personal health history as is possible. Patients are asked to perform common physical tests and movements to help identify the problem. A prognosis is made, taking into account general health habits, occupation, stress, and activity levels.

Radiographic studies (X-rays) may be indicated arising from the case history and presenting symptoms. An X-ray is invaluable but many chiropractors have been unduly influenced by patient cost concerns and the negative health warnings surrounding radiology. Utilization (radiation exposures per patient) is far higher among medical doctors and hospitals. Although a high percentage of chiropractic or spine conditions can be treated without the need of an X-ray, the assessment is always diagnostically beneficial to the understanding of structure and treatment options, and to rule out the presence of any pathological developments, particularly with respect to new patients. And, when symptoms indicate, or when patients do not properly respond to treatment, referrals are sometimes arranged for CT or MRI scans. Among the indicators of select conditions that may require referral are increasing neurological weakness of the patient and progressive loss of bladder and bowel function control.

The key determinant must be to ensure that the patient problem is not metabolic, vascular, or hormonal in origin, whether genetic or acquired. Some examples of such conditions include blood-related disorders, all forms of cancer, diabetes, and kidney failure, among others. There may be injuries requiring corrective action, either surgery or setting broken bones. Too often those describing the scope of chiropractic practice use the terms "organic condition" or "organic diseases" as the line between chiropractic and medicine. In fact, there is a substantial gray area in between, with collateral disorders arising from neuro-musculoskeletal origin.

Once a diagnosis is properly identified, a course of treatment will be proposed. This generally involves from 3–5 office visits provided within a short period, usually within 5–7 days. Most people feel a sense that something positive is happening during that period, but further care may be required to ensure proper and lasting results. The chiropractic doctor should also be a good teacher, advising about lifestyle, work habits, and exercises.

Here are a few examples of the conditions patients present to chiropractic offices:

- neck pain with headache, shoulder and/or arm numbness and tingling
- mid-back or thoracic pain with mechanical spasm or tightness on breathing
- low back pain with traditional findings of muscle pain
- disk-related conditions, nerve symptoms which may include leg pain, numbness and tingling, and on occasion increased frequency of urination

While there may be more than one cause for these conditions, the diagnosis and treatment outcomes will determine whether another doctor is necessary. The challenge in understanding which problem might be best treated by a chiropractor is knowledge about the spine-related neuro-anatomy.

Doctors of chiropractic do not treat major illnesses such as cancer and heart disease, but once they are assured that patients are receiving appropriate medical attention, chiropractic care can considerably ease ancillary discomfort patients may be suffering. Relief from pain, reduced stress, and increased relaxation can indirectly assist the body in its own efforts to heal. Similarly chiropractors consistently help patients suffering from asthma, including children.

The optimal situation is the all-too-rare harmonious relationships between chiropractic and medical doctors. Only through open-minded consultation between them can the total health of the patient best be determined. And in the most troublesome cases, co-operation would evolve into the kind of evidence-based practices beneficial to all, and indicate where proper scientific research might blaze new paths for everybody. Increasingly, knowledgeable patients and health insurers are becoming informed about chiropractic practices and expected outcomes. Medical doctors, who deliberately or unknowingly divert patients away from the treatments that could do them the most good, may run the risk of legal liability for the consequences.

Back surgery, traditionally, has been serious business with statistical risks far higher than hospitals and surgeons ever like to admit. Yet for many patients it has been the best option. Spinal fusions have been the most common surgical procedures for patients suffering from back and/or leg pain caused by damaged disks in the spine, but laminectomies are now far more common. This is the removal of part of a vertebra. As the body ages, the disks in the spine "dehydrate or dry out", and lose their ability to act as shock absorbers between the vertebrae. This condition is so common that by the age of 50, 85 percent of the population will show evidence of disk degeneration. Although most people with degenerative disks never experience problems, in some cases, surgery is required to relieve pain resulting from damaged or ruptured disks as a result of vertebrae compressing nearby nerves or spinal cord.

Sports fans have become aware of the wonders of arthroscopic surgery for knees and other joints, microscopically-sized penetrations into the affected area. Advanced arthroscopic spinal surgery is now increasingly commonplace, a minimally invasive procedure showing considerable success. Typically, a disk becomes herniated (ruptured), somewhat like "jelly squeezing out of a donut." Disk surgery removes the jelly, but not necessarily what caused the effect in the first in place. Vertebral deterioration occurs as some people age. In the past, when narrowing of bone joint space would interfere with the nerves, causing acute pain, the solution was sometimes to screw two vertebrae together. Today, arthroscopic techniques can remove the offending piece of disk or spur.

The chiropractic argument is simply that drugs and surgery should be recommended only after conventional and conservative treatments are found to have failed. At the primary care level, no one in the health field comes close to the detailed neuro-musculoskeletal education and experience required of doctors of chiropractic.

Chiropractic discipline

Regulatory bodies in each jurisdiction, usually called Colleges of Chiropractic, are charged with the responsibly of ensuring standards of education, information and practice. Patients are advised where to direct any concerns. In most provinces, there are public representatives on the College boards to help monitor the quality of patient care.

Exaggerated claims by some individuals in past decades, and undignified advertising, became issues requiring professional governance, because they impacted upon the image of all practitioners. In most jurisdictions, a typical advertising complaint focuses on the word "free." The professional standard does not want the basis of care, for any reason, to be primarily because it is free. As with other professions, billing irregularities and occasional sexual misconduct of practitioners comes under scrutiny. Publications and the web sites of chiropractic colleges and professional associations everywhere outline clear codes of conduct the public should expect, where to seek more information and how to properly register any complaints or concerns they might have.

Licensing boards are concerned about a few chiropractors who advocate unnecessary care. The vast majority of returning patients do so on an episodic basis as symptoms arise. The profession does encourage occasional check-ups, a quality and proactive approach for people of all ages, but the majority takes a dim view of colleagues who try to sign up all patients to long-term contracts without any demonstrable evidence to suggest the need.

Patients have a good sense about the care they need, and, in fact, the Canadian health system should demonstrate respect for them by placing far more trust in their judgment. Patronizing government is a disease in itself. Let people choose their preferred care providers rather than effectively railroading them in specific directions, through manipulation of public medicare and private insurance coverages, irrespective of whether it is the best choice for the condition.

Politicians have learned from the research of health economists that medical doctors will generate whatever business volume they need, irrespective of patient health, and therefore have feared that expanding coverage to other professionals would similarly invite business development excesses.

If 100 percent covered by medicare, would chiropractors do that? Human nature being what it is, we could assume that chiropractors and their patients would be no better or worse than anyone else, and likely drive up the frequency of service, perhaps beyond what is necessary. Aside from the obvious argument that chiropractor care is cheaper and more effective than the medical doctor alternative, Canadian experience presents a curious example. Until 1992, Saskatchewan residents had 100 percent coverage for chiropractic under medicare. Despite this, Saskatchewan's chiropractic patients averaged just eight visits each per year. The national average, irrespective of coverage, is between six and nine visits per patient per year. Cutting back coverage in Saskatchewan did not stop the long-term growth of the profession in that province and its patient base, but because far too many went to medical doctors after the restriction, Saskatchewan costs increased, rather than diminished, as a result of lessening chiropractic coverage. Medicare and private insurance records in other provinces demonstrate that patient access to chiropractors tends to be on a need basis, irrespective of coverage, and does not lend itself to the supplier-generated demand that concerns health economists about medical doctors.

Patients should study public information, including chiropractic web sites. Compare notes with friends. If it seems as if you or your family members are being asked to visit the chiropractor more often than what is necessary, you may be right. If so, you may be seeing a less than competent professional; a victim of excessive marketing; or, getting unnecessary care. Try a different chiropractic doctor.

Patients of all ages

There is an old joke of a doctor comforting the mother of a four-year-old child who had just suffered breaks and abrasions in a serious accident. The woman anxiously asks the prognosis and the physician replies, "We find that at that age, if all of the pieces are in the same room, they tend to grow back together just fine."

This is what concerns mainstream chiropractors about relatively recent marketing practices, in which families are encouraged to make indefinite numbers of office visits, beginning regular and contracted chiropractic care, even for young babies, where there is no clinical condition. While the concept of a "family chiropractor" is to be encouraged with the occasional check of all concerned, barring specific symptoms, the role ought to be an overview. Young children are remarkably healthy and pliable, and easily overcome routine health challenges.

But spine injuries or conditions occur at all ages. A difficulty impairing good care for the very young is the lack of meaningful communication about symptoms. While the majority of back conditions occur between the ages of 25 and 60, studies of younger populations are increasingly being done. A common example today is the prerequisite backpack carried at all times by school-aged children. Watch young people walking today, with or without their packs. A slight stoop has become habitual. Another factor is the highly physical life of the young, too frequently leading to sports injuries and accidents of varying origins. Periodic check-ups can be helpful in detecting correctable issues before permanent damage is done.

The consequences of these events are sadly too often dismissed with phrases such as "it's just growing pains" or "it will go away." Sometimes a professional consultant — if not treatment — is advisable. Too many adults, misled by medical folklore, also believe that all back problems will eventually heal themselves. A concept that is shown to be fundamentally flawed by health literature — which identifies that approximately 80 percent of persons experience back conditions during their life and at least 30 percent experience it daily — is the far too narrow view of "the back" rather than the neuro-musculoskeletal system. For years, medical associations and even distinguished journals advised doctors to inform patients that "research" had proven that most back problems go away in four weeks. No one ever stated where this so-called "research" had taken place. Certainly millions of back patients were mystified by it, particularly those who had unnecessarily been afflicted with inconsequential drugs and therapies waiting for this phantom cure to evolve.

In fact, a high percentage of back pain does go away. But whatever caused the difficulty in the first place remains like a time bomb. Since the "authorities" for the mysterious "research" accepted as gospel by the medical profession had never been identified, a chiropractic team in more recent history went out to trace the roots, sequentially working back through a number of medical journals asking each for the source of this quote. It was like the proverbial police search for truth, hearing only from the suspects, "some Dude done it!" Finally, one source was uncovered. It turned out to be a comment by one English physician, quoted in the *British Medical Journal*, that in his experience, most patients with back problems don't return after four weeks duration. It never dawned on him that a high percentage of these people didn't come back because they were not getting any benefit.

It also demonstrates how irresponsible much of the so-called "expert" health information can be. The proper advice is that any back condition that does not show improvement within three days should be referred for chiropractic examination. And the best advice to a chiropractor, if symptoms indicate or the patient does not satisfactorily respond to treatment, is to seek the help of a medical doctor in further assessing the problem.

Other controversies

Chiropractic neck manipulation has been the subject of widespread media, and grossly exaggerated criticism. This is dealt with at length in chapter 3, "Adverse Events," but the ill-researched critics unnecessarily alarmed the public suggesting a risk of stroke as a result of chiropractic care. Widely recognized as one of the safest, drug-free, surgery-free therapies available for the treatment of whiplash, neck pain, headaches, and other musculoskeletal conditions, one article published in the *Canadian Medical Association Journal* put the risk of stroke following neck adjustment at one in every 5.85 million adjustments. The most conservative study in the world established the risk at one in every 400,000 patients. Compare this to routine medical statistics: the risk of stroke from taking birth control pills has been determined to be one in 25,000, a risk considered too low to be publicly reported; the overall mortality rate for spinal surgery is one in 1,400; and, between four and nine out of every 1,000 patients entering an acute care hospital in Canada will die because of a preventable medical mistake.

Which of these facts should be the focus of alarmist media headlines?

Typical neck adjustments carried out by a qualified chiropractor are very safe and effective. In each case, the chiropractor will evaluate the need for the adjustment. It is estimated, that over a 10-year period, chiropractors in Canada performed over 134.5 million neck adjustments.

During the same 10-year period, only 23 reported cases of stroke could possibly be associated with the treatment. This extremely low occurrence cannot be matched by any medical procedure.

Middle ear infections – "Otitis media" is a generic name for several conditions that can affect the middle ear, including inflammation, ranging from acute to chronic and with or without symptoms. Acute otitis media is characterized by symptoms of pain and fever. Otitis media with effusion is typified by the presence of fluid in the middle ear without signs or symptoms of infection. Otitis media is the leading reason for visitation to a pediatrician's office. Millions of North American children up to the age of 15 visit physicians each year with these conditions. The predominant group is under the age of two. The usual course of treatment is a 10-day regimen of antibiotics, but increasing numbers of frustrated parents are bringing these children to chiropractors.

The condition requires a thorough chiropractic examination to first discover a subluxation, if any. If a problem is apparent, adjustment can frequently achieve relief. There is insufficient science to explain why, but it seems clear in these positive cases that the patient recovers in part due to fluid draining from the eustachian tube, which connects the neck and the middle ear. This would be a valuable area of medical-scientific-chiropractic research.

Migraines, sinusitis, and so-called "Type O" disorders – There is insufficient study and information to explain the relief many chiropractic patients get from a vast assortment of difficulties and it is improper to advertise that all persons may experience "cures." But when medical doctors criticize the profession for the unexplained, they fail to see that much of what they do that is successful cannot be explained either. Why does the body do what it does? And why does the same procedure work in some patients and not in others? At least chiropractors usually have an anatomic explanation based on considerable experience and both medical and chiropractic case histories — the body's nerve system interacting with organic processes.

Sticking one's head in the sand and trying to pretend what medical case histories confirm, is a disservice not only to the patients involved, but also to society itself. The challenge ought to be to document occurrences that cannot adequately be explained by science, and to then vigorously investigate the how and why to see if positive results can be consistently duplicated. Doctors of chiropractic and doctors of medicine often see the same patients with the same conditions. When successes occur, the facts are known in each doctor's files. Why deny results?

Immunization and vaccination – It is incorrect, as many prominent spokespersons for medicine allege, to state that the chiropractic profession is against immunization. The official position of the Canadian Chiropractic Association reads in part:

> Vaccination is well-established and widely mandated in public health policy. The public responsibility for vaccination and immunization is neither within the chiropractic scope of practice, nor a chiropractic specific issue. Public Health programming and literature provides additional sources of information for patient education dealing with protection, screening and promotional public health issues assisting with patient health and lifestyle concerns.

The elimination of major plagues has been among the greatest health victories of all time. Smallpox, polio, cholera, and many other genocidal calamities have been virtually eliminated. Widespread immunization against measles, chicken pox, mumps and influenza has also been effective, but against less deadly or threatening enemies. Many chiropractors believe so passionately in natural processes and the body's immunization system, they see these mass preventative efforts in a less than positive light. Immunization has created huge challenges for science, as viruses mutate to render ineffective many of the conventional cures. Chiropractors are citizens too, and they have a right to a personal opinion as individual citizens. In some circles, it is as bitter a debate as what invariably surrounds fluoridation of the water supply.

Miracles or, research yet to happen?

The biographies of just about every great scientist in history are replete with stories of how the affluent professional establishment of their day did everything in their power to make discoveries difficult. There is a responsibility of scientists and expert professionals in all fields to be cautious, protecting the public from fads, quacks and exploitation, but it is equally true, in any review of history, that the majority of the membership within each discipline were highly mediocre minds, who viewed any change as a.personal threat. They obviously worked hard to obtain whatever credentials they possessed — their key to success — and they lived careers of denial about any advance that may have happened around them.

All health professionals have witnessed mystifying situations, both positive and negative. Oncologists routinely see remissions of tumors defying all science and logic. Researchers in Alberta and British Columbia hospitals demonstrated a few years ago that comedy could achieve measurable improvement in the rates of healing. It was not the humor, obviously, but the positive mental attitude that enhanced healing. A researcher in the southern United States grew bored by the soft background music universally used to calm patients suffering from Alzheimer's and other dementias. She wondered if music could play any role at all in managing the disease. Her idea was to research the music these individuals loved best when they were vigorous and healthy. By systematically playing this personalized music, a double-blind study earned her world attention. Not only were her patients calmer than the placebo group, in time, measurable positive statistics were recorded to demonstrate that the pace of debilitation had slowed.

As old as time, parents have taught children mind over matter. On a more startling level, universities have conducted research on the great psychics such as Peter Hurkos, David Young of England, Uri Geller, and others. Phenomena beyond the ability of scientific explanation were satisfactorily demonstrated — repeatedly — to skeptical and learned scientists. Vancouver psychologist, professor, and businessman Dr. Lee Pulos once had a public encounter with the Israeli Uri Geller, in which Geller demonstrated kinetic power to bend spoons. Thousands of people phoned a radio show to report that clocks that hadn't worked for years jumped ahead or behind an hour, or simply started ticking without batteries, winding or apparent reason.

It was great entertainment, but was it real? In a public debate years later, a gleeful academic confronted Pulos with the report that Uri Geller had been caught faking on a British television show. Pulos replied, "so what?" His adversary was perplexed. Pulos explained to the effect that if Geller faked his trick thousands of times, the failure would still be meaningless. "If he was able prove it once — just once — and confirmed by science to be so, it would mean that everything you believe about the force of nature to be wrong." Pulos then explained that Geller and many other examples of paranormal abilities have had it scientifically confirmed not once, but many times over, proving only that existing science was, at best, incomplete.

Scientists ridiculed faith healers, gypsies, mystics, and Chinese therapists when they described an energy field around the human body. It was great fun to debunk these people until the Russians invented Kirlian photography and captured the aura, which abruptly ceased to be a phenomenon. Modern imaging has taken this light years further.

Great minds view the unknown as an opportunity. The weak ones are challenged by anything they cannot explain. Any medical doctor who is honest with himself must admit a sense of awe about the amazing, indefinable things that happen with frequency within health care. Because chiropractors work with the essence of the nerve system, the most skilled among them see these startling circumstances, if not every day, then certainly with frequency. And medical doctors who see these same patients are also fully aware of these results. Leaders within the chiropractic profession have consistently advocated a much better job of systematically recording these events, not merely as anecdotes to tell the next patient in similar circumstances, or to make small talk at professional conventions, but to parcel the thousands of anecdotes into solid research assignments.

How beneficial it could be to patients and society if all health care disciplines and the university-based scientists would work together to explore the mysteries for the benefit of future generations. Instead, the medical associations use all of their influence, assisted by the bottomless pockets of the pharmaceutical industry, to block the development of the chiropractic profession, and to oppose efforts to merge chiropractic colleges with mainstream universities, where they could work with the greatest scientists and laboratories.

Unfortunately, if there is not a wonder drug at the end of the road these days, there is usually little research money available. Big Pharma and their medical colleagues call the shots at too many universities.

"The biographies of just about every great scientist in history are replete with stories of how the affluent professional establishment of their day did everything in their power to make discoveries difficult. There is a responsibility of scientists and expert professionals in all fields to be cautious, protecting the public from fads, quacks and exploitation, but it is equally true, in any review of history, that the majority of the membership within each discipline were highly mediocre minds, who viewed any change as a personal threat. They obviously worked hard to obtain whatever credentials they possessed — their key to success — and they lived careers of denial about any advance that may have happened around them."

Dr. Pran Manga

15.

The Health Economist

*Those with no knowledge of history shall
be children forever.*

— ARNOLD TOYNBEE, *British historian*

On April 9, 1984, the day the House of Commons unanimously
passed the *Canada Health Act*, a government limousine pulled up
in front of a modest Ottawa town home. Mr. Speaker had sent the car to
bring a special guest to witness the proceedings that day, one who had
been intimately involved in the process leading to the legislation.

Coincidentally, during the gestation period and passage of the
Canada Health Act, Mr. Speaker was an economist with a Master's
degree from the University of Toronto, a PhD from the University of
Wisconsin and several years service as a senior economist within Health
and Welfare Canada. Dr. Lloyd Francis was among the most respected
Parliamentarians ever to be elected Speaker of the House.

Terms as an Ottawa city council member and Deputy Mayor were
followed by a strange career path in federal politics. Francis ran in an
Ottawa riding dominated by civil servants, winning precisely every second election over a considerable span of history. Liberals and the New
Democratic Party alternated victories in the riding. Francis, far more
accomplished than most MPs, hurt his Liberal cabinet chances by
speaking forthrightly on issues, even if his views were contrary to those
of the government. But he won the respect of all, and became an enthusiastic unanimous choice when his name went forward to become
Speaker in 1983. (A postscript to his all-party appeal came after the
Brian Mulroney sweep of 1984, when he again lost his Ottawa seat. The
Conservative Prime Minister appointed him to be Canada's Ambassador
to Portugal).

In the national political scheme of things, the Speaker is thought to
somewhat of a eunuch in the harem, occupying a largely ceremonial

position, but in biographical notes prepared by Gary Levy for the Library of Parliament, the Ottawa status of the Speaker is "the Mayor of Parliament Hill." He commands at least six major buildings, all Parliamentary staff and resources, a restaurant, five cafeterias, a magnificent library, a printing plant, a broadcasting service, a computer network, a security force, a barbershop, a messenger and minibus service and, most vitally, the assignment of offices and infrastructure (whether an MP is at the heart of things or in a distant Siberia). He or she lives like royalty within the Parliamentary complex and at a country retreat in Gatineau Park, across the river in Quebec.

Dispatching a limousine for a guest of the VIP section of the Public Gallery was a simple gesture, but also a measure of Dr. Francis' thoughtfulness. He had a health economist's view of the work that had gone on within Health Canada leading to this vote. Some cabinet ministers and MPs must have wondered that day, whom this distinguished guest might be and what was his role in the story. Small in physical stature, dark-skinned and of obvious East-Indian extraction, Pran Manga had been in Canada for over 20 years. Never had he been so proud. Francis had told him that unanimity in a social policy matter as profoundly important as the *Canada Health Act*, was virtually unprecedented.

Little did the parliamentarians know that the visitor had been an important cog in a big wheel, reporting to Dr. Rick Van Loon (now president of Carleton University), then a deputy to super-minister Jean Chretien, who was responsible for the government's social agenda; as well as Health Minister Monique Begin. When Dr. Maureen Law was the Deputy Minister of Health, one of her tasks was to convert the Hall Report to a new national health policy, essentially a consolidation and revision of the 1966 statutes. The Act followed bitter federal-provincial disputes during the late 1970s and the advent of balanced-billing by many medical doctors. Government once again appointed Justice Emmett Hall to study the issues and propose solutions. During this critical 1979–81 period, Dr. Manga served as Acting Director General for Health and Social Policy within Health Canada, and continued this work as a national research fellow at the University of Ottawa. He left Canada for several months in 1982 to advise the Health Minister of Zimbabwe, but he was back at the University of Ottawa to see the research he had assembled and the original policy papers he had drafted metamorphosize into the historic legislation of 1984.

Manga's outline had been a 32-page brief that can be seen today to be the core of the *Canada Health Act*, but he credits Dr. Van Loon with principal authorship: "Rick was a masterful writer. Shrewd. He knew the politics behind everything, including the health crisis in Canada. A trusted advisor to Chretien, he had a significant role in the preparation of the cabinet document that laid out the need for the CHA."

But Speaker Lloyd Francis made sure that Pran Manga's vital role was at least acknowledged.

Health economists

Canada's medicare was bold in design and deliberately experimental in operation. It was initially an attempt to synthesize hospital insurance programs that varied from province to province, but which had a long history, with the younger and less consistent approaches to cover medical services, including doctors. It fascinated the world. Canada set out to provide blanket coverage to everybody, irrespective of financial ability, without any fees attached and, furthermore, to make it impossible to purchase VIP standards of care for all "covered" items. What made it so unique was the determination to make sure this apparently socialist nirvana remained essentially free-enterprise. Doctors would still be independent practitioners, business centres within themselves, and they would negotiate fees on a province-wide basis just as in any labor contract. But there would be one common national insurer, eliminating considerable overhead and uncertainty about payment.

The paradox between socialized and private medicine fertilized a profession in which Canada would attain global significance. We spawned a generation of health economists who are among the foremost practitioners in the world. For 25 years, the research and conclusions of these experts, most university-based, helped evolve health policy.

The earliest chink in the medicare armor came in the funding formula. Initially, the sharing used the *Canada Assistance Act* model, a 50-50 federal provincial split of covered services. The regulations under the act determined what was covered. Provinces could then structure services. Anything in a hospital was covered. The challenge to bureaucrats at the provincial level then became a game of moving uncovered items under the roof of a hospital. A notable example was psychiatric services, which were not initially covered by the federal plan. Whole mental hospitals were moved to acute care facilities in order to obtain the 50-50 arrangement.

Once this flaw was properly diagnosed, health economists, including Dr. Pran Manga, went to work on a better system. Legislation laid the framework for what exists today. General guidelines were established for an evenness of care from coast to coast and per capita estimates of costs, region to region. An annual allotment to each province was agreed upon and the provinces would be free to manage the money as they saw fit and augment service wherever they wished. Penalties were established for non-compliance by any province in the national standards.

Good management prevailed throughout the 1970s. There were few complaints. Canadians became the envy of the world. Doctors, who initially opposed medicare as a socialist plot, started to become the greatest supporters. But they demanded more money and the freedom to charge extra for their services to patients if they so desired. A series of major national studies led to the *Canada Health Act* of 1984.

The "father" of the health economist profession in Canada was — indisputably — Dr. Malcolm Taylor of York University, who worked with Justice Emmett Hall from the beginning. For more than a generation, the acknowledged "Dean" has been Dr. Robert Evans of the University of British Columbia, who has also authored countless numbers of papers and who has served on a Royal Commission. Evans and his protégés Dr. Morris Barer of UBC and Dr. Greg Stoddart of McMaster have categorically demonstrated — repeatedly — the validity and impact of supplier-induced demand. They prove the utilization of doctors' services has more to do with the physician business development interests than it does with either patient health or community need. Stoddart is also an acknowledged expert in the economic factors related to epidemiology.

Other "stars" of the profession include Dr. Peter Ruderman, a Harvard-educated University of Toronto professor who has advised the World Bank, the World Health Organization, and several nations; and, Dr. John Horne, an economist with the School of Medicine at the University of Manitoba, who also served several years as Chief Operating Officer of Winnipeg's large Health Sciences Centre. Dr. Raisa Deber of U of T is an expert in health policy and Dr. Richard Plain of the University of Alberta has done valuable work with respect to physicians' user fees. Dr. Lee Soderstrom of McGill and Dr. Andre-Pierre Contandriopoulos of the University of Montreal are prominent in Quebec. Dr. Jack Boan was Saskatchewan's leading health economist and his expertise was invaluable when economic considerations forced the government of that province to close 150 hospitals and replace them with some of the most comprehensive and effective community health centres anywhere. Dr. Boan was instrumental in the formation of the

Canadian Health Economics Research Association, during the early 1980s, to share ideas and matters of common interest.

In the field of pharmaceuticals, Dr. Joel Lexchin, a professor in the U of T School of Medicine, who occasionally still does shifts as an emergency room physician, is the leading economic authority on the pharmaceutical industry. He has consistently decried Canada's abandonment of compulsory licensing of pharmaceuticals, which negotiated national deals for the sale and manufacture of all prescription drugs in the country. As a small nation, he argued that we should not be granting multinationals 20-year exclusive patents. His reports demonstrate that a high percentage of drugs paid for by government and individuals go into the toilet or the garbage; or, worse still, these drugs get improperly prescribed, or dangerously mixed with other chemicals.

Dr. Manga heralds Lexchin's work and takes it a step farther. He describes the so-called "Shamrock Summit" in Quebec City when President Ronald Reagan and Prime Minister Brian Mulroney sealed the North American Free Trade Agreement, as "The Sham Summit." Manga said that Mulroney's sell-out to Big Pharma was a national disgrace, based on phony evidence of promised jobs and research. Like other experts, Manga points out that any investment Big Pharma makes in Canada is for research cheaper than they could do elsewhere, subsidized by Canadian tax write-offs. We were far better off as a nation before the pharmaceutical patents deal.

These are but a few of the leading names. Paradoxically, along with medicare itself, the prominence of health economists within the planning and policy process seems to have eroded. Since 1990, the political agenda began to suffocate expertise. In his first day as finance minister, Paul Martin viewed the national debt and deficit as the nation's highest priority. Unchecked, this would kill all programs. He assessed provincial fiscal health as superior to the federal position, and unilaterally made huge cuts in transfer payments. Martin's success rescuing Canada from the basement of G8 national economies to become best in the world, has been an undeniable triumph, but intelligent management of health and social programs was the principal casualty.

Martin's war on the deficit set off a domino effect beginning in every provincial treasury and then down through the system. An era of crisis management began, everybody desperately clinging to the lifeboat, trying to salvage as much as possible in terms of routine operations. Since suppliers (doctors, hospitals) and consumers (patients) had unlimited scope to generate demand and costs, system managers have been in a defensive shock for 10 years or more, cutting and constraining wherever possible. Instead of reasoned studies of experience and options, our health policy became — and remains — a knee-jerk war between governments, ill-informed politicians, self-serving professionals, bureaucrats, health unions and various insurers. Every debate boils down to who pays how much to whom. Despite disingenuous speeches about concern for the public, the angst is really just territorial. It serves the purpose of all vested interests to have ignorant and dependent leadership.

This country's small community of health economists — some of them with a world reputation — sat angrily on the sidelines while medicare sank into public ignominy and chaos. Pran Manga has been among them. From his first Canadian mentor, the father of Canada's medicare, Tommy Douglas, to his friend and fellow health economist, Dr. Lloyd Francis, Speaker of the House of Commons, no one had been closer to the intellectual framework behind Canadian policy.

Rebel with a cause

Pranlal Manga was born in the Legislative capital of South Africa, Pretoria, in 1944. His ancestors had been shipped from Gujarat Province, on India's west coast, midway through the nineteenth century to become indentured workers on sugar plantations in the Zulu homeland, Natal Province. By the time Pran was born, the family had relocated and his father had progressed to the status of merchant, albeit a very humble one, a "hawker" with a small truck selling fruit and vegetables door-to-door in Pretoria. It was a great occasion during his childhood when his father acquired a treasured "licence" from the Afrikaner government, able to open up a permanent store in a market location. In the apartheid world of South Africa, Indians were officially categorized as "Asians" or "coloured," along with various communities with mixed or ambiguous pedigrees. While victims of discrimination with carefully controlled limits in opportunity, the "coloureds" were a step above blacks (more than 80 percent of the national population).

Pran Manga began work in his father's market stall at the age of 10 and credits his years of work experience as vital in his later career as an economist. He attended Pretoria Indian High School and set records in two areas: the poorest attendance and the highest grades. His teachers, not one of whom had ever attended university, could not command his attention. It was too easy. Much to the distress of his father, Pran's hero was his uncle, Nana Sita, a legendary name in the South African independence movement, possibly the most famous of all of the disciples of Mohandas K. Ghandi, who had first attained world prominence resisting the British in South Africa. Sita was a fearless adherent to the Ghandian culture of passive resistance, and became, in later years, among Nelson Mandela's most important mentors, and a partner in "the long walk to freedom." Nana Sita was jailed several times for resistance activities.

Through Sita, and with Sita's children — his cousins — daughter Maniben Sita and son Ramlal Bhoolia, the student Pran Manga remembers attending a rally at which Mandela was a speaker. "Nelson was a Xhosa chief, aristocracy by blood, and he was treated with reverence and great respect. He wasn't a very good speaker in those days, but everybody applauded anyway, because he was so important." Manga was disappointed that his fellow students, who suffered the racist government policies, were not more vocal. "The students were not very active because they were afraid." Matters became increasingly brutal after South Africa was humiliated by a relentless series of United Nations sanctions during the early 1960s and condemnations within the British Commonwealth for apartheid. The country quit the Commonwealth in 1961. Pran's cousin Ramlal Bhoolia studied law with Nelson Mandela, and for many years provided a huge amount of pro bono legal work for the African National Congress.

During Pran's formative years, there was but one rich Indian doctor for a community of about two thousand, and he callously overcharged the population. On one occasion, after treatment by this doctor for tonsillitis, Pran later learned that the fees paid by his father equaled a month's income for the family. He subsequently tried to suffer in silence and hide symptoms, rather than be the cause of such a financial burden. But injuries attained when police broke up a protest rally were impossible to hide. One day he was sought out by a group of policemen, and badly beaten. When he returned home he was bleeding from the ear.

Manga's father was typical of the successful Indian and Jewish merchant communities all around the world. They learned to live quietly, appear to accept the status quo, and get on with their lives. "My father said that democracy is when they leave you alone," Manga recalls. It was not surprising then, that the family was not only worried about young Pran's increasing interest in politics, but also the impact it might have upon the family and the business. It was suggested that Pran might follow others — including his brother — who had sought opportunities abroad. The situation was such that it was unlikely that he would be permitted by the Afrikaner authorities to attend a post-secondary institution.

Fresh with stellar graduation results from Pretoria Indian High School, he applied to emigrate to the usual targets for his countrymen: the Netherlands (Afrikaans is similar to Dutch), Germany (close to Dutch), France (often welcoming), England (shared history, also a familiar language, and the country that took most of the refugees), the United States and Canada. Only Canada, where a brother had preceded him and could act as guarantor, responded positively to Pran Manga's application.

He arrived in Canada and became lost at Toronto airport. He and his brother couldn't find each other. But he had the address and set off in a cab, realizing too late that he had insufficient funds to pay the fare. Pran offered the driver his meagre goods in payment, but the cabbie declined, accepting the loss in good cheer and wishing him luck. Although he had no money, he had an introduction from Uncle Nana Sita to a famous Canadian who would appreciate the significance, Rev. T.C. Douglas. Not only was Sita one of the international icons of social struggle and justice, studied by the most learned of Canada's New Democratic Party philosophers, (and pre-1960, the Co-operative Commonwealth Federation), but the respect was mutual. Tommy Douglas was greatly admired by the South African rebels as a model for putting philosophy into social action, particularly medicare in Saskatchewan in 1947.

Pran Manga's concerns were more immediate. His brother was a school teacher, and he helped Pran find work as a laborer in various jobs, from auto salvage to window cleaning. When he finally had a chance to meet Tommy Douglas, the 1963 election campaign was in progress and Manga was dispatched to go canvassing in the Kitchener-Waterloo area on behalf of Max Saltzman, a prominent member of NDP, who was successful.

It didn't take him long to realize that he had come to a special place. "My first experiences in Canada were marvellous — you fall in love with this country instantly," he said in a 2004 interview. "You grow up in a racially segregated health system where no Indians could go to a white hospital, although there was a much inferior Indian wing in one of the local hospitals. This was one of the worst things a person can experience, but then you meet someone like Tommy Douglas, whom I've always regarded as the father of medicare."

Serendipity

The timing of his exit from South Africa, the welcome to Canada, the strategically located and established brother, the generous taxi driver, the relationship to an international icon and the personal introduction to a legendary Canadian, were fortuitous circumstances for the 19-year-old immigrant, but what was to follow in efforts to obtain an education proved to be positively serendipitous.

South Africa was "big" in the public mind of that era. Canada had been playing a leading role in international affairs, never more proudly than in the years following the Nobel Prize awarded Lester B. Pearson for his work ending the Suez Crisis. Within the British Commonwealth of Nations, it was Prime Minister John G. Diefenbaker who led the charge against racist South Africa. Diefenbaker, sometimes a mean-spirited conservative in terms of fiscal policy, had always been a renowned champion of human rights and the dignity of each individual. Diefenbaker's pressure coerced South Africa's resignation from the Commonwealth.

Pran Manga was a curiosity everywhere he went, pumped for stories about his homeland. But he worked hard to eke out a living. He couldn't afford to even dream of paying university tuition. However, a family friend, also a South African Indian, was studying electronics at Ryerson College. He knew of Pran's outstanding academic record from Pretoria and started the process of getting him enrolled there. He could afford this if he lived with his brother and did some work on the side. But while this was going on, he heard of an open house at Hamilton's McMaster University and he took advantage of the opportunity. During the course of this visit he met and conversed with an engineering professor, Dr. Ernst Gadamer, who took a liking to the enthusiastic newcomer. The professor urged Pran to take the university's general "Aptitude Exam," a procedure used in those years to assess individuals with unconventional academic backgrounds, and to subsequently invite the best candidates to enroll. Manga passed with flying colors, among the highest scores recorded, and his sponsoring professor was very persuasive.

Money was an issue. Tuition was $150 at the time. Books could double that. He wouldn't be able to live with his brother. During the course of these worries, Professor Gadamer arranged for Pran to attend a meeting of the McMaster Engineers' Wives Association, where he gave a little talk about South Africa and his advent in Canada. At the conclusion of the meeting, the Association voted to give him a $300 bursary, a fortune at the time. He enrolled in first year engineering, delighting his sponsoring professor, and he started scouting the area for part-time jobs.

But everything was a worry. Books could cost as much as tuition but there was no choice. As he stood in line at the campus bookstore, with a large pile of second hand textbooks, waiting to pay, he conversed with an obviously affluent American student. At the cash register, Pran was stunned when the American paid for all his books. "For me, it was a big embarrassment," he recalls. But the young American became a friend and the gratitude for that moment remains to this day.

Manga settled into first year engineering and he got a job at Hamilton's largest employer, the Steel Company of Canada, becoming a member of the United Steelworkers of America union. He did well in all his courses, but had little feeling for the sciences so essential as an engineering foundation. He excelled in math and the social sciences, particularly economics where he recorded the highest grade among several hundred students. Following the first year, he was encouraged by his economics professor to pursue that discipline, rather than engineering. He was very relieved when his mentor, engineering Professor Ernst Gadamer, concurred with and supported the shift.

A valuable sidelight to the undergraduate years at McMaster was the work at Stelco and later Dofasco, where he learned about worker safety and health issues, frequently involved in matters related to injury and workers' compensation. After an Honors Bachelor's degree in economics, several scholarships and fellowships and a Master's from McMaster, Manga acquired the first in a series of endowments and fellowships to work toward his PhD at the University of Toronto. From the outset, he derived income from U of T as a part-time lecturer.

Once again, in 1970, Tommy Douglas was to play a pivotal role in his life. He had finished all of his comprehensive course work and examinations leading to the PhD, but Douglas suggested that Pran concentrate on health economics, "because we have lots of macropolicy experts and too few in social policy, especially health." Manga recalls that he then read "a few thousand pages on the history of medicare and health policy/economics generally to teach myself the subject." Douglas also suggested that Manga should go to Manitoba and work in the NDP government of Premier Ed Schreyer. But that attempt failed because a highly placed American in that government who interviewed him thought, "I was not left-wing enough."

A bigger opportunity came along soon after. Health and Welfare Canada hired him to work in Ottawa as a "Hospital Cost Analyst" in a project he intended to be his PhD thesis. He was verbally assured at the outset that this would be proper. For two years he studied all hospital economic issues and public finance implications, hospital insurance programs, the nature of hospital cost inflation and the cost-benefit analyses of expenditures. In 1973 he moved to Treasury Board as a policy analyst. But when he sought to submit his thesis to the University of Toronto in 1974 he was denied permission by his government superiors, because the work was "confidential." Pran was angry at the time, but it was a valuable lesson: "I learned to get things in writing."

He quit the federal post for an exciting challenge that was to dominate his time. This ultimately led to another PhD thesis. He was retained by the Ontario Economic Council to head-up the health portfolio. The Ontario assignment grew to involve many of the best health economists from coast to coast in Canada, including most who would become superstars in this specialized field. "We initiated about 20 major studies in social policy," Manga remembers. "It was a wonderful opportunity for me to meet all of the experts. We seemed to hire them all, for one project or another." Finally, in 1976, he published a thesis on the topic of the utilization of hospital and medical insurance programs in Ontario, earning his PhD in economics from U of T.

And then there was another fascinating side-trip. Manga had an opportunity to spend a year working in Ottawa's most controversial office, the Anti-Inflation Board. Inflation had become the number one political issue in Canada during the early 1970s and Prime Minister Pierre Trudeau implemented wage and price controls. Manga worked for David Dodge, then a rising star in the bureaucracy, who later served as deputy minister in both finance and health, now the Governor of the Bank of Canada. "David was the best of the best. Intelligent. Honest. Fair, and determined to do every job right. It was a privilege to have worked with him," Manga says.

Following this assignment, Pran Manga joined the business faculty of the University of Ottawa, exclusively engaged in research projects with funding from Health and Welfare Canada. National Research Scholarships were renewed for 12 years in succession, along with many other assignments. Manga has been at the university ever since, a full professor since the mid-1980s, and one of the two most widely published academics in a faculty of 80 professors. As a consultant, he has worked all around the world. There have been 11 separate assignments in the Peoples' Republic of China, including one for the World Health Organization. He has worked in Egypt, Zimbabwe, Ghana, India, Hungary, Costa Rica and Hong Kong and lectured to prestigious groups in countless numbers of countries from Australia to the United States, and from the United Kingdom to other European centres. But he has never stopped being a student. Pran Manga obtained a Master of

Philosophy Degree from the University of Wales in 2001, with a thesis making a case for physician-assisted suicide in Canada.

The coincidences in his life never stop. In 2004, the professor in the office next to his within the School of Management at the University of Ottawa was Monique Begin, who was the Minister of Health during the passage of the *Canada Health Act* in 1984.

What's wrong with medicare?

Dr. Pran Manga cites a number of serious malignancies that have sapped the potential of medicare, largely creating today's crisis:

- **The senior people do not put the public interest first and foremost.** They put the special interests first. Federal and provincial leaders fight for budget. Once acquired, every bureaucratic interest has a bite at it. Then follows regions, hospitals and professional associations, each with an insatiable shopping list. It is amazing that anything ever gets to the patient, always the lowest priority in a real sense. The patients' most useful role is to justify the building of empires and bank accounts.

- **From the outset, the phrase "medically necessary services" was never intended to be the exclusive domain of medical doctors.** The Act does not preclude coverage of other health professionals and each of them, within their special niche, would save money and improve results — dramatically so. But, from the beginning, the Canadian Medical Association has put its own definition on the CHA wording. They and the provincial associations seem always able to hijack the process and secure relative exclusivity, a system that guarantees the most expensive approaches possible for each problem, no matter how minor, and duplication of costs as the MD gatekeepers hand off to others.

- **Governments can't seem to grasp the word "substitution"** when different services are considered. Study after study shows that if nurse practitioner, optometric, chiropractic and other highly specialized regulated professions are used, costs per patient go down and outcomes improve. Drug utilization and rates of surgery decline. Yet politicians and bureaucrats see these as "additional" costs if they are not now covered and potential cost-cutting targets, if they are currently part of the program.

■ There is far, **far too much bureaucracy.** Each health practitioner seems to carry an army of paper pushers on his or her shoulders.

■ There is **insufficient competition because of medical, dental and pharmaceutical monopolies.** Manga often cites the fact that British Columbia has the lowest rates for dental hygiene services than anywhere in Canada, simply because it is the only province which doesn't give dentists an absolute monopoly on their services. B.C. hygienists are the only ones permitted to have an independent practice. In dental colleges, hygienists are professors. Manga says, "the dentists say to the hygienist that you can be my professor, but in the real world, you have to be my employee." The notion that there is any vital health prerogative for teeth-cleaning to be a monopolistic preserve of dentists is preposterous, a political gift to an already wealthy profession.

■ Despite overwhelmingly positive statistics from multidisciplinary community health centres employing nurse practitioners, physicians (usually on salary) and other health professionals as needed, **there has been too little progress on expanding the mode of care**, again because of opposition from the medical profession.

■ **Home care, convalescent hospitals and small surgi-centres should be dramatically expanded**, each with the aim of restricting acute care hospitals to only the most serious of all cases, but this must be done with political courage, eliminating all unnecessary personnel and infrastructure as soon as they become redundant. Acute care hospitals and trauma centres are not in the health and healing business, but focused on procedures, serious illness and emergencies. Convalescent patients or those with minor conditions simply get in the way and become vulnerable to the adverse events that haunt big hospitals.

■ **Pharmaceutical utilization and costs are out of control**, with about half of the $22 billion annual expenditure a complete waste. "You cannot possibly consider a pharmacare program if you have a bad system. ...the system has to be fixed first." Any consideration of pharmacare before addressing core issues would be profoundly stupid with predictably devastating consequences.

- Manga says **good policies work if the leaders are prepared to be tough.** Lamentably, that is too rarely the case. It is easier to coast along tinkering with the status quo. There has been no shortage of good ideas for health reform, but a lack of political will.

- Too often, the search for ideal, unanimous and even perfect solutions prevents any improvements from taking place. "The best is always the enemy of the good," he said. **"Progress gets lost in minutiae."**

Manga says the health economists of the country have diverse opinions, sometimes opposed to one another:

> While we don't always agree, there is a commonality of viewpoint about good health policy. We believe that medicare is basically good and could be improved through health care reform. And I am sure all of the economists would agree that the 'comprehensiveness' clause in the Canada Health Act is the one the government failed on hopelessly. That is that services other than medical doctors should be viewed as 'substitution' not simply an 'addition'. The best evidence we are right is the determination of medical associations to prevent this expansion of coverage — they know that it means a shift of business away from them. But the policy makers just don't get it! Cost-effective human resources substitution is the most neglected health care reform in Canada.

The Manga Report

When Dr. Pran Manga accepted an assignment from the Ontario Ministry of Health in 1993, he had no idea that this routine contract would become his Passport into the health industry's version of apartheid, a professional blacklist of those who do not conform to the medical associations' self-proclaimed supremacy, enhanced by a sycophantic bureaucracy in Ottawa and the provincial capitals.

Manga's conclusions in the 1993 report, prepared with the help of Doug Angus and others and updated in 1998, are reported in chapter 11, "Outcomes or Incomes?" He constructed a professional matrix to incorporate every study that had ever been done into the outcomes related to medical doctors treating patients with a range of neuro-musculoskeletal problems within the normal scope of chiropractic, and the results of chiropractic care. The report exhaustively explained the methodology. The bottom-line was that Ontario could save anywhere from $380 million to $770 million million a year (1998 version) if policies were established to encourage chiropractic care as the preferred treatment for neuro-musculoskeletal conditions. (Media were quick to use Manga's average Ontario number, described as a "likely" annual saving of $548 million, and calculate that this policy could mean $2.2 billion savings if adopted nationally). Before this report was released to the public, the highly respected Tom Wells, a former health, education and intergovernmental affairs minister of Ontario, chaired a committee to review the study, with inputs from unbiased expertise. *The Wells Report* became an unsolicited but powerful endorsement of both the research and the chiropractic profession.

The Manga Report as it became known, was a cause celebre. Dr. Manga was not surprised that it upset the medical profession. He was amazed that bureaucrats and policy makers did not enthusiastically take it further, either an attempt to thoroughly test his conclusions or to embrace its findings, particularly since the special committee which reviewed and assessed the work, found it to be substantially sound and defensible. Subsequent studies confirmed these basic findings. But the biggest surprise of all was that it thrust him into a distracting international stardom. He became a hero to chiropractors worldwide, invited to speak at conventions and seminars everywhere. There hasn't been any serious work about chiropractic anywhere in the world — nor any professional Internet web site — since 1993, that does not quote Canada's Pran Manga.

The absurdity is best demonstrated by a 2003 event in which the Canadian Centre on Health Technology Assessment commenced a study on chiropractic. It was proposed that Manga, the leading health economist in the world with respect to this topic, be part of the review. The appointment was opposed by just one person, the Deputy Minister of Health from Newfoundland, a medical doctor. All provinces were involved and the sponsoring agency decided to avoid a confrontation on any one appointment. Manga, who has consistently turned down honors, financing and assignments that might impugn an appearance of impartiality, said, "I am acutely concerned that everything associated with my work be seen as objective, scholarly and professional, because anything I write or say will be very thoroughly critiqued by the critics of chiropractic."

Dr. Robert Cushman, the medical health officer for the City of Ottawa, describes Dr. Manga as ""a gifted teacher. . .thanks to this classroom experience, I have been able to construct sound and comprehensive arguments for the cost-effectiveness of specific disease prevention interventions."

But the following testimonial from a distinguished colleague underscores the respect Manga has earned during his long career. Dr. Gilles Paquet, a professor emeritus at the University of Ottawa, author of over 30 books and hundreds of papers, a member of the Order of Canada and president of the Royal Society of Canada, had this to say:

> I have known Pran Manga for over 25 years. He was National Health Research Scholar before I hired him at the University of Ottawa. His expertise ranges from economics to policy analysis, to ethics, and he has been one of the very few in Canada who have been able to combine these diverse perspectives and bring them to bear on a wide variety of thorny technical and moral issues that have plagued the health field. By tackling controversial and complex issues, he has at times ruffled some feathers. But he has never entered any issue area without throwing new light on such issues and without suggesting original responses to old and new problems. His work is highly regarded as objective, careful, impartial, and innovative scholarship. This has not prevented him from being deeply committed to the transformation and improvement of the health field. He has done it with passion but never to the detriment of his scholarship. Clear-headedness and courage are not incompatible in the life of a scholar. And I have never felt that his stand on controversial issues have tainted in any way the credibility of his scholarly endeavour.

Dr. Manga has developed a sincere respect for chiropractors since that first report and many personal friendships, but there has been a downside. He has never — then or now — viewed chiropractic as anything but a niche within the overall global health care system. Dr. Manga's passion is for the overview, not any sideshow, and, to some extent, the chiropractic relationship has limited his role in the mainstream. "Until 1993, I had a perfect record with respect to projects and assignments from federal or provincial governments in Canada — every year there would be a role for me to play and proper funding to do the job," Manga said. "There has been a perfect record since 1993 as well. Not one assignment."

Professional discrimination is a pale imitation of what he experienced growing up in South Africa and he takes some satisfaction from the fact that history has confirmed all of his projections. Warnings he and fellow health economists made a generation ago were ignored by policy makers, who seem never to be held to account for the disastrous financial situation they have created. Every few years, there seems to be a turnover of both politicians and bureaucrats, each of whom eager to repeat the mistakes of those who went before them.

Manga's latest study of the Ontario chiropractic situation (See chapter 1, "The Gatekeepers") portrayed provincial government decision making so daft it would embarrass an elementary school math class. In Premier Dalton McGinty's first budget, chiropractic services were delisted from medicare coverage. The bureaucrats noted that $100 million had been spent for these delisted services in the current fiscal year and then projected a 100 percent savings of these funds after the cut.

The absurdity was the presumption that these patients would either cheerfully pay for what they lost, including all new patients needing chiropractic care, or just plain suffer in silence. Manga did a report based on hard evidence to demonstrate that many of the prospective new sufferers of neuro-musculoskeletal problems and many of the former chiropractic patients, would seek help wherever it was "free", most likely from medical doctors. This would lead to more expensive fees, physiotherapy, wasteful drug prescriptions and, too often, surgery. Manga projected that it will cost Ontario at least $200 million to replace the $100 million the province thinks it is saving.

"Ontario is the first jurisdiction in Canada to delist chiropractic care and may well be the first in the world to do so." He acknowledged earlier cuts in British Columbia, but not so drastic. He characterized as "ridiculous," the mathematics and arguments of Ontario officials.

"Since 1993, no one has convincingly contradicted my methodology or my findings. We researched all of the literature. There are many dozens of studies that show improved outcomes from chiropractic care over medical doctors, for the same conditions, and patients are invariably more satisfied with chiropractic management of musculoskeletal conditions. Not one study — anywhere in the world — not one ever, shows the reverse," he said. However, he notes that some Canadian medical doctors have taken brief courses (five weekends) in order to learn how to do spinal manipulation, usually the exclusive preserve of chiropractic doctors. How good these quickie courses prove to be will be seen in time (chiropractors spend four years learning this and everything else related to their profession), but the political statement is profound. The medical profession does everything in its power to debunk chiropractic, but a growing number of MDs see no hypocrisy when they attempt to cash in on the proven techniques.

As is frequently the case, Manga's work attracted international attention. In a 2004 paper published in the *Chiropractic Journal of Australia*, his thoughts could apply to the entire health care debate, a tragedy of selfish motives, ill-informed leadership, defending monopolies and an appalling lack of political courage.

One of the hallmarks of democracy — sadly neglected and the one that constitutes the most important democratic deficit — is that government must explain and justify its decisions. Simply and repeatedly declaring that it 'is responsible for the decision' it takes is trite and quite meaningless. After all, who else is or can be responsible for the decision the government takes? Taking 'responsibility' for a decision is hardly the same as explaining it. As commonly used, politicians often profess responsibility for a policy position only to avoid explaining the decision, thus converting perhaps an innocent or excusable error into an outright farce. The public does not ask who is responsible for a particular policy, it knows that already. What the public or for that matter particular groups in the public want to know is how the government can justify the decision it has taken. The government loses legitimacy and credibility when it cannot do this. . . . .there is surely an economic imperative not to jettison cost-effective care and replace them with less effective and costlier care? Indeed, there is a moral and economic obligation on government to promote cost-effective care.

"Martin's war on the deficit set off a domino effect beginning in every provincial treasury and then down through the system. An era of crisis management began, everybody desperately clinging to the lifeboat, trying to salvage as much as possible in terms of routine operations. Since suppliers (doctors, hospitals) and consumers (patients) had unlimited scope to generate demand and costs, system managers have been in a defensive shock for 10 years or more, cutting and constraining wherever possible. Instead of reasoned studies of experience and options, our health policy became — and remains — a knee-jerk war between governments, ill-informed politicians, self-serving professionals, bureaucrats, health unions and various insurers. Every debate boils down to who pays how much to whom. Despite disingenuous speeches about concern for the public, the angst is really just territorial. It serves the purpose of all vested interests to have ignorant and dependent leadership."

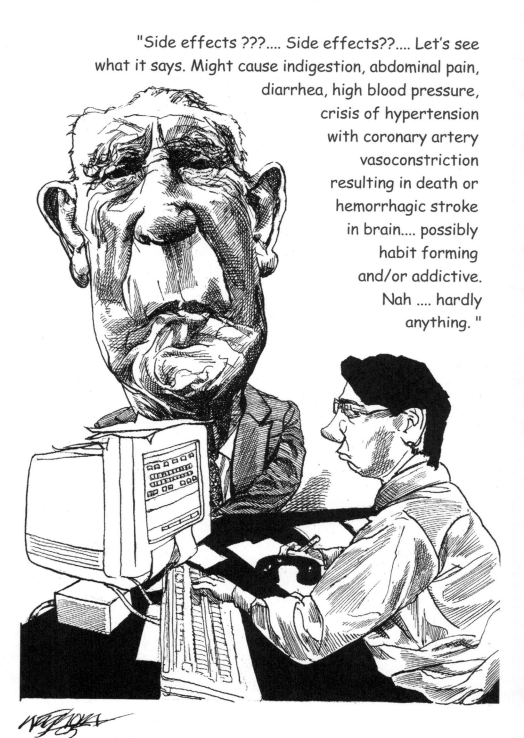

16. Budgets and Restructuring

Please try to stay the course of equal access. . .as a system, as a country, I have to applaud you . . . stay the course because to be forewarned is to be forearmed and we definitely have a stratification of the quality of health care services available in the United States based on your economic ability to pay. And it definitely compromises the quality of care and that is a tremendous social cost.

— LINDA ELDRIDGE, B.SC., MBA
American health management consultant

There is a common theme to most speeches by those in politics, government, and financially guaranteed positions within the health system, all of whom enjoy secure income and optimum extended health benefits courtesy of the taxpayers. They emphasize that despite current challenges, we are in great shape. This was parroted by Roy Romanow in the introduction to the final report from his national enquiry: "We have the greatest health system in the world, but we need to tweak it a little bit. The utilization of resources in the future must be more evidence-based."

Marvelous sophistry.

Canadians used to proudly assume and proclaim the supremacy of the health system, but know this is untrue today. Our country is number one in absolutely nothing in terms of international health care comparisons irrespective of where one fits on the demographic or socio-economic scale. Rich, middle-class and poor people have one overwhelming common denominator in Canada — with respect to health care, each of them would be better off just about anywhere else in the industrialized world. Arguably, the middle class and poor in the United Kingdom share Canada's frustration and the poor are definitely worse off in the United States.

Yet through this agonizing period of comparative decay, health costs have risen dramatically, from 30 percent of provincial budgets to as high as 48 percent. The norm is about 40 percent today, severely curtailing resources for every other public imperative, including programs that will improve the country tomorrow: education, economic development and social services. Perhaps we should only blame ourselves. Survey after survey has demonstrated public support of more health spending, and the most attentive readers of this data are those who prepare political plat-forms.

Political propagandists did everything in their power to hype the first ministers health summit in September 2004, with Prime Minister Martin determined to get a "deal" and the provincial premiers equally committed to restore fair play in the federal-provincial sharing formula. They demanded and received more funds from Ottawa. The final agreement will result in $41.2 billion more federal money over 10 years, on the basis of a six percent per annum increase in transfer payments. But the deal is front-end loaded to add a special $3.5 billion in transfers during the first two years and $4.5 billion over six years to cut surgery wait times.

There was also considerable discussion about more evidence-based management, but little detail as to how this would work. Virtually every political speech during the months preceding this event and every news-cast before, during and since, focused on little other than money, imply-ing that more money means better health care. No one seriously believes that. Furthermore, there is not one expert within health care, or govern-ment or at universities who does not believe that there are serious struc-tural problems and that we mismanage a considerable portion of the funds invested. Unfortunately, the exercise was more a matter of Prime Minister Paul Martin, in a minority government situation, trying to ful-fill his principal election promise, face-to-face with premiers who unan-imously believed that most of their financial distress had been caused by Finance Minister Paul Martin a decade earlier.

While the politicians all went away relieved, if not happy, Premier Dalton McGinty of Ontario was among those who speculated that the cri-sis may repeat itself before much time goes by. They may have to go back to Ottawa for more. In fact, if structural changes do not take place within the system, the September 2004 accord will prove only to have been an exercise in political posturing, inflation and avoidance of responsibility. The current inefficient system has an inexhaustible appetite to consume dollars.

"Federal" should mean strings attached!

Many Canadians fail to understand the basic nature of the country, a federation of legally-equal partners who cede to central management, issues that make the most sense for all. It is a federation, not a republic. The individual members are paramount. To use the vernacular, when push comes to shove, the provinces win. In fact, each province, with respect to its own interests, is theoretically superior to the "umbrella" organization. There have been few disputes about the federal supremacy in national defense, foreign affairs, central banking, the monetary system, the criminal code, federal policing, offshore fisheries, aviation, the railways, shipping and a number of other more obvious responsibilities.

The history of health care is entirely provincial. In fact, the provincial administration of health care was a consolidation of ad hoc services provided by churches, universities, charitable foundations, municipalities and even large industrial employers. The role of the federal government until after World War II principally involved research, public health, communicable diseases, aboriginal peoples, the military and the vast northern territories.

A more sophisticated and more mobile population in the postwar years discovered the tremendous discrepancy of services and health coverages as they moved from town to town and province to province. Gradually, the provinces started insisting upon a greater federal role, and this metamorphosis grew through provincial hospital programs, private insurance plans, and ultimately medicare in 1968. But it was the *Canada Health Act* of 1984 that marked the maturity of federal provincial relations.

The provinces continued to insist that the delivery of health services was exclusively their domain. Ottawa did not argue with this, but made it clear that the federal money came with strings attached. The provinces would have to buy into a standardized program from coast to coast, so that Canadians who moved from one jurisdiction to another would not encounter substantial differences in basic programs.

It would be good here to review, once again, the five basic tenets of the *Canada Health Act*: public administration, comprehensiveness, universality, portability, and accessibility.

The CHA has been a resounding success in terms of public administration, universality, and portability. Accessibility has become a serious
failure in recent history, but it is thought to be a correctable situation. The
principle works. It simply needs more money to erase the backlogs. The
overwhelming failure, as noted by economist Dr. Pran Manga and others,
is the "comprehensiveness" clause. The phrase "medically necessary
services" is too vague. The discrepancy of what is covered from province
to province threatens the founding philosophy of the act.

The *Act* defines "comprehensiveness" as follows:

> In order to satisfy the criterion respecting comprehensiveness, the
> health care insurance plan of a province must insure all insured health
> services provided by hospitals, medical practitioners or dentists, and
> where the law of the province so permits, similar or additional services
> rendered by other health care practitioners.

In practice, dentistry has only been covered when performed in hospitals. But the tag line "additional services rendered by other health care
practitioners," is where the negligence resides. The intent was that if a
"service" — a specific treatment — is covered by the insurance plan,
then the fees of any accredited, regulated and licensed health professional should be covered in the performance of that service. It can aptly
be demonstrated that medical doctors are the least well trained to perform some health functions.

Provinces have wide latitude to determine what services they wish to
cover, but the act insists that when a treatment or condition is included,
it must be 100 percent covered. This stipulation was made to prevent
practitioners or even provincial medical plans from separately billing
patients for portions of fees. However, in the letter of the law, some
provinces have consistently violated this clause in the reverse. They have
decided that they will pay to some practitioners, most notably chiropractors and optometrists, a portion of the negotiated fee for a specific treatment, requiring the doctor to collect the balance from the patient. It is this
kind of deceptive and contradictory practice that assaults the credibility
and effectiveness of medicare. Ottawa never acts to prevent or discipline
offending provinces, unless the oxen being gored are medical doctors.

Too often, the medical profession has been able to hoodwink politicians into believing "medically necessary services" is solely for medical
doctors to define. None of the authors of medicare, from Emmett Hall to
Taylor, Manga, Van Loon, and many others, ever intended that. It was

assumed that all government-regulated health professions would come under the act.

In fact, medical propagandists have successfully inserted a new phrase into the health vernacular, and that is "core services." These words appear nowhere in the *Canada Health Act* nor in any of the foundation documents that comprise the medicare legacy. How gullible the public officials appear to be. They swallow this new term like salmon chasing bait, and then find it odd that they are stuck inside yet another net designed to secure the dominance of hospitals, doctors and pharmaceutical companies.

And this remains the big flaw in "The Deal" as announced in September 2004. Unless Ottawa adds some definition to either the "comprehensiveness" principle within the CHA, or the government regulations under it, there will be no progress in terms of the much-ballyhooed (but little understood) new era of "evidence-based" policies. Federal authorities should define and insist upon coverage of nurse practitioners, chiropractors, optometrists and possibly — if realistic guidelines could be established — naturopaths, acupuncture and other demonstrably valuable services.

The "single national insurer"

Increasingly, it is not Canada's medicare that attracts the admiration of outsiders, but rather the fact that we have a "single national insurer." In the rhetoric of United States politics, critics of the system focus upon the 45 million Americans who do not have health insurance. Insured Americans do rather well.

Dr. Robert Wolber, a prominent British Columbia pathologist and laboratory physician is a native of Detroit with a Master of Science and a medical degree from the University of Michigan, and his specialty beyond that. He has worked in both worlds, including major hospitals and a university professorship. "The single national insurer is an outstanding advantage. You cannot believe the confusion and complexity faced by doctors, hospitals and patients in the United States, first trying to determine what coverages exist, and then the different systems of paperwork, administration and payment for over 3,000 different insurers in the country."

In fact this was the subject of a 2004 report by Senator Michael Kirby and noted heart surgeon Dr. Wilbert Keon for the Montreal-based Institute for Research on Public Policy. They argued that we fail to maximize the advantage as defined by Wolber because we prevent market forces from achieving optimum value, both in terms of cost and quality. There is an acute need for competition throughout our health care system and far more accountability.

Doctor knows best

The phrase "doctor knows best" may be the greatest single impediment we have to sensible health planning. This is pounded into us as children, both in the lessons of parents and in the relentless barrage of media. If something is wrong, the doctor can fix it. We feel confident that we can take any risk or avoid the development of sensible health habits. Parents feel no shame in allowing their personal and often reactionary attitudes to prevent the public schools and public health officials from developing adequate health and sex education programs. Each time progress seems to take place in a school district, some parents' protest or a campaign by a minority religious sect will impose their views. It doesn't take much to kill off embryo programs, particularly since every other education need is so starved for funds. As British humorists Jonathan Lynn and Antony Jay observed, "government operates with the engine of a lawn mower and the brakes of a Rolls Royce."

After all, if something is wrong, we can go to the doctor. It takes but a whisper of intellect and research to demonstrate that, on many topics, doctors most definitely do not know best. In fact, about some things, they are among the most uninformed people in society. Medical doctors did everything in their power to oppose the evolution of the nutrition movement, vitamins and other health supplements. The leaders in this field proved conclusively that medical education was almost devoid of anything to do with nutrition. Similarly, those who oppose school sexual education, often suggest that the matter is best left to the family and their physician. Parents, who suggest their children take advice from doctors on sex issues, might as well send the child to a garage mechanic. Perhaps romantic adventures during medical school evolved some insight, but what other qualifications does the doctor have?

Allopathic medicine is the business of cures, not prevention; injury and disease, not health. Ours is, unfortunately, limited to an allopathic medical system. Doctors' incomes depend upon diagnosing problems. Our system provides no reward for educating patients. Over 30 percent of all visits to medical doctors are for back and spine related problems. The spine and nerve network represent 60 percent of the human body.

Aside from elementary anatomy, medical schools teach nothing about spinal adjustment. Yet the profession greedily accepts all patients and fights to maintain exclusivity, even though they know that they can do little or nothing to treat the patient. They accept the fee anyway and make sure the patient doesn't go anywhere near the chiropractic profession, where they ought to have gone in the first place, and, of course, where quality help would be immediate.

Too many doctors and patients believe the advertising and propaganda that there is a miracle treatment available for everything, if not a cure, then certainly a way to make the symptoms less uncomfortable. The walls of monopoly make sure that neither irrelevance nor ignorance can be a serious impediment to medical business development, and the unlimited free access ensures that patients never have to think twice before abusing either themselves or the system with irresponsible behavior.

Since "doctor knows best," we make sure that doctors never get tested. Unlike some regulated health professions, there is no mandatory process to ensure that medical doctors' skills and knowledge are maintained at an acceptable standard. Astonishingly, a doctor who gains a license at age 27 is still assumed to be fully qualified 50 years later, without any evidence to prove competence. There is no other professional position in society, upon which the lives of others may depend, that would be permitted to take such a risk: pilots, air traffic controllers, race car drivers, firefighters, seamen, military personnel and amusement park workers, are among the many trades that require mandatory re-examination. Not medical doctors, the profession most able to either improve or endanger quality of life.

Every hospital-based doctor, surgeon and senior nurse knows that there is a hierarchy of competence among those who perform major procedures. Cardiac bypass surgery, for example, has now been around so long that charts can demonstrate the longevity of life that can be expected after surgery, depending upon where the work is done and by which surgeon. Your odds improve dramatically with volume, which means the hospitals that do the greatest number of procedures. But even within them, the institution knows that Dr. X's patients live 50 percent more years after the event than do the patients of Dr. Y. And professionals within hospitals know the physicians who should be avoided at all costs. But patients are never told. With luck, their general practitioner navigates their care to ensure the best specialists are aboard, but are they knowledgeable about relative competence of other physicians and specialists?

Why are doctors not obligated to be informed about all therapies related to a given condition, particularly non-drug, non-surgical approaches found to be more effective in specific situations. Will the day come when legal actions will be brought against doctors or insurers for routing people into inferior care, when it can be demonstrated that they knew or "ought to have known" there were better courses of treatment?

Discipline by Colleges of Physicians and Surgeons is nothing short of a farce. Aside from sexual misconduct and financial irregularities, the number of suspensions and license cancellations are insignificant. Rebates from government to doctors, to compensate for their malpractice insurance, remove even that threat from their daily lives. Since "adverse events" — accidents and malpractice by physicians and hospitals — may now be the number one killer in the country, would it be appropriate to consider the maintenance of professional standards, a periodic review of knowledge and qualifications, more determined discipline and greater levels of physician liability for malpractice? Governments should penalize malpractice, not subsidize it.

"Doc in a Box"

Dr. Wolber describes the modern walk-in clinics as "Doc in a Box." The waning role of the traditional family practice has generated impossible pressure on hospital outpatient departments. Impersonal clinics have sprung up in shopping centres and other convenient locations to fill this void. What has been lost is the doctor with a holistic view of the patient and a sense of family history. "I think I'd rather go to a witch doctor than someone at a walk-in clinic," Wolber said.

As recently as 15 years ago, a retiring general practitioner could sell the practice for a tidy sum to an aspiring successor. With rare exceptions, these practices now have no value. The patient base has aged with the doctor and is now principally a geriatric practice. Families have splintered for any of a number of reasons and public mobility makes just about everything these days transitory. In fact, the GP has, in most instances, not kept with the times. Increasingly, they have become traffic controllers for lab services, diagnostic centres, pharmacists, specialists, and physiotherapists, brokers, not service providers. And, irrespective of incentives being offered to locate elsewhere, general practitioners have been disinclined to move. Therefore, there has been a surplus of them in the major cities and a scarcity in rural and frontier areas. Modern health administrators, conscious of doctors' abilities to invent patient issues in order to optimize income, know that physician surpluses are bad news for everybody.

Ontario has been the Canadian leader in just about every industry trend, not all of them positive. But in order to make services more even around the province, Ontario officials 25 years ago resurrected a technique founded after World War I in the United Kingdom, more commonly known in Canada today as "capitation" and "rostering." The concept was quite simple. Negotiations established what was considered to be a healthy optimum caseload for a physician, usually between 1,200 and 1,500, depending upon the population concentration and geographic size of area served. The government provided, equipped and staffed the clinic. An appropriate annual salary was determined for the doctor. The physician's income would remain secure as long as the patient-base retained the optimum number. While growth of patient volume was discouraged, measures existed for fees and bonuses for extra work. If, however, patients chose to go elsewhere, pro rata deductions would be made from the doctor's income. This was designed as an incentive to make people happy and healthier, with the focus on wellness and not disease.

The concept got off to a rocky start, faced with the frequently open hostility of the Ontario Medical Association. Aside from the remotest of locations, where there was no alternative, growth was slow until Dr. Martin Barkin, a medical doctor and orthopedic specialist, became Deputy Minister in 1987. Barkin pushed forward vigorously and, to the surprise of most physicians, the program was uniformly successful. The doctors, nurses, support staff and communities were all happy. Barkin, who resigned from the government in 1991, is now Chief Executive Officer of Draxis Health Inc., a Quebec-based pharmaceutical company.

Many of these "capitation/rostering" prototypes evolved into an even more effective service delivery vehicle within Ontario, the Community Health Centre. Pioneering centres such as the Sault Ste. Marie Group Health Centre (founded in 1963) and the South Riverdale Community Health Centre (1976) have become world famous, large organizations with multidisciplinary services. Both are Canadian icons, and Riverdale has an added dimension of community development, uplifting from its origin an economically deprived area of Toronto. It has reached out to establish partnerships with major corporations and the University of Toronto. The Sault centre, Riverdale and the many that have followed in their image in Ontario, have taken an all-encompassing view of health care, beginning with receptionists and nurse practitioners as primary gatekeepers, professional administrators and adding medical doctors, surgeons, pediatrics and child care services, specialists as needed, dieticians and various counselors.

Riverdale, in a partnership with Canadian Memorial Chiropractic College, added chiropractic in 1999. Ontario, with respect to chiropractic, is a paradox. Its new government has been zealous in delisting coverage despite hard evidence that this will result in a net extra cost of at least $100 million for taxpayers, as patients with back and spine problems seek more expensive, and less successful remedies, all covered by the medical plan. But Ontario also has the most advanced approach to community health clinics and "rostering." Clinics that receive a gross annual sum based on total care for a set number of patients, benefit greatly from keeping people healthy. Many of those have found significant savings and improved outcomes by using alternate care approaches, such as nurse practitioners, chiropractors and other alternative caregivers. In addition to Riverdale, there are chiropractic services and/or research projects at Sherbourne Health Centre, St. Michael's Hospital, Anishnawbe Native Health Centre, Muki Baum Adult and Children's Centres and St. John's Rehabilitation Hospital, among many others around the province.

There has been a disturbing undercurrent throughout the history of Community Health Centres. Both Sault Ste. Marie and Riverdale had to overcome brutal, big-money opposition, and the intimidation of potential clinic doctors, from the Ontario Medical Association, and every centre since has been greeted with grudging acceptance at best. They have tended to overcome the opposition only if they stick to poor neighborhoods or remote areas where fee-for-service doctors don't want to go. And since most Canadian decision makers in government, business, media and the professions, do not live in remote or economically depressed areas, they have little or no experience with these outstanding operations.

But they are the models for the future — coast to coast in Canada. Just as in the structure for capitation and rostering of doctors, these centres negotiate annual budgets from government based on the communities they serve, and they are then free to manage the funds as they see fit. Only on-call medical specialists and other infrequent services result in specific charges to the provincial medical insurance plan. If the patient-base and approved services grow, the budget increases. If numbers decline, so does the budget. The incentive for first class service to families is the top priority. The healthier the patient community, the greater is the surplus of revenues over expenditures, funds available for community-beneficial projects.

It is hard not to agree with B.C.'s Dr. Robert Wolber about the dangers of "Doc in a Box," the walk-in clinics, or obtaining care exclusively from impersonal outpatient departments of hospitals. Obvious symptoms can be treated, but not the person. Improved health data procedures and access will enhance the sharing of important patient history, but the human dimension should go far beyond that. This is why the excellent Community Health Centres may become increasingly important in the future. They will provide everything the best of traditional family practice ever offered, and much, much more. The Centres can add the full gamut of all accredited health professions and counselors.

Bottom up priorities

Governments and the principal organizations involved in health care have clung to "top down" styles of management. By the time a policy or financial resource reaches the patient, it has been mauled into pulp by federal and provincial bureaucrats, regional health authorities, hospital administrators, medical associations, and health unions. Each takes a huge run at the issue to ensure that none of its sacred cows get sacrificed.

Obviously, elected representatives, public officials, professionals and experienced staff must assess information and establish priorities. But before anything is implemented, the question must be asked: "how will this benefit the patient?" Competent health economists and managers could easily create a decision-making model which could test fire each policy from the patient up. What happens with the patient? How will that impact upon the care provider? What support infrastructure will be required? How does it fit the overall regional, provincial national service? Is it practical and affordable system wide?

Many experts believe that the only way that progress can be made toward more of a patient and community-driven system is to systematically disembowel the large acute care hospitals. For decades now, we have done exactly the reverse. There has been the feeling that in order to get the best of equipment, professionals and services, we would have to consolidate everything into the largest imaginable institutions. This has backfired spectacularly, measured not just in costs, but also in shocking rates of illness acquired in institutions and unforgivable, unnecessary death statistics. In addition, it has put far too much power into the hands of large professional organizations and unions, eliminating much of the flexibility essential for good management.

The preponderance of expensive beds far from a patient's home has also added to the decline of the general practitioner and to hardships faced by surgeons. For GPs, instead of placing most of their patients in a facility near home, they either have to obtain privileges at a central hospital and travel long distances to see one or two patients at a time, or hand off the business to someone else. Surgery in the acute care hospitals has become so expensive, more because of support staff and union contracts than because of physician costs. Also the operating rooms can't affordably run long enough each day to handle the demand. Surgeons in major cities often find themselves rationed to a few hours of operating time a week at the only available hospital.

The priority in the future must begin at the bottom.

- **The patient** must be empowered more than ever to chose the professionals and services they need and if the choice is a regulated, approved care provider — professional or organization — at rates negotiated with the Medical Services Plan of the province, it should no longer be the business of government to say "no." Respect for patients, and the encouragement of informed free choice, should be an anchoring principle of professional ethics and government policy.
- **The Community Care Centre** with receptionists and nurse practitioners as gatekeepers and primary patient contact, and professional administration, should be the focal point of all care in the area. As demand dictates, this centre can place on salary physicians, more nurse practitioners, pharmacists, dieticians, chiropractors, psychologists, counselors or therapists, and co-ordinate a long list of on-call medical specialists and health professionals such as psychiatrists, optometrists, naturopaths, acupuncturists, podiatrists, and others.
- Perhaps using the facilities of the Community Care Centre as a head office, from there would fan out the **home care** and **home hospital services**, with a complete range of nurses, technicians, therapists, home care support and physicians as required.
- Nothing in the model would prevent **independent fee-for-service professionals** from building a client base in the area, but market forces would dictate their success or failure.

- **Long Term Care facilities** for seniors and others needing specialized care (such as Alzheimer's and other dementias) would evolve much as they have today, but supported by the Community Centre with all other infrastructure.

- **Convalescent hospitals** where "healing" and not "cure" is the mission. These would have small outpatient and paramedical services to augment Community Health Centres, but the potential population of these small and medium facilities could be two-thirds of today's total acute care hospital population. Good management should make it possible for them to operate at a cost 50 percent per bed less than the acute care cost. More importantly, the "adverse events" that haunt the big hospitals would drop precipitously, saving lives and substantial amounts of money.

- Where **private investors** are willing to pay for the capital costs, there should be no discouragement in the growth of **Magnetic Resonance Imaging, CT-Scanners, surgical clinics** or **other specialty services** throughout each community. They could perform non-covered items, as they do today, for whatever price they wish to charge, and any Medical Plan services as long as they charge no more than the established public sector insurance fee.

- **Specialty hospitals** for pediatrics, cancer, rehabilitation medicine, psychiatric care or other high-volume and specialized fields may always be the preferred option.

- Each province or region should attempt to develop a **diagnostic centre** of a quality approaching that of the Mayo Clinic, with the best of technology, facilities, and professionals. This could be linked with major universities or acute hospitals, as long as there is clear separation between the "centre" of diagnostics and the "centre" for treatment. This superior facility must replace and not duplicate the most advanced diagnostics elsewhere in the region served.

- **Acute care hospitals** should provide the major emergency departments, trauma centres, epidemiology and the most advanced of surgical procedures. But the operational culture must be to evacuate patients as soon as they pass from the need for critical care and treatment into a recovery mode.

■ In planning for any facility requiring expensive technology, technicians and support services, care must be taken to ensure a long-term need, and a financial plan that can **maximize utilization, up to 24 hours per day year round.** If these public facilities cannot be optimized, private sector contracting should be explored to provide the service on an ad hoc basis. The public facility should be closed and the support positions eliminated.

The possible principal irony as we go forward is the increasingly obvious need for mid-level, wellness and recovery hospitals, ironic in that governments in Canada have been closing small, older hospitals for years now, concentrating ever-increasing numbers of beds and facilities in the largest institutions. Many of these old abandoned buildings may have new life but even if new construction proves desirable, from an operational point of view, the capital cost is the smallest part of the health care pie. Building modern facilities, cheaper to operate with less high-powered personnel than at whatever institution they replace, would justify its cost within a year or two of savings per bed, based upon the acute care alternative.

Postscript

If the foregoing list came from a deputy minister's office as a statement of future goals, the attack would begin immediately. All unions, managers and professionals would think first about how this would disrupt their lives and their business. Opposition would mount. History indicates that obstructionism from doctors, hospital administrators and unions may not always be completely successful, but it never fails completely. Which means that meaningful reform ALWAYS FAILS COMPLETELY, because it has to be a package deal.

Therefore, from the outset, strong government must include all of the stakeholders in the discussion and respectfully so. An organized, professional workforce is far more desirable than ad hoc chaos where the supervision of working conditions, benefits, and qualifications become more confused and inconsistent. Professional associations, health care and hospital unions could have a significant role to play in reform. The future should mean more and better jobs, but it cannot possibly mean more of the same jobs, protecting all of the existing institutions. That, more than anything else, will make increased privatization the most attractive option. Higher quality service, faster and cheaper.

Government must deliver the ultimatum. Wherever possible, existing personnel should be protected and, if specific jobs or institutions become redundant, they should have the right of first refusal if they are qualified to fill other openings. But they must be prepared to move and to accept sensible and efficient working conditions.

The patient comes first — a revolutionary concept.

"What are we going to do Mr. Prime Minister?"

"Let's have a Royal Commission"

"Will that help?"

"Of course not, but it will take years and by then the election will be over. Worry not."

17.
Squandering Billions

The management of our health care system is so inefficient that we not only fail to put patients in the hands of those professionals most qualified to give the best treatment, we actually ensure that the most expensive and least qualified person provides the care. . . . the structure of health management in Canada makes the squandering of billions unavoidable.

— PRAN MANGA, PhD, M.PHIL.

The Prime Minister and Premiers began their Ottawa summit of September 2004, convinced that medicare was in crisis, and that the current 4–5 percent annual growth in total cost was unsustainable. In fact, the anticipated $125 billion total public and private spending on health in 2004 would grow to $163 billion by 2010. The government share of that increase could be as much as $35 billion more.

What the premiers gained was a deal in which at least half of the growth in costs in years to come will be borne by the federal treasury through increased transfer payments. Unfortunately, the numbers reflect only a continuation of current cost increases, but no funds for system and service improvements. Since the consensus is that national health care has deteriorated, bold strides are necessary to manage the funds better.

The Canadian Institute for Health Information analyzed actual expenditures from 1975–2002 inclusive, and projected these trends to arrive at 2003 numbers. Of the $121.4 billion expected to be spent in Canada on health in 2003, governments would spend $84.8 billion and the private sector (corporations and individuals) would spend $36.6 billion.

This 2003 total broke down as follows, in billions:

- hospitals and institutions   49.0
- drugs   19.6
- medical doctors   15.6
- dentists   9.0
- vision   3.1
- other care providers   2.3
- capital investment   5.6
- public health, administration,
  research and miscellaneous   17.2

Rx for tomorrow

To use a popular sports colloquialism, governments "hit the wall" in terms of health spending within the past few years. The 10 percent of Gross Domestic Product we now invest stands up well by any international comparison, but the services do not. We have been going backwards. The share of provincial budgets as high as 48 percent is an unconscionable assault on everything else government is supposed to do, and, to be brutally frank, spending 48 percent of resources serving the current population is grotesquely unfair to future generations, who have the right to expect a society made better as a result of our inhabitation.

Therefore, some severe surgery and reconstruction is required:

ADVERSE EVENTS

A study of a small slice of Canadian health care determined that 185,000 patients are victimized each year as a result of errors or diseases contracted within the system, and as many as 23,750 of these people die. The research focused on hospital records composed in somewhat of an "honor system" within the institutions where the problems occurred. A Harvard-based expert on this topic says that these records are never more than 5–20 percent accurate. The truth is definitely far worse.

And, since this evidence represented only a selection of acute care hospitals, and not the total field of drugs, surgery, doctors' offices, other institutions and clinics, it may be correct to project 50,000 unnecessary deaths each year as a result of medical mistakes. The cost of treating errors must be multiple billions of dollars.

Various initiatives have more recently recommended third party review of all incidents.

This is a tragedy and a crisis beyond imagination.

DRUGS OUT-OF-CONTROL

Every professional study demonstrates that 50 percent or more of all drugs prescribed is a complete waste: incorrect prescriptions, over-prescribing, dangerous conflicts with other medication and unnecessary in the first instance. Experts advise that we consume two or three times per capita the amount of antibiotics used in Europe, without supporting evidence of more disease requiring attention. The 2004 numbers show $18 billion in prescription drugs and $3.8 billion in over-the-counter remedies. Nothing has grown faster in health costs and there is absolutely no statistical evidence that any of the additional cost has achieved a system-wide benefit. Profits of drug companies have soared. Fees to prescribing professionals remain robust. How many billions of this total end up in toilets, garbage cans, gathering dust in medicine cabinets and causing more harm than good — sometimes fatal — within patients, no one really knows.

A parallel issue was Prime Minister Brian Mulroney's demolition of what may have been the best managed pharmaceutical system in the world. Canada's compulsory licensing made all of the latest and best drugs available, through negotiations with international and domestic pharmaceutical companies, and we also developed an enviable generic drug industry. By granting Big Pharma 20-year guarantees on patents, Mulroney achieved nothing for Canada except soaring prices. The fact that we have cheaper costs than the United States is evidence only that the Americans are being ripped off. Our mass purchasing by hospitals with a government-imposed policy favoring generic drugs if they are equally good as brand names, moderates all Canadian prices.

Government should consult experts such as Toronto's Dr. Joel Lexchin about a return to compulsory licensing and a national purchasing system such as that which operates so effectively in Australia.

This should be a top priority federal-provincial assault: fewer and more accurately dispensed prescriptions, and a national purchasing system.

COMPREHENSIVENESS

It is time to make the "comprehensiveness" clause of the *Canada Health Act* as it was intended by its authors. Vigorous policies to enhance the abundance and utilization of nurse practitioners, chiropractors, and all other regulated health professionals would improve service, increase the emphasis on health rather than disease, and significantly reduce the amount of unnecessary drugs and surgery. There is a vast body of evidence to support these claims.

An example of the savings possible is Dr. Pran Manga's internationally accepted methodology analyzing what might be possible if the Ontario Health Insurance Plan fully covered chiropractic for neuro-musculoskeletal problems (one third of all visits to the health system), rather than less effective medical doctors. Dr. Manga's 1998 numbers estimated a minimum annual saving of $380 million to a maximum of $770 million per year in Ontario alone. His average or "likely" estimate of $548 million, extrapolated nationally, would be $2.2 billion. Assuming an average inflation of 3 percent since 1998, it would indicate a potential national saving of $2.7 billion per year. Put another way, by not following his 1998 advice, the country has squandered $10 billion, completely irrespective of the hundreds of thousands of patients who received inadequate or inappropriate care, and suffered unnecessarily.

ADMINISTRATION

Sometimes it seems as if Canada's leading health statistics are all about the number of meetings, seminars, conferences, task forces, Royal Commissions, and parliamentary inquiries rather than treatment programs. And now we have a new category, A SUMMIT! Salaries in the managerial side of the health system are ridiculous, particularly in hospitals and regional health authorities, and cannot possibly be defended by any accountability process. Hospital managers typically earn $300,000 to $500,000, with every benefit under the sun, first class travel, and they often get more in wrongful dismissal damages when fired than when they are at work.

Because there are 32 million shareholders in the Canadian health network, a democracy in action, it is unrealistic to expect private sector efficiencies and accountability. Private firms can be selective about the work they do and how they report. Democracy is cumbersome. But need we have a daily airlift of federal and provincial bureaucrats travelling around inflating each other's sense of importance?

Here are some ideas to ponder:

- No salary of any taxpayer-financed official, including hospitals and health authorities, should exceed that of the Deputy Minister of Health within the specific jurisdiction. Excluded from this would be doctors and other health professionals whose compensation can be more easily determined by the market. The stars of the system must be the patient and those who serve the patient directly, not administrators.

- No public official — ever — should travel first or business class, unless they are accompanying a politician. First class political travel is a dubious perk as well, but politicians answer to a different court of judgement.

- Government should call tenders among airlines for bulk buying of excursion fares, including an assortment of "advanced" and "immediate" travel vouchers. Similar negotiations should take place with hotel chains.

- All but necessary travel should be discouraged. Far more effective use of telephone and video conferencing and web casting should be evolved.

- Top administration might be reduced significantly if decision-making is downloaded through the levels of service, particularly to the care providers and the patients themselves. Competition and choice among professionals would permit the market forces to regulate behavior.

- Discussions should take place with private insurers to explore whether economies and efficiencies could be attained by contracting out some or all of management of the Medical Plan fee schedule and payments within each province.

CO-PAYMENT

Nothing would impact more positively upon health resources than an effort to encourage responsibility among both doctors and patients. Co-payment — a modest user fee for professional visits — should be considered. The amount is almost irrelevant and the administration cost would be net zero. Half of whatever is charged would be debited from professional fees paid by the patient's medical plan. The other half would cover the administrative cost of the new process at the point of care.

Social services recipients would be exempt; seniors and the working poor would be refunded fully through tax credits. We are the only universal access nation in the world that does not have a user fee to encourage responsible behavior by both patients and service providers.

Despite all of the obstacles placed by the system to divert patients from chiropractors, optometrists, naturopaths, podiatrists, acupuncturists, physiotherapists, massage therapists and others, for whom the patient or their insurer must pay some or all of the fees — as opposed to the "free" medical doctor competition — these professions demonstrate every day that people will pay for value received. It is high time medical doctors earned the same respect for their "free" medical services to patients.

CLOSER TO HOME

The best investment in better and lower cost future care would be a determined program to evolve small convalescent hospitals, multidisciplinary Community Health Centres, and comprehensive home care infrastructure.

If this is pursued with vigor, wherever possible encouraging competition among professionals and provider organizations, including private sector firms and nonprofit organizations, it is likely to have heavy upfront costs, far in advance of any savings from current hospital-based systems.

However, if the individuals we elect have the strength to ignore the self-serving broadsides sure to come from today's monopolists, this cannot fail to provide better and more economical health care in the future. The up-front investment, if amortized like a typical business proposition, will prove to be exceptionally wise.

In search of respect

Big brother does not know best. This is the information age. If patients do not avail themselves of what can be found the Internet, in public libraries and in consultations with friends, professional and otherwise, they deserve whatever consequences come their way. The system must stop force-feeding the care it decides to deliver, empowering the patient wherever possible to think and choose for himself or herself.

It is the duty of government to manage funds wisely, to provide appropriate facilities and services, and to regulate the health professions. It is the business of each profession to make its services known to prospective patients. Before opening the floodgates to put all professions on an equal access footing with medical doctors, fee negotiations and market testing should take place. We have the experts in Canada to establish the research models to monitor the value of any new service. The tests should confirm that the changes substitute superior outcomes (cost and quality of care) for whatever exists now, rather than adding new self-serving business development processes for more professionals. Successful reform should be phased in system-wide as experience dictates.

Government must ensure truth in advertising and information and then get out of the way. Patients should be free to make their own choices about their own health care, without a stacked deck distorting the selection process. Not only should we respect the patient, it is high time all of the health professions started respecting each other.

In the words of Mr. Justice Emmett Hall, who wrote the blueprint for federal medicare:

> No good can come from warring factions between competitors in the health field. It is, in our view, fundamental to good health care, that all who labour legitimately in the field should do so in harmonious cooperation.

Glossary of Acronyms

AARN ....Alberta Association of Registered Nurses
ACA ......American Chiropractic Association
AHCPR ...Agency of Health Care Policy and Research
APN ......Advanced Practice Nurse
AMA .....American Medical Association
BCIT .....British Columbia Institute of Technology
BCMA ....British Columbia Medical Association
BSE ......Bovine Spongiform Encephalophy
CCA ......Canadian Chiropractic Association
CCAC ....Community Care Access Centre
CCE ......Council on Chiropractic Education
CCF ......Co-operative Commonwealth Federation
CHA ......Canada Health Act
CHC ......Community Health Centre
CHO ......Comprehensive Health Organization
CIHI ......Canadian Institute for Health Information
CIHR .....Canadian Institutes of Health Research
CJD ......Creutzfeldt-Jacob disease
CLC ......Canadian Labour Congress
CLSC .....Local Community Services Centre
CMA .....Canadian Medical Association
CMCC ....Canadian Memorial Chiropractic College
CMI ......Chronic Mental Illness
CMPA ....Canadian Medical Protective Association
COOP ....Health Cooperative Models
CSC ......Canadian Stroke Consortium

CT . . . . . . .Computed Tomography, *as in* CT scan
DC . . . . . . .Doctor of Chiropractic
DO . . . . . .Doctor of Osteopathy
DTCA . . . . .Direct to Consumer Advertising
EMP . . . . . .Extra Mural Philosophy
FDA . . . . . .Food and Drug Administration (US)
FSU . . . . . .Florida State University
GP . . . . . . .General Practitioner of medicine
HMO . . . . .Health Maintenance Organization
HRT . . . . . .hormone replacement therapy
HSO . . . . . .Health Services Organization
ICA . . . . . . .International Chiropractic Association
IHF . . . . . .Independent Health Facility
JD . . . . .Doctor of Laws (US)
LabCorp . .Laboratory Corporation of America
MD . . . . . .Medical Doctor
MRI . . . . . .Magnetic Resonance Imaging
NCAHF . . .National Council Against Health Fraud
NDP . . . . . .New Democratic Party
NP . . . . . . .Nurse Practitioner
NSAIDs . . .nonsteroidal anti-inflammatory drugs
OD . . . . . . .Doctor of Optometry
OHIP . . . . .Ontario Health Insurance Plan
OMA . . . . .Ontario Medical Association
PBS . . . . . . .Pharmaceutical Benefits Scheme (Australia)
PhRMA . . .Pharmaceutical Research and Manufacturers
                        of America
RPN . . . . . .Registered Psychiatric Nurse
SFU . . . . . .Simon Fraser University
TMJ . . . . . .Tempero Mandibular Joint
UBC . . . . . .University of British Columbia
UCLA . . . . .University of California Los Angeles
U of T . . . . .University of Toronto
UVIC . . . . .University of Victoria
VSC . . . . . .Vertebral Subluxation Complex
WHO . . . . .World Health Organization

Bibliography

The following is a partial list of books and reports that proved helpful in this project. See also "Authors' Note."

Angus, Douglas E., and Pran Manga. *Co-op/Consumer Sponsored Health Care Delivery Effectiveness*. Ottawa, ON: Canadian Co-operative Association, 1990.

Bayne, Lillian. *BC Laboratory Services Review*. Victoria, BC: Lillian Bayne & Associates, Government of British Columbia, 2003.

Butler, Andrew and Stan Dubas. *Chaos and Crisis, the Current State of Health Care in British Columbia*. Victoria, B.C.: 2001.

Canadian Institute for Health Information. *National Health Expenditure Trends*. Ottawa, ON: 2003.

Chomsky, Noam. *Media Control*. New York, NY: Seven Stories Media Control Press, 2002.

Decter, Michael. *Healing Medicine*. Toronto, ON: McGilligan Books, 1994.

Evans, Robert G. *The Role of Private and Public Health Care Delivery in Alberta*. Keynote address to Alberta Congress Board, 2000.

Goozner, Merrill. *The $800 million pill: The truth behind the cost of new drugs*. Berkley, CA.: University of California Press, 2004.

Gordon, Robert. *The Alarming History of Medicine*. London, U.K.: Sinclair-Stevenson, 1993.

Graedon, Joe. *The Peoples' Pharmacy*. New York, NY: St. Martin's Press, Inc., 1976, 1985.

Haines, Judith. *The Nurse Practitioner, A Discussion Paper*. Ottawa, ON: Canadian Nurses Association, 1993.

Hamowy, Ronald. *Canadian Medicine: A Study in Restricted Entry*. Vancouver, BC: Fraser Institute, 1984.

Illich, Ivan. *Limits to Medicine: Modern Nemesis*. London, UK: Marion Boyars Publishers, 1976.

Inglis, B.D. et al. *Chiropractic in New Zealand*. Commission of Inquiry into Chiropractic. Wellington, NZ: 1979.

Kelner, Merrijoy, Oswald Hall, and Ian Coulter. *Chiropractors, Do They Help?* Toronto, ON: Fitzhenry & Whiteside, 1980.

Kirby, Senator Michael J.L. *State of the Health Care System in Canada*. Standing Committee on Social Affairs, Science and Technology, Senate of Canada. Ottawa, ON: October 2002.

Kirby, Senator Michael J.L. and Wilbert Keon. *Why Competition is Essential in the Delivery of Publicly Funded Health Care Services*. Montreal, QC: Institute for Research on Public Policy, 2004.

Manga, Pran, D. Angus, C. Papadopoulos, and W. Swan. *The Effectiveness and Cost-effectiveness of Chiropractic Management of Low-back Pain*. Toronto, ON: Kenilworth Publishers, 1993.

Manga, Pran, and Doug Angus. *Enhanced Chiropractic Under OHIP as a Means of Reducing Health Care Costs, Attaining Better Health Outcomes and Achieving Equitable Access to Health Services*. Ottawa, ON: 1998.

Manga, Pran. "The Perverse and Discriminatory Policy: The De-Listing of Chiropractic Care in Ontario, Canada." *Chiropractic Journal of Australia*. Wagga Wagga, Aust.: 2004.

McIver, Susan B. *Medical Nightmares: The Human Face of Errors*. Toronto, ON: 2001.

McTaggart, Lynne. *What Doctors Don't Tell You*. New York, NY: Avon Books, 1996.

Mendelsohn, Robert S. *Confessions of a Medical Heretic*. Chicago, IL: Contemporary Books, Inc., 1979.

Muse & Associates. *Utilization, Cost and Effects of Chiropractic Care on Medicare Program Costs*. Washington, DC: July, 2001.

Null, Gary, Carolyn Dean, Martin Feldman, Rasio, and Dorothy Smith. *Death by Medicine*. Access: http://www.nutritioninstituteofamerica.org. New York, NY: Nutrition Institute of America, October 2003.

Postman, Neil. *Technopoly: The Surrender of Culture to Technology*. New York, NY: Alfred A. Knopf, 1992.

Richardson, Jeff and Stuart Peacock. *Will More Doctors Increase or Decrease Death Rates? An econometric analysis of Australian mortality statistics*. Victoria, Aust.: Centre for Health Program Evaluation, 2003.

Robinson, Jeffrey. *Prescription Games*. Toronto, ON: McLelland & Stewart Ltd., 2001.

Romanow, Roy. *Building on Values, The Future of Health Care in Canada*. Ottawa, ON: Government of Canada Commission, November 2002.

Schaller, Warren E,, and Charles R. Carroll. *Health, Quackery & The Consumer*. Philadelphia, PA: W.B. Saunders Company, 1976.

Smith-Cunnien, Susan L. *A Profession of One's Own, Organized Medicine's Opposition to Chiropractic*. Lanham, MD: University Press of America, 1998.

Smith, J.C. *How to Avoid Back Surgery*. Chiropractic Paradigm Systems, Warner Robins, GA. 1996.

Strabanek, Petr, and James McCormick. *Follies & Fallacies in Medicine*. Glasgow, Scotland: Tarragon Press, 1989.

Torrey, E. Fuller. *Nowhere To Go: The Tragic Odyssey of the Homeless Mentally Ill*. New York, NY: Harper & Row Publishers, 1988.

Wilk, Chester A. *Chiropractic Speaks Out*. Park Ridge, IL: Wilk Publishing Company,1973.

Wilk, Chester A. *Medicine, Monopolies, and Malice*. Chicago, IL: self-published, 1996.

York, Geoffrey. *The High Price Of Health*. Toronto, ON: James Lorimer & Company, 1987.

Index